IN THE SHADOWS
OF VICTORY II

America's Forgotten Military Leaders, the Spanish–American
War to World War II

THOMAS D. PHILLIPS

CASEMATE

Philadelphia & Oxford

Published in United States of America and Great Britain in 2017 by
CASEMATE PUBLISHERS
1950 Lawrence Road, Havertown, PA 19083, USA
and
The Old Music Hall, 106–108 Cowley Road, Oxford OX4 1JE, UK

Copyright 2017 © Thomas D. Phillips

Hardcover Edition: ISBN 978-1-61200-546-1
Digital Edition: ISBN 978-1-61200-547-8 (epub)

A CIP record for this book is available from the British Library

Printed and bound in the United States of America

For a complete list of Casemate titles, please contact:

CASEMATE PUBLISHERS (US)
Telephone (610) 853-9131
Fax (610) 853-9146
Email: casemate@casematepublishers.com
www.casematepublishers.com

CASEMATE PUBLISHERS (UK)
Telephone (01865) 241249
Email: casemate-uk@casematepublishers.co.uk
www.casematepublishers.co.uk

CONTENTS

PREFACE

As was noted in the opening words of the first volume in this series, *In the Shadows of Victory: America's Forgotten Military Leaders*, "history plays tricks sometimes."

During the course of America's existence, history has enshrined an exceptional few military leaders in the nation's collective consciousness while sometimes ignoring others often equally as deserving, relegating them to footnotes at best. Though the nation owes them considerable debts, the military history of the United States is replete with examples of leaders whose singular leadership is now little remembered. *America's Forgotten Military Leaders* is about those who have been overlooked: military leaders whose accomplishments have been too little acknowledged and too seldom celebrated.

Throughout the book, examples are also noted of leaders whose major renown is associated with a specific war—John J. Pershing, America's towering military figure during World War I, for example—who also rendered exemplary though largely forgotten service during a different conflict (in Pershing's case, the Philippine Insurrection).

At the end of each chapter, a "Deeper in the Shadows" segment with accompanying brief biographies identifies officers whose contributions, while perhaps less consequential than those of colleagues chronicled elsewhere in these pages, are deserving of far more recognition than has thus far been accorded them.

Volume I covered "forgotten leaders" during essentially the first one hundred years of the nation's existence, from the War of Independence through the Indian Wars of the American West. This book continues the story over the next turbulent decades, from the Spanish-American War, through the Philippine Insurrection, World War I, and World War II.

This volume includes an added feature: a "Road to War" section at the beginning of each chapter that traces the roots of the conflict and discusses the paths that led to America's involvement.

I am again beholden to comments and recommendations solicited from the military history departments at the United States Military Academy, the United States Naval Academy, the United States Air Force Academy, the Virginia Military Institute, The Citadel, and the University of Nebraska–Lincoln. Once again, I am especially grateful to Lieutenant Colonel Douglas Kennedy (Air Force Academy), Lieutenant Commander Jourdan Travis Moger (Naval Academy), and Dr. Peter Maslowski (University of Nebraska–Lincoln) for so graciously investing their time to provide detailed, thoughtful, comprehensive responses while identifying candidates for consideration.

As with the initial volume, there was nothing approaching a unanimous recommendation for any leader in any war. That outcome is altogether to be expected considering the different experiences, interests, and areas of expertise brought to the project by historians who contributed to it. It also accurately reflects the breadth of opinions regarding a most subjective, and at times highly controversial, issue.

Ultimately, though, the choices were mine alone.

This book tells the stories of more than 20 individuals and chronicles their activities through conflicts spanning almost five decades. Space limitations in a work of this scope preclude the listing of a bibliography in the traditional sense. I have instead compiled individual bibliographical lists, each focusing on a specific leader. These condensed lists may also serve as recommended readings for those interested in adding to their understanding of the individuals who led forces during these extraordinary periods in our nation's history.

Similarly, traditional footnoting would have required the numbering of every third or fourth sentence and added scores of pages to the text. Therefore—as have Robert Leckie (*The Wars of America*) and others who have written in this genre—in the interests of space and readability, I have confined reference notes to directly quoted material. In those instances where different opinions exist regarding facts or numbers, the contending views are noted in the text.

This volume covers forgotten leaders from the four major conflicts the United States engaged in from the end of the 19th century through the middle years of the 20th. A third and final volume will take us from the onset of the Cold War to the present day.

As with my previous books, I am again indebted to Jeanne Kern for her superb editing, friendship, and wise counsel.

CHAPTER 1
THE SPANISH–AMERICAN WAR

THE ROAD TO WAR

In a letter to his friend Theodore Roosevelt, John Hay, America's ambassador to Great Britain, called it a "splendid little war." To Hay and others who shared his view that the war with Spain was an affirmation of America's growing role in the world, "splendid" was perhaps an apt characterization. Others saw it differently. Although public sentiment was generally supportive, the conflict was not universally popular. Some Americans, such as Mark Twain, regarded it as a shameful exercise in imperialism. Military observers were discouraged by the army's abysmal preparations and by the confusion that attended almost every major movement of forces.

Cuba, 90 miles from American shores, had long been of special interest to the United States. Two attempts, one by President James K. Polk in 1848 and a second by President Franklin Pierce in 1854, had been made to purchase the island from Spain. Both were declined by Spanish governments that regarded Cuba as a valued outpost, an extension of Spain and Spanish culture. To most inhabitants, though, the island was a restless, unhappy place. Multiple rebellions had broken out over the years: 1868, 1879, 1883, 1892, and 1895. All had withered away or been crushed by Spanish authorities. Massive population resettlements—*reconcentrados*—to thwart guerrilla activity had resulted in economic hardships and thousands of deaths. Slavery had only been abolished in 1888. While many strains fed the eventual American decision to intervene, sympathy and humanitarian considerations were prominent among them.

Unquestionably, there were other factors as well. An influential faction viewed a prospective conflict as an occasion to extend America's reach around the globe—even, perhaps, to begin constructing an American empire. Some in the business community envisioned economic advantages from a war. Others professed to see an opportunity for reconciliation, a chance to heal national wounds still remaining from the Civil War. Indeed, when war came, one of the senior commanders would be Major General Joseph Wheeler, formerly a general officer in the Confederate army.

Historians continue to debate the effect of "yellow journalism," particularly as practiced by William Randolph Hearst's *New York Journal*, on America's decision to enter the war. Hearst allegedly instructed a *Journal* staffer, "You supply the pictures, I'll supply the war." Whatever its impact among a multitude of other colliding pressures, the *Journal*'s almost daily recitations of atrocities, starvation, and disease—often exaggerated and at times totally fabricated—kept Cuba at the forefront of American awareness.

As the situation between Spain and the United States grew increasingly strained, two events brought the smoldering relationship to the flash point. The first was a letter written by Enrique Dupuy de Lôme, Spain's ambassador to Washington. Sent to the editor of a Madrid newspaper who was visiting Havana, the letter was stolen by a member of the Cuban revolutionary junta. Leaked to the American press, de Lôme's letter expressed contempt for President William McKinley and inferred that Spain's outward attempt at conciliation in Cuba was a sham.

The second event, on February 15, 1898, was an explosion aboard the USS *Maine* in Havana harbor. The *Maine* had been sent to Havana in January, ostensibly to protect American citizens and property. The loss of the ship and 270 members of the crew under ambiguous circumstances provoked an immediate outcry. Spain proposed a joint investigation of the incident. The U.S. Navy, however, decided on a three-officer court of inquiry. The court concluded that because of the way the *Maine*'s keel was bent into an inverted V, the explosion had occurred external to the ship, caused by an undersea mine. Seventy-five years later, a formal investigation by the navy (led by Admiral Hyman Rickover) determined that a coal fire on the *Maine*, followed by an internal explosion, had most likely caused the loss of the ship.

Driven by de Lôme's letter and the destruction of the *Maine*, public sentiment and political pressure pushed McKinley, a reluctant warrior, toward war. A month after the *Maine* incident, he obtained a joint resolution from Congress, declaring Cuba independent and demanding the withdrawal of Spanish forces. A later amendment disavowed any

The sinking of the battleship Maine *in Havana harbor in the evening of February 15, 1898, led to a U.S. declaration of war against Spain. Though the circumstances surrounding the incident remain murky, prowar advocates used the event to shape public and political opinion in favor of military action.*

U.S. intention to permanently occupy the island. Blockades of Cuba's northern coast and the port of Santiago followed. Rather than concede to the American ultimatum, Spain declared war on the United States on the 24th of April. The U.S. declaration, made retroactive to the date of the joint resolution, came the next day.

LEONARD WOOD

Commander of the U.S. First Volunteer Cavalry, the "Rough Riders," Wood was of the few notable American combat leaders during the Spanish-American War. Later, as military governor of Cuba, he led successful efforts to combat Yellow Fever.

Properly memorializing the scope of Leonard Wood's accomplishments would require the invention of a separate, distinct category of leadership. Wood's achievements were unique, transcending strictly military matters and combat leadership. Spanning decades, his military service took him from chasing Geronimo's Apaches to preparing America's armies for World War I.

Wood's life was an extraordinary mixture of professional disciplines and exceptional responsibilities. A Harvard-trained medical doctor, he was the White House physician to Presidents Grover Cleveland and William McKinley. He was a recipient of the Medal of Honor for his service during the army's final campaign against Geronimo. In the Spanish-American War, Wood organized, trained, and successfully led in battle the 1st Volunteer Cavalry Regiment (popularly known as the Rough Riders). His later achievements as military governor of Cuba brought him international fame. Success there was soon followed by similar duties in the Philippines. He later served as chief of staff of the U.S. Army. In 1920, he was nearly nominated as a candidate for the office of president of the United States.

During the fighting in Cuba, Wood emerged as one of the few notable American combat leaders. The senior American commander, Major General William Shafter—chosen primarily for his lack of political ambitions—was obese, gout-ridden, and incapable by inclination and infirmity of exercising close leadership over his forces. Major General Joseph Wheeler, a feisty former Confederate general, was periodically ill during the campaign, as was Brigadier General Samuel Young, whom Wood was called upon to replace before a key battle. Another senior leader was alleged by some contemporaries to have had a drinking problem.

In that milieu, Wood's achievements shone brightly indeed. The administrative and organizational abilities that later made Wood famous were first in evidence even before American forces set foot on Cuban soil. Wood carefully screened and selected the thousand-man cadre that would eventually become known as the Rough Riders. The training regimen that he and his deputy, Theodore Roosevelt, instilled at the Rough Riders' encampment near San Antonio, Texas, made the unit one of the most effective of the hastily thrown-together volunteer units. In comparison to the leadership of much of the deployed force, Wood's foresight and planning, combined with the aggressive manipulation of the army bureaucracy that would characterize the remainder of his career, admirably prepared the Rough Riders for the forthcoming campaign.

Wood went directly to the chief of ordnance to secure modern Krag-Jørgensen smokeless rifles for the regiment. Sabers were not available, so Wood procured machetes to chop through the jungle growth. Whereas most of the American forces went to Cuba wearing blue wool uniforms, Wood, realizing the discomfort heavy apparel would pose in the tropics, bought lightweight brown canvas clothing for his troops.

In the mass confusion that surrounded the embarkations at Tampa—it was left to each commander to clothe, train, and transport his troops to Florida—Wood's efforts made the Rough Riders a model of order and discipline. The regiment's tent city was neat, well constructed, and thoroughly organized. Within a day, Wood policed the area, laid out streets, and began drilling his men. Field kitchens were quickly available. Sanitation, a quality generally lacking in the neophyte units but a focus of Wood's throughout his days in the army, was exemplary.

Wood's professionalism—one colleague called him a "dynamo of organization"—was clearly an exception. Few things about the coming invasion, including ship assignments and loading arrangements, had been thought through. Wood commandeered an empty freight train to carry the unit to the port area. Then, when it appeared that in the catch-as-catch-can atmosphere a ship might not be available to carry the Rough Riders, Wood personally rowed out to a vessel in the harbor and confiscated it for the regiment while his troops held space at the dock.

Amid scenes of general confusion, the American units, many of them separated from their provisions, made an unopposed landing at Daiquirí on June 22, 1898. Fourteen miles to the west, over a rutted, often muddy track sometimes not much more than a path, lay Santiago de Cuba, the invading force's initial major objective. America's first great overseas expedition was under way.

In furnace-like temperatures, tormented by late-day downpours, the American force pushed slowly inland. The plan called for Brigadier General S. B. M. Young to take a contingent of regular troops and Cuban insurgents along the trail that constituted the area's major road. Meanwhile, Wood and the Rough Riders would move generally parallel

U.S. forces disembark at Daiquirí, Cuba, in June 1898.

along a jungle path higher up on a ridgeline. The two forces would come together a few miles west. There, at a pass known as Las Guásimas, a force of about 1,500 Spanish regulars waited, dug in along a defensive line that shielded the passage. Las Guásimas was a key position: Spanish possession of it would prevent an attack on Santiago and bottle up the Americans on a pestilential strip of land vulnerable at all times to malaria and soon, with the full advent of the rainy season, to yellow fever. Wood's 574 Rough Riders would attack along the right flank while Young's larger contingent would strike from the left.

As the Americans approached the pass, the leading units ran into an ambush and immediately started taking casualties. Wood's coolness under fire—his men called him "Old Icebox"—became quickly evident. He and Roosevelt remained exposed to shots from the Spanish soldiers' Mauser rifles throughout the fight. Wood calmly gave orders, directing Roosevelt to take a squad into the bush to the right of the American advance and clear the Spanish sharpshooters. Soon after, he repositioned the Rough Riders to higher ground and a generally open area shielded by timber along the left side of the battle zone. From there, he intended to sweep the Spanish towards Young's approaching force. As the fighting progressed, Wood's troops were joined by other American units moving up along the main road.

The difficult fight lasted for an hour and a half before the Spanish began breaking ranks as a force of a thousand Americans pushed up the hillsides. Although a few observers conjectured that the Spanish commander's plan was to make a fighting withdrawal, Las Guásimas was an important milestone for the inexperienced, hastily formed American volunteer force. In the war's first significant land combat, they had made a successful, disciplined attack against a well-entrenched force and captured important ground. At a cost to the Rough Riders of 8 killed and 34 wounded (out of a total American loss of 16 killed and 52 wounded), Las Guásimas was in American hands. The road to Santiago was open to further advance.

A day after the battle at Las Guásimas, General Young was stricken with fever. Wood replaced him as commander of the force's entire dismounted cavalry and subsequently, with near lightning speed, was promoted to general of volunteers. What lay next before them would make the Rough Riders immortal. The area collectively known as San Juan Heights consisted of San Juan Hill and a smaller elevation named Kettle Hill by the Americans. Running north to south, at its closest point the heights were not much more than a mile from Santiago.

As the Americans prepared for battle on July 1, 1898, the most prominent defensive positions visible to them were large blockhouses atop San Juan Hill. Other Spanish fortifications were well hidden, though not all were ideally placed to observe and bring attacking forces under fire as they approached the heights. Coming up the slopes, however, the Americans would remain visible and exposed to Spanish shells.

The Spanish defenses shielding Santiago were more extensive than General Shafter had anticipated. Four thousand yards of trench lines, some three deep, ringed approaches to the city. Behind of a series of breastworks, General Arsenio Linares, the Spanish commander, had placed row after row of barbed wire around and between the stone blockhouses visible to the American troops as they moved up the ridges.

SANTIAGO, CUBA AREA
July 1–16, 1898

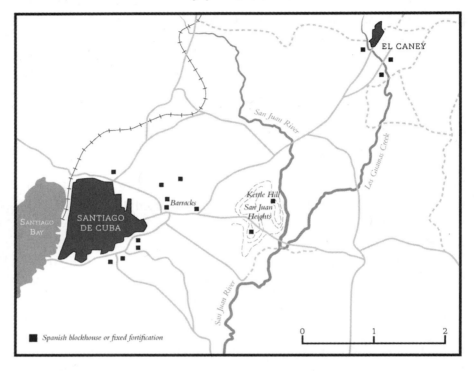

1 JULY
U.S. Forces begin Santiago Campaign. Rough Riders advance east to west across Kettle Hill. El Caney, Kettle Hill, and San Juan Heights taken by Americans. Spanish fall back to inner defenses which are then closely invested by U.S. units.

3 JULY
Spanish fleet attempting to escape from Santiago Bay is destroyed by American naval forces under the overall command of Admiral William T. Sampson.

16 JULY
Santiago surrenders. U.S. forces enter city the following day.

North of the heights, blockhouses anchored a fort near the village of El Caney. Kettle Hill stood on the northern edge of San Juan Heights on key terrain overlooking the site where two tracks of the main road emerged from the jungle. Linares knew that the Americans would have to use those dual paths to sustain an attack on Santiago. Spanish weapons atop Kettle Hill were trained on the spot where

American units would appear as they moved out of the jungle onto open ground.

General Shafter's intention was to attack San Juan Heights with two divisions while sending a third division under General Henry Lawton to eliminate the strongpoint at El Caney. Opposition at El Caney was expected to be overcome within two hours. Lawton's troops would then turn south and join the rest of the U.S. force in a combined attack on the heights.

The American assault units began taking losses, several unit commanders among them, as they moved to positions near the ridges. Casualties continued to mount as the force halted at the base of the elevations awaiting further orders. The area at the bottom of the hill became known as "Hell's Pocket" as the American units waited under fire for Lawton's division to arrive from El Caney.

The plan called for Wood's contingent to remain in reserve and then join with Lawton's troops as they moved back south after securing the fort at El Caney. Lawton, however, was in trouble. After hours of difficult fighting, the Spanish still held control of the stronghold.

As the American units waited under fire at the bottom of San Juan and Kettle Hills, repeated requests from Wood and others asking permission to attack were met with directions to hold position. Eventually, with his entire force under fire and his potential line of retreat exposed to Spanish artillery, Wood felt his only choice was to move in a direct assault against the Spanish positions ahead of him on Kettle Hill.

Slowed at times by heat exhaustion and withering fire, Wood's lines pushed steadily upward. Occasionally, units became mixed together as they moved, fired, sought cover, and moved again. Aided by supporting rounds from Gatling guns that swept the Spanish trenches, the Americans pushed ahead, breaking into an all-out charge about 150 yards from the crest of the hill. Near the trench lines brief episodes of hand-to-hand combat erupted before the Spanish retreated.

At about the same time Wood began his move, American commanders on San Juan Hill made similar decisions to advance. As on Kettle Hill, the Americans waiting under fire at the base of San Juan Hill started to move up the slope. The initiatives in both places were in large measure spontaneous, made without the direct orders, or with ambiguous directions at best, from General Shafter and his division commanders Brigadier General James F. Kent and Major General Joseph Wheeler.

The American attacks on the two hills occurred almost in tandem. Both were carried out by troops advancing steadily up the slopes in the face of heavy fire. Kettle Hill fell first, taken by Wood and his force of dismounted cavalry at about 1:30 in the afternoon. Wood's situation remained unsettled, however, as the Americans found themselves exposed to fire from the west and vulnerable to counterattacks from three sides. Wood called for reinforcements. Told there were none—they had been sent to El Caney to help Lawton—Wood moved a Gatling gun to the top of the hill and dug in. Still in precarious straits from Spanish fire from higher ground to the left on San Juan Hill, Wood determined that another charge would be necessary to clear the right end of San Juan ridge and help General Kent's troops gain control of the heights.

Moving across a saddleback terrain feature that connected the two hills, Wood's dismounted cavalry, "Buffalo Soldiers"—African-American troopers who gained fame during the Indian Wars of the American West—of the 10th Cavalry and the Rough Riders among them, struck the flank of San Juan Hill and with Kent's forces began pushing towards the crest. Aided by supporting fire from the small contingent of Gatling guns, the Americans finally reached the summit. At about two o'clock, Spanish troops were cleared from the trenches, the blockhouses were overrun, and the Spanish flag was pulled from the flagstaff.

The position on the ridge remained precarious through the remainder of the day, exposed to fire and counterattacks by Spanish units in Santiago. A weak Spanish attempt to retake the hill came fairly soon after but was quickly broken up by American units now entrenched near the summit.

Later in the afternoon, a force of six hundred Spanish infantry launched a stronger attack against Kettle Hill. Devastating fire from Gatling guns and American sharpshooters tore apart the Spanish assault, throwing it back with heavy losses. Anticipating further attacks, the U.S. forces worked through the night to strengthen lines and build breastworks. For reasons unknown, the Spanish commander chose not to counterattack with the full strength of his garrison quartered nearby in Santiago city.

A widely reported anecdote from an incident during the fight further enhanced Wood's reputation among his troops. When a young officer was struck in the leg by rifle fire, Wood noted that the wound had been less than expertly dressed by the attending medic. Wood reverted to his medical training and in the middle of the battle used his own medical kit to properly clean and bandage the wound.

The Americans' success on July 1 enabled them to place Santiago under siege, though General Shafter, stunned by the extent of American losses, at first wavered in his convictions. Two days later the U.S. Navy's victory over the Spanish fleet in the waters near Santiago sealed the fate of the Spanish garrison. On July 17, the Spanish surrendered the city.

Although months of negotiations followed, the Spanish surrender of Santiago effectively ended hostilities in Cuba. With the French acting as intermediary, the Spanish government requested a cease-fire the following day. All Spanish forces were off the island by January 1, 1899. The Treaty of Paris, officially ending the war and defining the international status of Cuba, Puerto Rico, Guam, and the Philippine Islands, was signed on April 11, 1899.

On July 20, 1898, three days after the Spanish surrendered the city, Wood received orders to serve as military governor of Santiago. Subsequently, those duties would be expanded to cover all of Cuba. It was a role that would bring him worldwide renown. While it is unusual to single out a senior officer for primarily administrative accomplishments, more than one hundred years later Wood's achievements as military governor continue to defy comparison.

When General Shafter met with Wood to appoint him military governor of Santiago, Shafter told him that he was to maintain order, feed the poor, and reestablish industry. Wood found himself the absolute ruler of a dirty, pestilential city inhabited by 40,000 hungry people, a least a third of whom suffered from some form of fever. Nearly 20,000 emaciated refugees from fighting in nearby areas also crowded the town, as did 4,000 Spanish soldiers captured during the war, many of whom were also fever-stricken.

Wood began immediately, pardoning Cuban prisoners who had been held by Spanish authorities under dubious circumstances, meeting with

Cuban leaders, and punishing misbehavior and infractions of rules. It was a pattern Wood would follow: he ruled with an open, but iron, hand.

Wood set about cleaning up a city notable for its general squalor, finding it in places knee-deep in garbage and excrement. Realizing that commerce could never thrive under those conditions and that the filth contributed to the diseases that wracked the population, Wood divided the city into districts, each with assigned medical and sanitation officers. Disregarding social status, Wood formed hundred-man work crews on which Cuban and Spanish grandees found themselves working side by side with the desperately poor. The latter were given food in return for labor; the rich were drafted. Wood confiscated every wheeled vehicle and draught animal in the city and used them to haul garbage.

At first, bodies—human and well as animal—littered the streets. When local cemeteries could not cope with the numbers, Wood established crematories. When the kerosene necessary to burn the bodies ran short, local businesses attempted to raise the price. Wood called the merchants into his office, berated them at length, and reset the price to the original level.

Wood's sanitation crews visited every home and courtyard in the city and ordered owners to move the piles of manure and garbage into the street where the refuse could be picked up. Every privy in the city was inspected. Those beyond repair were removed; all others were cleaned.

The city's 1830s water system was inadequate for the tasks at hand. Lacking sufficient water, Wood had contaminated surfaces scraped clean and scrubbed with abrasives or lime. Cesspools were emptied bucket by bucket. Sometimes working crews up to 16 hours a day, a month after Wood was appointed military governor, every house in Santiago had been sanitized.

Streets, water, and food supplies came next. Wood paved the city's formerly dirt streets, shaped them for drainage, and installed gutters. Weeks were spent repairing or rebuilding the ancient water system. Until the work was finished, water was rationed section by section in amounts sufficient to assure survival.

Grocery stores, markets, and butcher shops were inspected, then either cleaned or closed. The food situation in and around the city remained desperate, however. In an attempt to quell the insurrection, the Spanish had resettled much of the rural population into concentration camps. Fields had been neglected and farm buildings destroyed by both sides during the fighting. Left unattended, large swaths of agricultural land were rather quickly reverting to jungle.

Wood confiscated food stockpiled by the Spanish authorities to stave off disaster, passing it to hospitals, churches, prisons, and directly to private citizens at ration stations. Within a month, he had distributed 935,000 meals (50,000 a day on peak days) secured from requisitioned supplies as well as from private donors.

Wood used food to control and rehabilitate the city. Only those who worked received food rations. Those who helped clean Santiago were given food for a day and a small stipend or rations in an amount tied to the number of hours they worked. Food distribution proceeded so efficiently that the Red Cross shifted its efforts elsewhere on the island.

Having averted catastrophe, Wood focused next on making the Santiago area self-sufficient. Many of the missing workers had fought with the insurgent forces against the Spanish. They needed to be found, returned to their families, and provided supplies and food until farms could be restored and crops began coming in. To help make that happen, Wood paid the returning *insurrectos* to help clean the city, anticipating that they would use the cash to rebuild their farms. He then positioned food depots in rural areas so farmers would not need to journey to the city for supplies. Wood rotated farmers through about two thousand paid jobs, stabilizing three times that number of families financially while putting them in a position to grow the crops that would feed the city. By January 1899, produce and livestock were flowing from the reestablished farms to Santiago markets. Concurrently, the amount of distributed rations needed to feed the city was reduced by three-fifths.

With Wood increasingly in command, one of the few remaining prospective threats to American authority came from a group of nearly 25,000 armed *insurrectos* still roaming the countryside around Santiago. Wood got large numbers of them to trade their weapons for food and sent them back to their farms. Others who did not wish to become farmers were trained as policemen in a newly formed Rural Guard.

Those who refused to farm or do police work and declined to turn in their weapons were declared bandits, hunted down, and shot.

Accolades and recognition for Wood's accomplishments began to capture the public's attention. By fall, Santiago, whilst not prosperous, was generally self-supporting. Wood apportioned a sizable amount of Santiago's tax revenues for sanitation, transforming the place from one of the world's most squalid cities into one of its cleanest. The death rate from various epidemics dropped from 100 a day to 30 or 40 per week. Despite the many demands on the city's treasury, Wood actually achieved a budget surplus through efficiencies and scrupulous honesty in administering taxes and tariffs.

When Major General Henry W. Lawton, military governor for the entire Santiago province, was recalled to the United States, Wood inherited his responsibilities as well. He found conditions throughout the region to be as bad as or worse than those he had faced in Santiago city. A fourth of Guantánamo's population had starved. The city of Holquín alone had three thousand active smallpox cases. Wood divided the province into sectors and started feeding programs. American doctors vaccinated the entire population. Smallpox was controlled within a few weeks. As in Santiago, healthy citizens were put to work cleaning the cities and burning decades-old accumulations of garbage. By early the following year, houses had been cleaned and shops were open for business.

Although Wood doubted the Cuban people's ability to fully govern themselves if given independence, he began organizing municipal administrations. Wood or one of his staff officers appointed all officials based on lists submitted by local elites. All decisions were initially subject to American authorities. Conversely, Wood gave the people of Cuba an unprecedented degree of personal freedom, publishing a list of universal rights based on the U.S. Constitution's Bill of Rights.

In winning Cuban trust, Wood complemented his own absolute authority with grants of personal liberty and his own transparent honesty. In Cuba—unlike his later experience in the Philippines—he visited extensively, touching all parts of the province, counting on his personal presence to secure support for his goals.

Wood inherited a judicial system that was corrupt and inefficient. Cases were backlogged for years. Those accused of crimes were held in atrocious conditions. Wood replaced every judge in the provincial court system and reformed the judicial process, operating the courts at half the costs of those sustained in the Spanish colonial system. Justice became quick and fair but remained harsh. Cattle theft and similar crimes were rampant. Wood had Cuban police shoot on sight anyone caught stealing or resisting arrest.

Wood's several months' stretch of operating a benevolent autocracy with almost complete freedom of action officially ended on January 1, 1899. Although several senior officers aspired to be named military governor of the island, the position went to Civil War veteran Major General J. R. Brooke, an ultraconservative martinet appointed solely on the basis of seniority.

Many officials in Washington, Teddy Roosevelt and Senator Henry Cabot Lodge among them, expressed concern that Brooke's appointment might jeopardize progress then being made on the island. Typically, Wood was not shy about writing directly to President McKinley, the secretary of the army, and other officials expressing his views about how the place ought to be administered.

The change made Wood subordinate to Brooke. Brooke's tenure brought a year-long period of restlessness and frustration for Wood, that fueled frequent, acrid exchanges of correspondence between the two generals and their staffs. Charges and countercharges about the use of public funds and administrative matters were hurled back and forth. For a time, Wood considered leaving the army for a position in private industry.

In the meantime, his Washington friends, Roosevelt foremost among them, lobbied on his behalf, seeking his appointment as governor. Wood's wife, the ward of a Supreme Court justice, buttonholed officials from the president on down, making Wood's case to be named to the position when Brooke departed. All the while Wood continued to pull strings, writing with such frequency that McKinley, among others, became agitated.

Nonetheless, likely through a combination of circumstances, in December 1899, Wood was named governor-general of Cuba. The appointment was greeted with general enthusiasm throughout the island.

Wood, then 39 years old, remarkably young for a general at the time, was in essence the absolute ruler of Cuba and its million and a half citizens. Aside from Santiago, the rest of the country faced enormous challenges. The long insurgency against Spain and the resettlement policy that accompanied it had killed a fifth of the population. Farms were burned out. As much as a third of the island's agricultural land lay fallow. Eighty percent of the cattle were gone. Tobacco and sugar production was only a fraction of previous years. The coffee industry was essentially destroyed. More recently, the American naval blockade had left portions of the island's population near starvation, a condition from which it was only now recovering.

Wood's task was not made easier by the animosity from Brooke's remaining staff, who believed Wood had engineered Brooke's removal. Other veteran officers and civil servants with far more years of service were openly jealous that a young former physician—and until recently an officer of volunteers—had been promoted over them. Wood's personality did little to win them over.

As always, Wood forged straight ahead. On his first day in Havana, he secured the resignation of the intensely unpopular Cuban civilian cabinet that had been appointed by Brooke. His legendary capacity for work was now in daily evidence. His day typically began at 5:00 a.m. and ended around midnight, consumed with meetings, speeches, visits, and paperwork.

Despite periodic problems with backbiting from some of his inherited staff, Wood, as in Santiago, plowed forward with a series of necessary reforms. He began by consolidating segments of the Cuban government, a task that took about two months. He made reform of the island's penal system and its horrific prisons a priority, summarily firing the Cuban administrators responsible, including the attorney general. Wood ordered that untried prisoners be brought immediately to trial or freed. Time remaining on adjudicated sentences were posted so prisoners would know their dates of release. Women and children were separated from the general prison population, and minimum standards of sanitation were introduced. Wood went so far as to establish schools to train court reporters. He put all officers of the court on salary, replacing a floating scale of fees previously paid by litigants.

Reforms in other areas followed. He funded, built, and staffed an insane asylum of impressive quality for the time. He constructed temporary hospitals throughout Cuba, using American military surgeons to supplement Cuban medical staffs.

Wood turned his formidable energy to education reform as well. When American forces landed in Cuba there was not a single building devoted exclusively to primary education. Wood invested heavily in education, spending nearly a quarter of the government's operating budget on classrooms, teacher training, and teacher compensation. Wood paid teachers at salary levels exceeded by only three districts in the United States and spent considerably more per student than the American average. Under the Spanish, fewer than 21,000 Cuban youngsters were enrolled in school. Through Wood's oversight, enrollment peaked at 256,000.

Higher-level education benefited similarly. The once-proud University of Havana had more than 100 faculty members, but most neither worked nor contributed to educating the institution's tiny student body. One department had 15 professors but only seven students. Wood directed that the entire faculty be fired. He quickly rehired the 25 most productive performers, consolidated departments, installed a new curriculum, and conducted competitive exams to fill sufficient positions to bring the total faculty size to 70. Money saved from chopping more than 30 faculty salaries enabled tuition rates to be lowered. Enrollment increased by more than 600 the following academic year. In the meantime, he built science laboratories and opened a medical school.

Concurrently, though, he had created a powerful and implacable enemy. Soon after becoming governor, Wood began hearing rumors of fraud in the Cuban postal department. Allegedly officials were paying personal bills out of government funds. Internal postal audits were strangely incomplete. Although post office operations were outside of Wood's direct authority, he ordered that department, and all others in the Cuban government, to undergo a comprehensive, independent audit.

Running postal operations in Cuba was an influential American named Estes Rathbone. Rathbone, in turn, was a protégée of Senator Mark Hanna, the "King Maker," who had gotten William McKinley elected president of the United States. Wood tried to be circumspect in his investigation, but the facts were irrefutable: postal accounts were at least $100,000 short, and Rathbone was using a considerable portion of the Havana post office's monthly budget for personal purposes. The postal department never complied with Wood's request for an internal audit, as the auditor—who had been diverting $500 a week to a personal account—had fled Cuba, taking his records with him. Hearing that Rathbone intended to flee also, Wood had him arrested.

Coming as they did in an election year, Wood's actions created a firestorm. While perpetrators were convicted and the American public was generally supportive, Wood's political enemies, joined by army critics and officials envious of his advancement, would be unforgiving.

Through the disturbance brought on by the postal crisis, Wood worked to shore up the Cuban economy, left in a shambles first by Spanish rule and then by Brooke's administration. Wood imported oxen and with spotty results provided public service jobs to farmers, eliminated several agriculture-related taxes, cut import duties on farm equipment, and assigned Rural Guardsmen to protect cane fields from exploitation by arsonists.

Believing that literacy, among other conditions, should be a prerequisite for voters, Wood favored a limited form of suffrage that would likely assure a more conservative electorate. Secretary Root, however, insisted on broader voting rights that resulted in electoral outcomes Wood was sometimes less than comfortable with. Nonetheless, after four hundred years of subjugation, Cubans voted for the first time. Starting from scratch with no election machinery and an entirely inexperienced electorate. Wood had brought it off within a period of months.

A massive outbreak of yellow fever struck Cuba in the summer of 1900. Despite strenuous efforts to clean, scrub, and sanitize, the disease swept through the populace, striking down American servicemen and members of Wood's staff. For a time, a nasty dispute erupted between Wood and General James Ludlow, the previous governor of the Havana region. Fought in newspaper articles and official correspondence, the quarrel was over reported data and the extent of responsibility for the outbreak. Many observers believed that Wood tried to shift the burden of responsibility toward Ludlow.

Nonetheless, the outbreak led to a breakthrough in modern medicine and a personal triumph for Wood. In June 1900, a commission led by army physician Major Walter Reed examined several potential causes for the disease before eventually testing the notion that it was spread by a type of mosquito. Confirmation would require experiments on humans. Tests on team members appeared to validate the hypothesis, but proving it would require more extensive trials. Reed went to the army's surgeon general for help. The surgeon general went to Wood. Wood agreed immediately, allocating funds to the effort although realizing the tests, though well designed, would likely provoke a public outcry.

For test subjects, Wood decided to draw primarily on recent immigrants from Spain, reasoning that the new arrivals would not have been previously exposed to the fever and would likely be receptive to the generous amount of money being offered. There would also be less public reaction in the event of their deaths than there would be if American soldiers or Cuban citizens died whilst taking part. Wood first got approval from the Spanish consul, Madrid's senior representative in Cuba, who agreed to let the immigrants participate so long as they volunteered, were at least 24 years old, and were suitably paid. Indeed, the payment was sufficiently high that American soldiers also asked to be allowed to participate.

By late fall, Reed's team had definitively proved that yellow fever was spread by mosquitoes. The results were irrefutable, but Wood, along with Reed, was subjected to withering criticism in the press.

From his earliest days on the island, Wood had made eradication of the disease a major goal. He immediately began to wage war on its carriers. Screens were installed on barrack windows and doors, standing water was drained, water barrels were shielded or sanitized, and buildings were fumigated. The effort began on military installations, then spread to the civilian population. Homeowners who violated the "mosquito regulations" were fined. (The fines were remitted when the infractions were corrected.) By fall of the following year—1901—yellow fever had essentially ceased to exist in Havana and, as it disappeared, malaria vanished with it. By 1902, the death rate from yellow fever among American soldiers in Cuba was lower than at any post anywhere in the world. Ironically, it was only a third of that of soldiers stationed in the United States. Wood regarded the benefit to the world from the conquest of yellow fever as having been "worth the cost of the war."

Meanwhile, Wood's ongoing efforts to streamline the Cuban government had achieved a surplus in the treasury while funding courts, hospitals, schools, and paying municipal debts from previous years. Wood's structuring of government operations was accompanied by a steady accretion of power and authority. Appeals regarding his executive actions and administrative decrees were prohibited.

When the United States declared war on Spain, the Teller Amendment had disavowed American intentions to retain control of Cuba, promising that governance of the island would be passed to the Cuban people. Now with the war in the past, sentiment in Congress began to shift toward ending the occupation and transferring power to Cuban authorities.

Wood had grave misgivings, believing that the occupation should be prolonged, otherwise the risk was that more unstable, revolutionary factions might gain control. Wood's uncertainty regarding full self-government was shared by several influential Congressional leaders. Oregon Senator Orville H. Pratt introduced an amendment to the 1901 Army Appropriation Act that restricted Cuban sovereignty and allowed the United States to intervene to protect Cuban independence. A treaty with Platt Amendment provisions came into effect in May, 1903.

Despite his personal feelings, during his last months in Havana, much of his time and energy were expended in putting a foundation for elections in place and admittedly, when his schedule allowed, striving to shape the outcome. Wood never wavered in his belief that control by an educated, efficient conservative elite would better serve the interests of both Cuba and the United States.

Although preparing for elections and transfer of power consumed large portions of his work days, Wood found time to deal with two issues involving the Catholic Church. To the apparent satisfaction of all parties, he decided that both civil and church weddings would be regarded as legal, and he resolved a thorny problem regarding church real estate and payment for use of church property. Moreover, with Secretary Root's assistance, when the island was opened to railroad construction,

Wood established an organization similar to the Interstate Commerce Commission to regulate rates and charges.

Still, the looming presence of the Teller Amendment overshadowed other business. Though Wood had been surprised by the extent of nationalist victories in recent municipal elections, the process had gone off without major problems. Wood and Root were in agreement that a constitutional convention should be the next step. They disagreed, however, on its nature and provisions. Wood continued to believe that the United States should remain in control, initially pressing for a document that would retain the American governor's absolute veto power. Wood spent considerable time on the road advocating his beliefs to Cuban audiences but eventually failed in his attempt to apportion the delegates in a way that would provide a greater voice to the Cuban intelligentsia.

His travels across the island had persuaded him that the constitution should stand alone and not be weighed down, as some U.S. officials insisted, with clauses involving Cuban-U.S. relations. At issue was the Platt Amendment, an act that superseded the Teller Amendment. Passed in 1901, the amendment effectively limited Cuban sovereignty, providing that some decisions of the Cuban government could be overruled by the United States. Wood believed that the Platt provisions should be addressed separately in a format distinct from the national constitution.

Root overruled Wood on the major issues involving the Cuban constitution. Regarding the governor's role, Root believed Cuban independence meant Cuban administration and, more so than Wood, saw both happening in the near term. Wood, however, was probably more correct in his view that provisions of the Platt Amendment should be left out of the constitutional document. Root, guided by his personal convictions and influenced by domestic political considerations, insisted that the Platt clauses should be part of it. Including them made passage more difficult. When the document was initially rejected, Wood had to forcefully intervene to overcome opposition and secure a favorable vote. Finally passed by reluctant delegates, the amendment all but assured U.S. intervention in Cuban affairs—a condition that would continue into the 1930s.

For much of his time in Cuba, Wood was confronted professionally not only by daunting administrative challenges but also by uncertainty regarding his military status. Technically, Wood began his tenure in Cuba as a brigadier general in the volunteer army. Looming as an uncomfortable backdrop was the possibility that when the volunteer army was disbanded, Wood's rank would revert to his regular army grade of captain—perhaps he would even be returned to the Medical Corps.

Wood wrote repeatedly to senior officials reminding them of his dilemma and requesting assistance. Once again, Wood's Washington supporters actively intervened on his behalf. Eventually President McKinley kept a promise to make him a brigadier general in the regular army.

While Wood's nomination to brigadier general was approved by the Senate, the action was not universally acclaimed. Some in Congress believed that Wood's limited time as a combat leader was insufficient to justify his advancement. Critics inside the army railed at this promotion, noting that it jumped him ahead of scores of more seasoned officers. With his relative youth and early date of rank, the promotion would almost assure that Wood would eventually become the army's senior officer.

Wood left Cuba in 1902 proud of the many accomplishments that had made him famous around the globe. His experience on the island had changed him, however. Scrupulously honest but notoriously thin-skinned, Wood bristled at challenges to his methods and decision making. As he was confronted by persistent questions concerning his iron-fisted leadership, carping from political opponents, and backbiting from within the army establishment, Wood's management style turned increasingly inward. Although his later administration in the Philippines would also be noted for its achievements, his governance there would be more closed and rigid, never again as transparent or inclusive as it had been during his earlier days in Cuba.

Before and After

Wood was born in Pocasset, Massachusetts, on October 9, 1860. After attending Pierce Academy, he entered Harvard Medical School, graduating with a degree in medicine in 1884.

The following year he took a position as a contract physician with the army and was later commissioned as an officer in the Medical Corps.

Wood's first posting was at Fort Huachuca, Arizona, where he served under Major General George Crook and Major General Nelson Miles and took part in the army's final campaign against Geronimo and his Chiricahua Apaches. He was later awarded a Medal of Honor for carrying dispatches 100 miles on a night trek through hostile territory and for taking command of an infantry company in the absence of other officers.

General Miles recommended Wood, a protégée, for the medal, which was awarded in 1898, 12 years after the action described in the citation. The somewhat thin justification provoked hard feelings from some fellow officers, particularly those who had served on arduous campaigns under Crook and Miles.

Assignments at Fort McDowell, near Phoenix, and the Presidio of Monterey, California, followed. Always in outstanding physical condition, at the Presidio Wood was placed in charge of physical training and at one point organized a race around the installation's 17-mile perimeter, which he won easily.

In August 1893, after four years in California, Wood was transferred to Fort McPherson near Atlanta. Bored by life at the post, he coached and played football for the Atlanta institution that later became Georgia Tech.

In 1895, after going over the head of his supervisor, Surgeon General George Sternberg, and permanently alienating him, Wood, with the assistance of highly placed friends, secured a transfer to the Surgeon General's staff in Washington, DC. Wood eventually met President Grover Cleveland at a social gathering. The two quickly became friends. Wood found himself attending White House functions, traveling with the president on leisure outings, and assisting with medical care for the first family.

In 1897, William McKinley was elected president. McKinley's wife, Ada, who as a young mother had lost two children, was a hypochondriac. She became somewhat dependent on Wood, calling on him frequently for care and consultation. That summer, Wood met Theodore Roosevelt, then assistant secretary of the navy. They were kindred spirits: adventurous, physically active, hard-charging personalities who shared a fascination with outdoor challenges, sports, and all things military. They soon became inseparable friends.

In 1898, with war looming on the horizon, Wood and Roosevelt, with influential supporters and Washington platforms, were well placed to raise the volunteer force that became the 1st Volunteer Cavalry Regiment—the Rough Riders. Soon after he arrived in Cuba, Wood received a field promotion to brigadier general of volunteers when the brigade commander, General Samuel B. M. Young, became ill. Aided by his stellar performance as combat commander and military governor, Wood's years-long attempts to transfer from his Medical Corps commission and become a line officer in the regular army eventually came to fruition. In 1901, before leaving Cuba, Wood was promoted to brigadier general in the regular army. Promotion to major general came two years later in the Philippines.

With his duties in Cuba completed, Wood went to Europe for an extended period to vacation, meet with military leaders in Britain, France, and Germany, and to observe maneuvers.

In the meantime, on the other side of the world, widespread violence had erupted in the Philippines. Acquired as a result of America's victory over Spain, the islands remained in turmoil in the unsettled aftermath. An abortive Filipino independence movement would soon be followed by a bloody Islamic extremist uprising, the Moro Rebellion. Theodore Roosevelt, now president, asked Wood to reprise his role as military governor. Wood agreed, serving first at the provincial level before taking command of the Philippine Division.

Chronicled in detail in the following "Philippine Insurrection" chapter, Wood's governorship in the Philippines took a different form than his administration in Cuba. While he continued to introduce reforms in education, infrastructure, and other areas, he placed less emphasis on nation building. More of his time and attention were devoted to military activities, a circumstance driven by disillusionment over criticism of his humanitarian efforts in Cuba, bitter opposition to his promotion, and, mostly, by the fact that the Moro uprising had transformed into a bloodbath.

Controversy, pitched at decibel levels even higher than those he faced in Cuba, followed Wood's aggressive, counterinsurgency campaigns in the Philippines. Although he had effectively shut down major outbursts by the time he left in February 1908, sporadic flare-ups continued until 1913.

After again meeting with French and German officials in Europe, Wood returned to Washington for a prolonged tour of duty. In June 1909, President William Howard Taft appointed him commanding general of the U.S. Army, a position he assumed in the summer of the following year. With tensions increasingly evident in Europe, Wood became on outspoken advocate for military preparedness. Alarmed that in the first decade of the 20th century the army of the United States consisted of only 25,000 regular troops ostensibly augmented by National Guard units whose caliber was generally abysmal, Wood pushed for training, modernization, and increased manpower.

In his Washington duties he worked equally hard at restructuring and reinvigorating a general staff establishment that was disorganized and demoralized. He replaced old divisions with a fewer number of new ones, forced decision making downwards, and in 1911, by the secretary of war's estimate, saved the army a quarter of a million dollars in useless paperwork alone.

Europe was not the only international trouble spot festering outside of American shores. Indeed, a problem was developing much closer to U.S. soil: violence from a revolution in Mexico was threatening to spill over the border. Efforts to consolidate forces into a Maneuver Division to more effectively patrol the border greatly frustrated Wood, who was plagued by a military base system scattered across the landscape in tiny, company-sized packets. Transportation and equipment were lacking. None of the commanders had experience in leading sizable numbers of troops. The crisis was eventually averted, but Wood and Secretary of War Henry Stimson immediately began working to rectify the deficiencies revealed by the mobilization effort.

Wood was perhaps the least doctrinaire of the army's leaders. Open to innovation and change, he possessed energy and a restless intellect that forced a sometimes reluctant institution to accept new equipment and policies. When flight tests convinced him that airplanes had enormous potential utility, he worked the army's budget to accommodate the purchase of 20 aircraft. A chemist showed Wood an intriguing new metal for which he saw application in high-velocity projectiles and as lining for cannon and rifle barrels. With Wood's encouragement, the General Electric Company donated the process for making tungsten steel alloys to the army.

To the chagrin of many senior officers, Wood directed the super-intendent of the United States Military Academy to begin instructing cadets to handle enlisted soldiers as intelligent human beings, insisting as well that academic courses be made available to enlisted men. Drawing on his experience in Cuba, where he had trained an effective force within six weeks, and based on his success in the Philippines as well, Wood believed that the eventual model—an educated force treated with respect—would better fit the American culture. He rammed through changes to a military justice system that he regarded as best constituted for creating demoralized convicts. Again acquiring a bloc of Washington enemies, Wood forced the retirements of politically connected, obstruc-tionist officers.

The election of Woodrow Wilson as president in 1912 posed a new set of challenges. At a time when Wood was urging military prepared-ness and a larger force, Wilson opposed both with a pacifist zeal. In personality as well as political beliefs, the two men were polar opposites. Wilson was a liberal Democrat; Wood was totally Republican. Wilson, an academician, was put off by his vocal, visible army chief.

Foiled by Wilson's reluctance to increase the size of the army and create a reserve force, Wood hit upon the idea of army-run summer training camps that interested college men might attend on a volunteer basis. Wood wrote to several schools and spoke at many others, describing the program. By 1914, the program's second year, 600 students attended four camps. By 1916, there would be 16,000 at 10 sites. All volunteers paid their own way. Wood knew he could not produce professional officers in four weeks, but he believed he could instill an interest in the military that might serve the country well later on. Wood's volunteer program served as the forerunner of the Reserve Officer Training Corps.

Wood's tour as chief of staff ended in April 1914, when he returned to duty with the Department of the East. While in that position, he persisted in his campaign for universal military training and conscription.

Friction between Wilson and Wood continued to build as yet another flare-up with Mexico—whose army at the time was larger than that of the United States—again revealed the country's military shortcomings. Wood's outspoken criticisms twice drew official censures.

Meanwhile, events in Europe and the sinking of the *Lusitania* nudged the United States closer to war. Wood's public speeches and congressional testimony castigating the nation's lack of preparation continued to frustrate the Wilson administration.

On April 2, 1917, the United States declared war on Germany. At the time, Wood was the army's ranking general and the only American officer with a significant national and international reputation. (Frederick Funston, a hero of the Philippine Insurrection, had died of a heart attack in February.) Many observers thought Wood was the logical choice to command America's army in Europe. Instead, the position went to John J. Pershing. Although older than Wood, Pershing was the most junior of the army's major generals. Wilson, likely tired of Wood's persistent criticism and wary of his political ambitions, wanted no part in providing a larger platform for him.

Seething, Wood soldiered on, waiting for a call from Pershing that never came. Wood was to spend most of the war training troops in Kansas.

In October 1917, a visit to France to observe preparations and determine training needs resulted in friction with Pershing. Precipitated initially by differing views on how the newly arriving American units should be integrated into battle, Wood later openly expressed his opposing thoughts on subjects as diverse as artillery training and the rate at which American units should flow to the front. As was often the case, whether the audience consisted of leaders of foreign governments, Allied general officers, or groups of American soldiers, Wood was unable, or disinclined, to control his tongue.

During the tour, Wood was wounded and several high-ranking observers were killed during a trench mortar demonstration conducted by the French. After the bleeding was stopped on the wound above his right elbow, Wood refused treatment until others were cared for and then walked a mile to the nearest aid station so vehicles would be available to transport others who were injured. Convalescing three weeks later at Pershing's chateau, Wood criticized his host at length during a dinner gala.

Pershing's retribution for Wood's lack of grace was not long in coming. Wood was ordered to return immediately to his training duties in Kansas, ending speculation that he might command an American division on the Italian front or attached to British forces.

Shortly afterwards, his closed-door congressional testimony critiquing American preparations was leaked to the press, further infuriating President Wilson. When it subsequently appeared that, despite all that had happened, Wood might still be given command of a division about to deploy to France, he was reassigned at the last moment while waiting to board ship in New York City. Back in Kansas, Wood unknowingly presided over the outbreak of the world's most lethal flu pandemic. After a week, with deaths at Camp Funston in the hundreds, the disease moved on, eventually killing as many as 20 million worldwide.

In November 1918, Wood's aspirations for combat duty ended when Germany agreed to an armistice based on Wilson's Fourteen Points. Presaging the Marshall Plan three decades later, Wood advocated spending millions to help restore Europe's industry and commerce. He was equally ahead of his time in anticipating problems that might arise when soldiers transitioned back to civilian life. He established a program with a nearby college that enabled soldiers to take academic and vocational courses to prepare for civilian employment. In addition, veterans received direct monetary or other assistance.

Wood's great friend Theodore Roosevelt died on January 19, 1919. Preparations were well advanced for Roosevelt to make another run for the presidency in the 1920 election. With considerable backing and Roosevelt's imprimatur as close friend and confidant, Wood was asked, and readily agreed, to assume TR's mantle.

At first, national events conspired to aid Wood's candidacy. It was an unsettled time, and Wood's astute use of the army to put down riots and strikes and restore order was generally applauded by the public.

Ultimately, though, his weaknesses as a candidate were revealed. He disregarded advice to speak little, shield himself behind military duties, and run on his reputation as a soldier and humanitarian. After internal squabbles, a less competent adviser came to the forefront of his campaign. Wood spoke often, sometimes as many as three or four times a day, usually while in uniform, an appearance that many regarded as unseemly. On the campaign trail, forced away from military- and patriotism-related topics, many of his speeches had little substance or impact. As weeks went by, his inept chief adviser alienated many Republican Party regulars.

Despite the shortcomings, Wood went into the Chicago convention as the clear frontrunner. On the first day of balloting, Wood led with accelerating numbers throughout the initial four ballots. When voting resumed the following day, he led through the seventh ballot, but momentum had peaked. Eventually, a compromise candidate, Warren G. Harding, received the party's nomination—the choice, it was later said, of "15 men in a smoke-filled room."

Wood was gracious in defeat, but, as president-elect, Harding was anxious to have his outspoken recent opponent far away from Washington. He named Wood to the chairmanship of a committee being formed to investigate deteriorating conditions in the Philippines where public health had declined, roads went unrepaired, and there was widespread hunger. The Philippine bureaucracy had become grossly inflated, staffed by incumbents often ill-equipped or untrained to handle their duties. Corruption was rampant. Even many Filipinos were wary that if the Americans left, the country would come apart. Most assuredly, they would not be able to defend themselves against foreign intervention— and Japan's recent expansion of an already formidable navy was becoming particularly worrisome.

So ominous was the commission's report that Harding asked Wood to stay on as governor-general. Although prior to the commission he had expressed reluctance to take on the role, after seeing conditions firsthand he agreed to serve. On October 15, 1921, Leonard Wood became governor-general of the Philippines. It was a position he would hold until his death six years later.

In some ways Wood's first year was a replay of his time in Cuba: He funded medical schools, rehabilitated a mental hospital, began mosquito-control programs, vaccinated the population for typhus and smallpox, and built suitable housing for a leper colony. He divested the government of ownership of coal, cement, and other companies.

As time passed, though, his administration became increasingly closed and autocratic. To some extent the drift coincided with his deteriorating physical condition. In 1905, a surgeon had attempted to remove a lesion from Wood's brain. The operation resolved his symptoms but did not extract the entire tumor that was causing the problem. In 1910, Wood had been operated on to remove the tumor itself, a relatively revolutionary procedure at the time. His third such surgery came in 1923. Close family friends noted the gradual changes: ever more inflexible behavior, increasing forgetfulness, occasional tremors.

Wood's demeanor became icier. Throughout his life he had been frequently aggressive and overbearing; now those characteristics were further layered with increasing arrogance and tactlessness. His final years in Manila devolved into constant episodes of bickering, both petty and serious, with Philippine leaders themselves not immune from arrogance and intrigue. At one point the cabinet resigned en masse. Petitions flew from the Philippines to the U.S. Supreme Court and eventually to President Calvin Coolidge. Filipino delegations visited Washington seeking independence and removal or restraint of Wood. The courts, the Coolidge administration, and later an appointed commission generally upheld Wood's decisions.

Coincident with his fast-failing health, a series of foibles by two profligate sons further complicated Wood's life. By early 1927, he was unable to exercise and grew steadily weaker and obese. In May he drove a car into a ditch. The resulting minor hand injury provided the pretext for going home. On August 6, 1927, nearly blind and paralyzed on his left side, he was operated on for a fourth time for the recurring brain tumor. He died the following morning at age 66. Two days later, Wood was buried at Arlington National Cemetery.

With his passing, Wood left a complex and fascinating legacy. He was both an organizational genius and the pettiest of autocrats. He saved thousands of lives and improved the quality of countless others, yet waged military campaigns with ruthlessness devoid of quarter or compassion. His towering achievements were accompanied by a vaulting personal arrogance. His personal honesty was legendary, yet he was notoriously intolerant of criticism. Many of the great personages of his time—Roosevelt, McKinley, Root, Stimson, Miles, and others—recognized his extraordinary abilities, but his brittle personality and outspoken tactlessness created frequent and implacable enemies. He was, almost, president. One can only speculate on how history might have been different had Leonard Wood, not Warren Harding, been president of the United States.

Deeper in the Shadows ...

WILLIAM T. SAMPSON

Sampson led the U.S. Navy in actions off Cuba and Puerto Rico and was the architect of the American victory at Santiago Bay. His force destroyed the Spanish fleet, setting the stage for the Spanish surrender that soon followed.

The most-remembered naval figure from the Spanish-American War remains Commodore George Dewey, famous for his victory over a Spanish squadron in Manila Bay, as well as for his remark "You may fire when ready, Gridley." Aboard the USS *Olympia*, flagship of the navy's Asiatic Squadron, Dewey sailed from Hong Kong, reaching Manila on May 1, 1898. In the battle that followed, Dewey's fleet attacked and sank every Spanish ship anchored in the bay.

Less well-recalled are the exploits of another American naval officer whose force also destroyed a Spanish squadron and did so in a battle closer to American shores. During the course of the war, the flotilla commanded by Commodore William T. Sampson engaged in a variety of duties—conducting actions off Cuba and Puerto Rico, shielding the United States from potential attack by a Spanish fleet thought to be sailing toward American shores, and escorting invasion forces—that are little remembered today.

Sampson was well qualified for his wartime duties. In 1896, with Spanish-U.S. relations in a downward spiral, he served on a board that developed contingency plans in the event of war. In February 1898, because of his expertise as former chief of the navy's Bureau of Ordnance, he was chosen to preside over a court of inquiry to determine the cause of the explosion that sank the USS *Maine* in Havana harbor. Relying primarily on the evidence of a portion of the *Maine*'s hull that had been bent into an inverted *V* shape, the court concluded that the explosion had resulted from an external mine. That blast, the court determined, had in turn caused partial detonations in two or more of the ships' forward magazines. Over the years the court's findings have not been universally accepted.

Three days after the court adjourned, Sampson was named commander of the U.S. North Atlantic Squadron, replacing an officer stricken with malaria. Sampson was personally selected for the post over several more senior officers by the secretary of the navy, John D. Long. Promotion to the temporary grade of rear admiral accompanied the new position.

Even before the war began, Sampson had presented navy officials with plans to bombard, capture, and occupy Havana immediately on the outbreak of war. Sampson and many other observers, past and present, believed that such a strike could have enormous military and political consequences, perhaps even prompting an immediate end to the war.

Sampson's plan was rejected by Secretary Long, who did not want to risk American ships until Spanish naval power had been degraded. In any event, the army was not ready to take on the task of a major invasion. Pleading that additional time was needed to recruit, train, equip, and assemble forces, the army successfully advocated sending instead a small initial force to the island. Once ashore, the six thousand or so soldiers would rendezvous with Cuban rebels who had waged a years-long insurgency against Spanish authority. Meanwhile, the navy would blockade key ports along both coasts and shield the invasion force against a Spanish countermove. The latter was indeed a possibility. In late April a planned invasion was canceled when word was received that a Spanish fleet had left the Cape Verde Islands. Unsure of the intentions of the Spanish commander or the destination of his ships, Washington postponed the assault.

For a time, Sampson pulled away a portion of his blocking ships and, with little available information, positioned vessels at the most likely points of interception. Public fears of Spanish naval attacks along the eastern coast of the United States prompted the removal of additional vessels. Sampson maintained the tightest possible blockade, but the scarcity of ships allowed some Spanish supplies to reach ports along the southern coast of Cuba.

Anticipating that any arriving Spanish vessels would use San Juan, Puerto Rico, as a coaling station, on May 4 Sampson sailed east with a task force. After reaching San Juan and determining that the Spanish fleet was not in the area, Sampson shelled the city's fortifications, concentrating on Morro Castle, a massive structure overlooking the harbor. Having too few forces to take and garrison the city and concerned that that the Spanish fleet might still be headed toward Cuba, Sampson turned back toward Havana. While Sampson's bombardment did no major damage, news of it quite possibly dissuaded the Spanish admiral from using the port.

For several days the location of the Spanish fleet remained uncertain. Finally, on May 15, Sampson learned that it was near Curaçao, headed north. The most logical destinations were two of Cuba's southern ports, Cienfuegos, which was linked directly to Havana by railroad, and Santiago. On May 18, Sampson rendezvoused at Key West, Florida, with a squadron under the command of Winfield S. Schley. The following day, he sent Schley to Cienfuegos, believing that the Spanish would utilize that port because of its rail connection with Havana. Later Sampson learned that the Spanish ships were in fact in the harbor at Santiago. Schley reached Cienfuegos on May 22. Directed to move to Santiago, Schley delayed sailing and did not arrive until May 26. Sampson reached Santiago with the rest of the North Atlantic Squadron on June 1.

With General Shafter's army forces approaching the city and the navy blocking the Spanish fleet in the harbor, Santiago became the strategic focus of the campaign. After initial unsuccessful attempts to sink a ship in the narrow channel and obstruct the entrance to the harbor, Sampson set about sealing the Spanish fleet inside the port.

Sampson's approach to the blockade was innovative and not without risk. In daylight hours he arrayed his fleet in a semicircle about six miles from the harbor entrance. At night he moved his ships two miles closer but placed his battleships even farther in front where their massive searchlights—turned intermittently on and off during the night—could illuminate the channel and detect any Spanish ships that sought to break out. That technique risked exposing the positions of the American battleships to attacks by Spanish torpedo boats, but the Spanish admiral later acknowledged that his navigators were blinded by the lights and could not steer through the difficult channel at night. Indeed, a sortie on the night of June 7 had been turned back after the Americans inflicted damage to three Spanish vessels.

While maintaining the Santiago blockade, Sampson sent two ships to Guantánamo Bay to clear the way for eventual occupation by American forces. Once inside the bay, the ships destroyed a Spanish gunboat and leveled a fortification that protected the inlet. On June 10, a battalion of Marines ousted the Spanish garrison from Guantánamo city. Over the next four days, acting in concert with Cuban rebels, the Marines drove Spanish forces from the area.

The eventual establishment of a ship repair and coaling station at Guantánamo prevented Sampson's ships from having to backtrack to Key West for maintenance and fuel. For the Marines, the capture of a forward base for eventual use by the fleet was a historic first. In later years, the operation would become a centerpiece of the Marine Corps's mission.

On July 1, Sampson dispatched three ships to bombard the Spanish garrison at Aquadores. The navy's action was in support of a feint attack aimed at drawing Spanish forces away from the army's major thrust, the attack on San Juan Heights. The Aquadores action was a rare moment of cooperation between the two services.

Through the course of the campaign, communication between Sampson and Shafter was strained. In this first American overseas expedition, there was little tradition or experience for commanders to draw on. There was no joint service organization, no single focal point for campaign planning, and no supreme theater commander for final decision making. The commanders' personal staffs were small and ill-prepared to handle interservice issues. Sampson, like most of his naval colleagues, was impatient with the army's slow preparations and movements, believing that Santiago was vulnerable especially if assaulted quickly. Conversely, Shafter wanted Sampson to force his way into the harbor, destroy the Spanish fleet, and bombard the city's garrison. Sampson, though, wanted Shafter to first take the forts that guarded the harbor's entrance so he could clear mines from the channel and get his ships inside without losing some of them on the way to the fight.

Differences between the two were not helped by the fact that at times neither was in the best of health. On at least one occasion, Sampson had to send a surrogate to a scheduled meeting because he was too ill to attend. Shafter, obese and gout-ridden, drew criticism even among army officers for his lack of mobility.

Ironically, on July 3, Sampson was on his way to meet with Shafter when the Spanish fleet attempted to break out of the harbor. Hearing the distant fire, Sampson and his staff aboard the battleships *New York* and *Massachusetts* quickly reversed course but arrived on the scene after the main action had been completed. In the meantime, the Spanish fleet had been destroyed.

The Spanish sortie began at about 9:35 in the morning when four cruisers and two destroyers, vulnerable as they moved up the narrow channel, sailed toward an American flotilla under the immediate command of William S. Schley consisting of four battleships, two cruisers, and two destroyers. By a few minutes after one o'clock in the afternoon, every Spanish ship had been sunk, run aground, or had struck her colors. The cost to the Americans was one dead and two wounded.

Relations between Schley and Sampson had long been difficult. Sampson, though junior in service to Schley, had been promoted over him to command the North Atlantic Squadron. After the battle, Sampson, inadvertently by most accounts, compounded a dispute that would continue for the remainder of both officers' lives. Sampson's telegram announcing the victory stated: "The fleet under my command offers the nation as a Fourth of July present the whole of Cervera's [the Spanish admiral] fleet." Though Sampson's message was technically correct, Schley and his staff, already predisposed toward resentment, were offended that Schley's role had not been mentioned. The resulting feud over which officer should receive credit for the victory split much of the navy into "pro-Sampson" and "pro-Schley" camps for years to come.

Many knowledgeable authorities, including renowned naval theorist Alfred Thayer Mahan and Secretary of the Navy Long, believed Sampson's role was paramount. Like Mahan and Long, most who judged Sampson's case to be more compelling have cited his astute positioning of his ships, insightful preparations, and prescient standing orders as being the decisive elements in the American victory. Sampson himself observed that the marksmanship of the American gunners, a skill that he emphasized and developed through intense training, far surpassed that of the Spanish crews.

The navy's victory in Santiago Bay brought a request the next day from Shafter—worried about heavy losses and the onset of the yellow fever season—for Sampson to enter the harbor and shell the Spanish garrison. Sampson again refused, citing what he believed to be Shafter's commitment to first capture the forts at the harbor's entrance.

That night (July 4), the Spanish attempted to block the channel by scuttling a capital ship near the harbor's mouth. The attempt was foiled by Sampson's gunners, who sank the ship before it could be maneuvered into position.

American soldiers atop a Spanish fort on San Juan Heights, a few miles from the city of Santiago.

The destruction of the Spanish fleet all but assured the Americans of eventual victory. Still, the Spanish commander rejected initial truce feelers while awaiting guidance from Madrid. Although conditions in the trench lines were difficult in the extreme, Shafter further tightened the siege of the city. On July 10, reinforcements accompanied by Major General Nelson Miles arrived from the States, bulking up American units depleted by casualties and disease. On the same day, Sampson began a prolonged bombardment of Santiago.

The onset of the rainy season and the presence of 100 cases of yellow fever inside American lines—a number that was sure to grow—frustrated the Americans as the Spanish continued to hold out. However, the Spanish, the weather, and disease were not the only problems confronting the army in Cuba. Leonard Wood and other commanders complained of the overall mismanagement of the campaign. Wood called the army's lack of effort to provide necessary artillery, food, and ammunition "simply criminally negligent."

Horrific conditions in the field and a generally uncertain future finally prompted a plan for concerted action. Shafter and Miles proposed a major attack for July 14 that would have combined a landing west of the harbor entrance with an attack on the city from San Juan Heights. Meanwhile, Sampson and his ships would enter and take control of the harbor.

American troops pose on San Juan Heights after a victorious battle on July 1, 1898. Future American president Theodore Roosevelt is at the center near the flag.

Events overcame the need for the attack when the Spanish commander, meeting with Miles and Shafter, agreed to capitulate. The formal surrender took place on July 17. Shafter did not invite Cuban rebels and delayed Sampson's invitation until it was too late for him to attend.

Sampson's absence precluded him from including items of concern to the navy in the surrender document. Sampson had wished to specify that the Spanish clear the mines from the waters around Santiago and that the guns guarding the harbor be dismantled. Shafter had at first refused to turn over six Spanish ships that remained at anchor in the harbor, a dispute that was resolved (in Sampson's favor) only by the intervention of President McKinley.

Although the American victory essentially ended major hostilities, conditions elsewhere consumed Sampson's attention. For a short time, the presence of Spain's remaining fleet in the Mediterranean posed a worrisome threat. Sampson responded to the potential danger by preparing a squadron to sail to Spanish waters if the Spanish fleet moved in a threatening way toward the United States. That threat dissipated soon after when it became clear that any Spanish plan to attack had been abandoned.

Near the end of the month, Sampson's vessels escorted the army's invasion force to Puerto Rico. Landings commenced on the southern coast on July 25. Under the command of General Nelson Miles, U.S. forces moved northeast against sporadic opposition. With the army's troops ashore, Sampson proposed a naval assault on San Juan, believing he could take the capital with his own Marines and other resources. Miles's strong objection and his appeal through the secretary of the navy effectively killed Sampson's plan.

After suspension of hostilities, Sampson was appointed one of three U.S. commissioners for Cuba, serving until late 1898 before returning to his command duties with the North Atlantic Squadron. Later he served as commander of the Boston Navy Yard.

Sampson's retirement in February 1902 brought closure to a long and, at times, distinguished career that began in 1861 when he graduated first in his class from Annapolis. Amid a variety of shipboard assignments that followed over the years, he served as assistant superintendent of the Naval Observatory, superintendent of the Naval Academy, and chief of the Bureau of Ordnance.

Sampson's lasting legacy was as a premiere builder and innovator during a time of technological change. His focus on scientific education for naval officers and his contributions as chief of the Bureau of Ordnance did much to improve the firepower of American warships. Historians noted that from 1892 until the outbreak of the Spanish-American War, every gun built for the navy was constructed under his supervision. At the Bureau of Ordnance, Sampson personally designed the navy's largest weapons.

Sampson died on May 6, 1902, and was buried at Arlington National Cemetery.

CHAPTER 2
THE PHILIPPINE INSURRECTION

THE ROAD TO WAR

The Philippine Insurrection was an outgrowth of America's war with Spain. Admiral Dewey's defeat of the Spanish squadron in Manila Bay on May 1, 1898, and Spain's subsequent surrender left the islands' immediate status uncertain. The McKinley administration had given little thought to the consequences of victory. (At the outset, the president acknowledged that he would have trouble locating the islands on a map.) Eventually McKinley determined to annex the Philippines and administer the islands under U.S. control.

Several factors likely influenced that decision. Foremost initially was the concern that unless the United States maintained jurisdiction, the islands might fall into the hands of another power. Indeed, the sizable German Far Eastern Fleet had all but followed Dewey into the harbor at Manila. Economic pressures were present as well. Some business leaders saw the Philippines as the gateway to markets in China and Japan. Others feared the reverse if Japan, particularly, assumed provenance. There was widespread sentiment among American military and political leaders that the Philippines were not ready for independence. Those who held that view regarded the occupation as humanitarian in nature—benevolent colonialism that would prepare the Filipinos for sovereignty and security in the modern world. (Local self-government would be granted in 1916, full autonomy in 1934; independence—delayed by World War II—was achieved in 1946.) Militarily, the navy valued the islands as a repair/refueling station and saw it as a potential bastion in the Pacific.

Not all Americans agreed with annexation or occupation. Mark Twain and other American Anti-Imperialist League supporters were vocal in their opposition. The group's public protests continued as casualties mounted.

Indeed, casualties from the conflict far exceeded those sustained during the war with Spain. U.S. deaths numbered 4,163 (about three-quarters from disease), with another 3,000 wounded. An additional

2,000 Philippine Constabulary members fighting on the side of the Americans were killed or wounded. Deaths among Filipino insurgent fighters approximated 16,000. An estimated 100,000 to 200,000 (some place the figure higher) Filipino civilians died of famine or disease during the course of the conflict.

At its peak strength, the U.S. Army had more than 100,000 troops, a mixture of regular forces and volunteer units, deployed on the islands. The rebel army initially numbered between 80,000 and 120,000 core fighters, with thousands more serving as auxiliaries.

A Filipino insurgent movement had been active throughout the islands for several years prior to the Spanish–American War. In 1896, a full-blown rebellion had broken out against Spanish rule. By the time the United States became involved two years later, the rebels controlled a considerable portion of the islands' territory. When the United States intervened, the insurgent's primary leader, Emilio Aguinaldo, initially assisted U.S. forces in defeating the Spanish garrisoned around Manila.

On June 12, 1898, Aguinaldo declared the Philippines independent, a claim recognized by neither Spain nor the United States. In February of the following year, after President McKinley announced the decision to annex the Philippines, fighting broke out between American forces and Aguinaldo's army. A series of decisive American victories prompted Aguinaldo in November 1900 to renounce conventional combat operations and adopt guerrilla warfare tactics. Aguinaldo's decision foreshadowed a far more brutal phase of the conflict. Atrocities of the most hideous form were committed by both sides. Sizable portions of the rural population were put into camps, often under difficult living conditions inside protected "free-fire zones," to separate them from guerrilla fighters.

The capture of Aguinaldo on March 23, 1901, by troops led by Major General Frederick Funston precipitated the insurrectionists' formal surrender on April 19. Although some fighting lingered on for a time, most rebel units obeyed Aguinaldo's request that they lay down their arms and declare allegiance, as he had done, to the United States. The last major insurrectionist unit surrendered in April 1902. On July 4 1902, President

Theodore Roosevelt announced a full pardon to all Filipinos who had fought against the United States.

America's difficulties did not end with the surrender of Aguinaldo's army. Almost immediately a bloody, more complex, and in some ways even more horrific struggle erupted on the outer islands between U.S. forces and Muslim insurgents. Fought on larger southern islands such as Mindanao and Jolo and many smaller ones, the Moro Rebellion introduced suicide attacks and "water cure" torture—a forerunner of "waterboarding"—to the American public.

On Mindanao, Jolo, and other southern Philippine islands, Filipino Muslims—Moros—waged a prolonged insurgency.

Labeled in more recent days as America's first war against Muslim insurgents, the conflict cost 500 U.S. dead and wounded against 10,000 to 20,000 Muslim casualties. Notable large-scale battles were fought at Bud Dajo and Bud Bagsak before the insurgency was fully suppressed in mid-1913. The parallels with American involvement in Afghanistan in terms of length and conditions of combat are often striking.

FREDERICK FUNSTON

The foremost American combat leader during the Philippine Insurrection, Funston was most noted for two actions. The first, at Rio Grande de la Pampanga, earned him the Medal of Honor. The second, his audacious capture of guerrilla leader Emilio Aguinaldo, effectively ended Aguinaldo's insurgency.

At five feet, four inches tall, weighing at most 120 pounds, Frederick "Fred" Funston did not fit the usual image of a dashing combat leader. Indeed, physical considerations aside, other than a persistent quest for adventure there was little in his earlier life that would have foreshadowed that role. Funston had failed the entrance examination for West Point, and his restless energy had induced him to leave college before earning a degree. He spent the first decade of his adult life moving rapidly through an eclectic mixture of jobs. Eventually, a speech about the Cuban revolutionists' struggle to free the island from Spanish rule drew him into military life. As events would show, as a leader of soldiers in combat, he had few peers. Funston had discovered his calling.

The 20th Kansas, a volunteer regiment formed in Topeka and commanded by Funston, sailed from San Francisco on October 27, 1898. One of the early-arriving units, the 20th landed on Luzon before hostilities broke out. Anticipating duty as benign occupiers, within weeks they found themselves in combat. Although Funston led forces in numerous battles, it was his participation in two actions that would bring him renown. The first earned him the Medal of Honor. The second essentially ended the war.

On February 4, 1899, soon after President McKinley announced his decision to annex the Philippines, Emilio Aguinaldo resumed his attempt to secure the islands' independence. Conventional combat on a wide scale broke out immediately. Later, when Aguinaldo and the insurgents shifted tactics, the conflict was transformed into guerrilla warfare in its most appalling form.

When the scale of the uprising became obvious, the 20th was one of the first American units committed to battle. Led by Funston, they earned a reputation for exceeding their assigned objectives and attaining results greater than anticipated by planners. At the outset of the war Funston, leading from the front as always, conducted a successful weeks-long campaign to take Caloocan and the insurgents' capital at Malolos in south-central Luzon.

In late April, near Calumpit on the Rio Grande de la Pampanga, Funston's force came up against four thousand heavily dug-in insurgents facing them on the northern bank. Only a partially destroyed bridge spanned the four-hundred-foot-wide, fast-moving river. Several attempts to cross were driven back by heavy fire. Sometime during the course of the fight, the Americans found a small raft. Funston decided to use it as a ferry to cross and establish a beachhead. Two young privates volunteered to swim across the river and attach a tow rope on the opposite bank. With supporting fire, Funston and seven others made the first raft-ferry trip across the river.

With his small team holding a place on the hostile embankment, the raft made repeated trips across the river ferrying additional troops to Funston's position. When a sufficient force had finally been gathered, Funston drove the Filipinos from their entrenchments and cleared the entire shoreline.

For their heroism on the Rio Grande de la Pampanga, Funston and the two privates were awarded the Medal of Honor. Funston was promoted to brigadier general of volunteers while recuperating from a wound to his left hand sustained during the Malolos campaign.

Enlistments up, the "Fighting 20th," as it was now called in the press, was rotated back to the States in late 1899. In 11 months, Funston had led the regiment in 19 battles at a loss of only 34 killed in action. Thirty others died of disease.

Funston sailed back to San Francisco with the 20th but was almost immediately returned to the Philippines for further duty. His actions a few months later would effectively end Emilio Aguinaldo's insurgency.

From the time the first shots were fired in February 1899, U.S. forces had been attempting to locate and capture the insurgent leader. During the bitter months that followed, Aguinaldo had shifted his headquarters ever deeper into remote northern Luzon. With aspects similar to the tracking of Osama bin Laden 110 years later, the break came when an American unit captured Aguinaldo's chief courier. Brought to Funston, the courier, Cecilio Segismundo, revealed Aguinaldo's location—the village of Palanan in the extreme northern portion of the island.

When captured, Segismundo was carrying documents from Aguinaldo that, when decoded, disclosed a request for reinforcements. Using Aguinaldo's need for additional men as bait, Funston devised an audacious plan. Funston's proposal—approved with grave misgivings by his superior officer, Major General Arthur MacArthur—called for Filipinos loyal to the United States to pose as rebel soldiers on their way to join Aguinaldo while coincidently escorting five American "prisoners" (one of whom was Funston) into captivity. Funston believed the ruse was the only way to get past insurgent patrols that sealed off the area and shielded Aguinaldo's headquarters. Eventually, 81 Filipinos posed as the replacements requested by Aguinaldo. Funston and four other American soldiers feigned roles as captives.

On March 6, 1901, the USS *Vicksburg* ferried Funston's group to Casiguran Bay, where they were dropped off about 50 miles from Aguinaldo's fortified camp. Although the group was stopped occasionally by Filipino villagers, the deception was convincing, and at times it was given detailed instructions to Aguinaldo's base.

Although the slogging was difficult, all went well until a problem occurred about five miles from the pseudo rebels' destination. In response to a message they sent announcing their approach, Aguinaldo's camp sent back directions to leave the Americans behind. The leader of the contingent of loyal Filipinos, Hilario Placido, then forged a note reversing the first order and directing that the "prisoners" be brought to the rebel post.

Placido's sham order cleared the way to the insurgents' headquarters area. Aguinaldo, however, as a further precaution for keeping his location secret, had prohibited the presence of any Americans inside the town of Palanan. Funston and the four other Americans were momentarily left under a small guard detail at the edge of the city while Placido and his 80 men proceeded into Palanan to meet Aguinaldo. Both parties, Funston's and Placido's, moved expeditiously. Funston's group quickly overcame the guard detail, and Placido's men went after Aguinaldo. It was all over very quickly. A few minutes later, when Funston and his men arrived, Aguinaldo had already been taken prisoner. By nightfall on March 23, 1901, Funston's group, with Aguinaldo their captive, was on their way to Manila.

Aguinaldo was detained in Manila for three weeks. On April 19, after meetings and individual discussions with senior U.S. officials, Aguinaldo formally capitulated to the Americans. In a proclamation, he declared his allegiance to the United States and asked his generals to surrender.

Almost all did so, although for some time afterward small pockets of resistance continued in isolated locations.

With Aguinaldo's capture, the insurrection lost its primary leader and its driving energy. Within a year all major rebel units had surrendered.

Although editorials in some major American newspapers criticized the deceptive tactics that led to Aguinaldo's capture, Funston was hailed as a national hero and commissioned a brigadier general in the regular army. Ill and worn-out by his ordeal, Funston returned soon after to the United States for a lengthy convalescence. His time in the Philippines was over.

Before and After

When Funston was a toddler, his family moved from his birthplace in New Carlisle, Ohio, to Allen County, Kansas, where he grew up in and around Iola. It was because of his connection with the state and his combat experience with the Cuban insurrectionist army that he was chosen to lead a Kansas regiment in the war in the Philippines.

All that was 30 years in the future, however, and there would be several adventures in between. Although Funston eventually completed his high school education, he dropped out for a time to teach at a small rural school nearby. A voracious reader of math, economics, and science books, Funston in many ways was self-taught in major subject areas. His indifference to classroom education showed again a few years later when he dropped out of college before completing his degree. Along the way, Funston became proficient in Spanish, an ability that would serve him well in both Cuba and the Philippines.

After finishing high school, Funston tried to gain admittance to West Point. His grades on the entrance exam were not high enough, however, and instead for a time he attended the University of Kansas. Restlessness and, possibly, financial considerations prompted him to leave Lawrence after a year. Although he would return to the school sporadically, he never completed his degree.

Away from school, Funston filled the next several years with a remarkable variety of experiences. At various times he worked for a railroad as a surveyor, ticket collector, and deputy comptroller and as a newspaper reporter in Topeka, Kansas, and Fort Smith, Arkansas. For a time in 1890 and 1891, working mainly as a botanist, he joined Department of Agriculture expeditions to the Dakota Badlands and Death Valley, California.

Funston's first narrow escape from death occurred on a gorge in Death Valley when his horse stumbled near a precipice. As both horse and rider slid toward the rim, Funston managed to grab onto a small bush. The precarious handhold prevented him from following his horse over the edge to the canyon floor several hundred feet below.

Later he helped open a new trail in Yosemite National Park and lived for a time with a Native tribe in California. After the second of his newspaper sojourns, he moved to Alaska for a botanical study. The winter of 1893–94 found him wintering alone on the Klondike River. When spring arrived in 1894, he built a boat and paddled down the Yukon River to its mouth, where he sighted a ship on the open sea, climbed aboard, and sailed to California. A failed attempt to establish a coffee plantation in either Mexico or Central America ensued (the record is unclear), soon followed by another tour with the railroad, this time as deputy comptroller.

In New York City in 1896, purely by chance, Funston attended a rally sponsored by Cuban revolutionaries struggling for their independence from Spain. Enthralled by a speech given by Union Civil War general Dan Sickles, Funston enlisted in the revolutionary army. Commissioned as a captain of artillery, he found an instruction manual that he used to train himself and a cannon to practice on. After evading U.S. authorities, Funston and others set sail on a blockade runner bound for Cuba. When that ship was sighted by a Spanish naval vessel, Funston and another member of the party climbed into a small boat and rowed themselves two miles to shore.

Funston spent 22 months in Cuba. Most accounts cite his participation in more than 20 major battles and having had as many as 17 horses shot from under him. He was wounded in an arm, shot through both lungs, survived a near-fatal fever, and had large splinters penetrate one of his hips when his horse was shot or stumbled during the chaos of a cavalry charge.

On his way home to convalesce, Funston was taken captive by the Spanish but managed to destroy incriminating documents and talk his way out of immediate danger. Eventually, he was released. When he finally returned to the United States in early 1898, he weighed perhaps as little as 80 pounds.

Funston emerged from the conflict as a lieutenant colonel in the revolutionary army. Desperate as it was at times, his combat experience in Cuba sent him on the path that would consume the rest of his life.

Funston was back for only a short time when the United States declared war on Spain. In May 1898, he was appointed as colonel and commanding officer of the 20th Kansas Regiment. Funston went first to Washington, DC, and later to Florida to help plan the war in Cuba. However, the short four-month duration of the conflict precluded the 20th from being sent to the Caribbean.

Soon after, following President McKinley's decision to maintain American military forces in the Philippines, the regiment was sent to San Francisco for eventual shipment to Luzon.

Funston joined the unit there, finding the soldiers' physical conditioning, morale, housing, equipment, and marksmanship all less than satisfactory. For five busy months, he drilled his men, tested them on maneuvers, and sent them repeatedly to the rifle range—all the while working to improve their billeting arrangements. The 20th boarded ship on October 27, 1898, fit and well prepared for the conflict that awaited them within weeks of their arrival.

After returning from the Philippines and recovering his health, Funston embarked on a nationwide speaking tour to increase support for the war effort. In April 1902, he made a blustery, widely quoted speech that justified using extreme measures, including hanging, against insurgents and seemed to suggest that lethal measures were also warranted against Americans who supported the belligerents. Soon after, he made remarks insulting to a Republican senator who opposed the war.

The comments constituted a rare faux pas for Funston, who was regarded as an effective spokesman for the nation's expansionist policy. Unlike Leonard Wood and other of his army colleagues, Funston was generally diplomatic in his comments. Nonetheless, the blowback from

Mark Twain and other anti-imperialists was fast and formidable. President Roosevelt ordered Funston silenced and officially reprimanded.

With the insurgency dying and the full sweep of the Moro uprising yet to come, national attention shifted elsewhere. Funston's outbursts did not unduly damage his reputation, and Roosevelt's reprimand had little impact on his later career.

Beginning in the spring of 1902, Funston moved quickly through a series of influential billets. By 1906, he had commanded, in turn, the Departments of Colorado, Columbia, and California. Funston was in California, the ranking officer at the Presidio in San Francisco, when the massive earthquake struck the city on April 18, 1906. If indeed his reputation had been tarnished in any way by his outbursts in 1902, his performance in San Francisco redeemed it.

When it became immediately evident that the scale of the disaster vastly overwhelmed available civilian resources, Funston offered the army's assistance and in essence took command of the city. The army assumed responsibility for providing food, shelter, drinking water, and clothing to thousands of disaster-stricken refugees. Soldiers patrolled the streets to prevent looting, guarded government buildings including the U.S. Mint, and provided security at the city jail.

With water mains fractured, no water was available to fight the four-square-mile firestorm that swept through the city. Funston used dynamite to destroy buildings in its path, creating firebreaks that contained the flames. Four days later, the fire burned itself out.

By some estimates, San Francisco was left with as many as 300,000 homeless people and the near total loss of banks, lodging facilities, and food outlets. Funston established tent cities, provided rations, and built the final plan for recovery. Not until July did civilian authorities resume responsibility for the city. Funston was generally regarded as a national hero—"the man who saved San Francisco."

When American troops were withdrawn from Cuba in 1902, the Platt Amendment maintained the U.S. prerogative to intervene under certain conditions in the island's affairs. The first intervention under the amendment took place during the period 1906–9. Because of his fluency in Spanish and his standing as a hero in the Cuban revolutionary army, late in 1906 Funston was sent to the island as an emissary for the American government. His work with Cuban authorities helped quiet the hostilities. The five infantry and two cavalry regiments sent to keep peace on the island were withdrawn in 1909.

For a four-month period beginning in December 1907, Funston was in charge of three infantry companies, totaling about three hundred soldiers, dispatched to Goldfield, Nevada, during a labor dispute. With sketchy justification, local authorities sought to validate the intervention by asserting that violence had occurred and the potential existed for widespread unrest. In actuality, few clashes took place. Funston's troops were withdrawn and replaced by a newly formed state militia on March 7, 1908.

In August 1908, Funston began a tour of duty at Fort Leavenworth, Kansas, as commandant of what is now called the Army Command and General Staff College. He served in that position until January 1911, when he returned to the Philippines as commander of the Department of Luzon. Three years in Manila were followed by a similar position as commander of the Department of Hawaii, a tour shortened by the threat of hostilities with Mexico.

Events in Mexico found Funston back in the United States in 1914. Over the next 24 months, two episodes with international implications would again thrust his name into the headlines. During the chaos that followed the election of Victoriano Huerta as president of Mexico, several U.S. servicemen had been made captive in Tampico. Soon after, President Woodrow Wilson sent Funston to take command of U.S. forces being assembled along the border. However, as American units were massing in Texas, the initial flash point occurred elsewhere. Responding to reports that a German merchant ship was bound for Vera Cruz carrying weapons and ammunition to Huerta, Wilson ordered the city to be taken. After an encounter that produced casualties on both sides, navy and Marine units gained control of the city. Funston was then directed to take five thousand troops to secure the city and the surrounding area. That done, Funston was appointed governor-general of Vera Cruz.

By nearly every account, Funston handled the job admirably. He distributed rations, dealt fairly with the populace, set up an efficient city administration, and maintained order. Funston's astute diplomacy, aided by his fluency in Spanish, minimized confrontations between troops and civilians and resolved irritants before they festered into major disputes.

Starved of supplies and pressured both internally and internationally, Huerta left Mexico. On November 23, 1914, the last U.S. troops left Vera Cruz—a circumstance that, according to some American press reports, was regretted by many occupants of the city.

Huerta's departure did not end Mexico's political unrest. Conditions remained unsettled, and in 1916 cross-border raids by Francisco "Pancho" Villa again caused tensions to escalate. On March 9, Villa led more than a thousand guerrillas in an attack on Columbus, New Mexico, that killed 18 Americans. Funston was among those who recommended that American forces pursue Villa into Mexico. The Wilson administration agreed. Funston was instructed to designate a subordinate officer, Brigadier General John J. Pershing, to conduct the pursuit. Funston would provide overall supervision and support while handling security along the entire length of the U.S. border with Mexico. Thousands of National Guardsmen were activated for federal service, a process that would provide valuable lessons when the United States entered World War I in April of the following year.

The so-called Punitive Expedition was Funston's last substantive duty. On February 19, 1917, while dining with friends in San Antonio, Texas, Funston died of a heart attack at age 51. His body lay in state at the Alamo; he was the first person so honored. A few days later he was buried at the Presidio in San Francisco, forever a part of the city he had helped save.

Leonard Wood was the army's senior general when the United States entered World War I two months after Funston's death. However, Wood's frequent and public criticisms of President Wilson's policies ruled out his selection as commander of the American Expeditionary Force, the fledgling but soon to be enormous army that would contribute to the eventual victory in France. Funston, however, was liked and respected by Wilson. It is quite possible that had he lived, it would have been Frederick Funston and not John Pershing who commanded U.S. forces in World War I.

LEONARD WOOD

Wood led the successful counterinsurgency campaign that quelled the uprising of Filipino Muslims—Moros—on Mindanao and nearby islands in the southern Philippines. As in Cuba, he launched humanitarian programs on a large scale.

By the time Leonard Wood arrived in the Philippines, Frederick Funston's capture of Emilio Aguinaldo had effectively ended the guerrilla war waged by Filipino revolutionaries. Except for one region, the Philippines were essentially pacified.

The exception, though, was major in scope and substance. In Muslim-populated Mindanao and the surrounding islands, violence continued. Muslims constituted only five percent of the Philippine population but controlled 40 percent of the land area. The Filipino Muslims—Moros—based their livelihoods on piracy, raiding other Filipinos, stealing from British subjects on nearby Borneo, and capturing and owning non-Muslim slaves.

After battling their Muslim subjects for more than three centuries, the Spanish eventually wearied of the struggle and allowed the Moros considerable autonomy. The Americans, newly arrived, were less tolerant and were determined to stamp out incidents of piracy, slavery, and general banditry.

In 1902, Wood was appointed governor of Mindanao. He came to the Philippines somewhat a changed man. Despite his formidable record as an administrator in Cuba, he had undergone attacks that questioned his accomplishments, methods, and character. His bitterness now combined with a perceived need for strong measures to pacify an increasingly brutal and implacable opponent. In the Philippines, Wood would again introduce political changes and humanitarian measures, but unlike in Cuba military matters, law enforcement, and population control took precedence over civic reform. Having earned worldwide renown as an administrator, he was now determined to leave his mark as a military leader.

Wood moved into a position that for the first time combined military and civil authority. Like his superiors, he realized that long-term success depended on effectively accommodating the Moro culture and religion.

The 75,000 to 250,000 Moros—population estimates varied widely—were formidable opponents. Their weapon of choice was the *kris*, a long, single-edged, razor-sharp sword that could bisect a man or cut off a leg with a single swipe. Swung two-handed, it could cleave through skull and bone. A favorite technique was to cut the ropes of tents housing sleeping soldiers. The collapsed tent would reveal the profiles of the soldiers who would then by sliced to pieces in their cots.

In a foreshadowing of warfare Americans would face a century later in Iraq and Afghanistan, the most extreme of the radicals took a vow to kill Christians and were promised direct access to paradise as compensation. At times, such "martyrs" came at the Americans in waves. Women were sometimes armed and participated in attacks. Similar to the experience of some of the American veterans during conflicts with Natives on the Great Plains, troops had difficulty differentiating the apparel of Moro men and women during the chaos of a fast-moving encounter.

In the months ahead, both sides waged warfare with little quarter given. Wood found American captives sliced to pieces and left to be devoured by the islands' wild hogs. Prisoners of the Moros were sometimes buried up to their necks, a trail of honey leading thousands of ants to the prisoners' mouths which were propped open to allow access.

The Moros lived in fortified villages called *cottas*. Over the centuries many had been turned into killing fields. The villages were ringed by spiked parapets further surrounded by moats and earthworks. Most were accessible only by a single bridge. Inside the sole entrance, the passages were exceptionally narrow, allowing kris-wielding defenders to hack intruders to pieces.

Wood's approach, quickly put in place, was to not risk the lives of his soldiers in that type of fight. Most often, he used artillery and Gatling guns to blow the *cottas* apart and then followed with infantry sweeps to mop up whoever remained. His methods were both successful and controversial.

Before taking the offensive, Wood had tried negotiations. He called prominent Moro leaders—called *datos*—together and informed them that a new, very strong country now controlled the Philippines. The United States would, he said, insist on peace. Although the Moros might not like it, slavery, piracy, and banditry must stop immediately. If not, Wood told the *datos*, the result for the Moro people would be like committing suicide. He made it plain that he would go after the extremist imams who administered jihadi-like oaths to the radicals urging the slaughter of Christians. Wood told the assembled group that they—the *datos*—as well as the imams would be held responsible. After the group meeting Wood traveled around the island, meeting individually with nearly every *dato* on Mindanao. Wood's meetings and his show of force—he traveled with several companies of infantry and artillery—temporarily quieted the island.

In the meantime, as a civil administrator, Wood began establishing schools, developing a degree of local government and creating a constabulary force manned by Moros loyal to the United States. A legislative council, municipal codes, and antislavery laws were quickly put in place.

In the fall, after an initial period of relative calm, reports of renewed kidnappings and slave raids reached Wood at his headquarters in Zamboanga, Mindanao. Seeking to send a message to all recalcitrants, Wood took to the field. In the weeks ahead, he would fight a counterinsurgency campaign under exceptionally difficult conditions. Mindanao is an island the size of Ireland. Tribes in the deepest interior still practiced human sacrifice and cannibalism. Amid 36,000 square miles of jungle, there were 50 miles of roads. Some of the Moro combatants were well armed, having raided military arsenals during the interregnum between the Spanish withdrawal and the American takeover. Armed groups sometimes numbered 700 or more. Despite horrible conditions—swamps, snakes, jungle growth, mosquitos, and bats with five-foot wingspans—Wood, with seven infantry companies, 150 pack animals, three Gatling guns, and forty thousand rounds of ammunition, pushed forward with surprising speed, shifting his force temporarily to Jolo, a hotbed of extremist activity.

On Jolo, Wood's camp was immediately attacked by a group of the most violent radicals—called *juramentos*—who had sworn an oath to kill. Thirty of the attackers were killed and a considerable number were wounded. There were no American casualties.

That same night, three more companies joined Wood, bringing his force to about 1,250 men. Wood set out the next morning after a local Moro leader and his band. An extended chase killed a number of Moro fighters and in a larger, set-piece battle, one hundred or more were killed in a fight near the leader's palace-like complex.

The following day, 27 more Moros were killed as Wood maintained a relentless pursuit. In the days ahead, *cottas* thought to house hostiles were shelled, burned, and stripped of weapons. Although the estimates have varied from source to source, an official report at the end of Wood's initial campaign cited 1,500 Moros killed. Wood's losses were listed as 17 killed and a few more wounded.

The period of relative quiet that followed lasted until the early spring of 1904. Reacting to reports that insurgents were again gathering in a different region of Mindanao, in March Wood set out to disperse the Moro bands or hammer them into submission. After a brutal march, Wood's force came upon an enormous, heavily fortified *cotta* at Seranaya thought to contain several thousand Moro warriors. Wood shelled the *cotta* for two days. Eventually, the Moros raised a white flag. Americans entering the now nearly deserted village found near-total devastation. Multiple graves and a bloodstained landscape gave evidence of heavy losses. Along with other weapons and war-making matériel, 21 Spanish naval guns and seven tons of powder were captured.

Although the Moro leaders had escaped, Wood was pleased with the outcome of the expedition. The local Moros had regarded the leader of the village as being unbeatable and thought his compound impregnable.

When word of Seranaya reached Manila, the governor-general, William Howard Taft, sent a scolding, highly critical telegram to Wood ordering him to refrain from use of similar tactics. Wood replied that the measures were necessary, that it was his force that had been initially attacked (a questionable assertion), and that peaceful means would be used whenever possible. Taft chose not to pursue the issue.

With the victory at Seranaya, Wood believed that Moro bands in two of the three regions of major insurgent activity had been decisively punished. The third area, the Lake District, would require a final object lesson.

On April 1, 1904, Wood moved out with 16 companies of infantry, two troops of dismounted cavalry, and a battery of field artillery. Reaching a large lake after a two-day march, Wood's soldiers opened fire on Moros attempting to escape by canoe. There were no survivors. Wood then took his force from *cotta* to *cotta*. Advising his officers that the inhabitants of the villages had been intractable for generations and persisted in brutalizing their neighbors, Wood destroyed every *cotta* where there was even the hint of resistance. Through the entire region, villages were blown apart and burned, and war supplies were destroyed.

After several weeks back at his headquarters in Zamboanga, Wood took to the field again after an American infantry company was ambushed with the loss of two officers and 11 enlisted men. Wood's expedition found the bodies hacked apart and partially eaten by wild hogs. Four weeks later at a settlement called Cotabato, Wood's men caught and killed 26 Moro fighters. On Jolo a short time later, 21 Moros were killed after threatening an American customs agent.

By the end of summer 1904, Wood's scorched-earth policy, the mass destruction of *cottas*, and the heavy losses inflicted on the Moros began to show results. Small patrols could now freely move about the island. Piracy and slave trading were almost nonexistent.

Wood visited schools, asylums, and prisons in the intervals between insurgent flare-ups. He used his experience in Cuba to suggest methods for combating a tuberculosis epidemic among prisoners.

The subsequent peaceful interlude lasted almost a year. For a time, eruptions were put down by a show of force, but on Jolo the deteriorating situation caused Wood to move against a large gathering of Moro fighters. Hostilities began immediately. On the first day of the campaign, Wood's men killed 50 Moros at a loss of one of their own. A short distance away on the following day, Moros attacked an American column and killed three men before retreating to a fortified *cotta*. Wood moved his men and artillery to nearby high ground, destroyed the village with his field guns, and then swept it with soldiers converging from all sides. Wood lost seven men. The exact death count among the Moros was uncertain, though significant. Wood, anticipating criticism, noted that women were armed and that the village had refused his request to surrender. Another large *cotta* nearby was attacked the following day with the loss of additional significant numbers of Moro lives.

Wood's methods were not without effect. Soon after, a *cotta* located close to the coast surrendered without a fight when approached by Wood's force and threatened by two navy ships lying offshore.

In July 1905, Wood left the Philippines for several months, undergoing his first surgery for brain tumor at a Boston hospital, followed by recovery time and extensive travel in Europe. Back on Mindanao in late October, he was lauded by the governor-general, who pronounced the province the most progressive in the Philippines. Revenues were up twofold despite the absence of opium production and the lottery, previously the island's two main sources of income. Moros were paying taxes for the first time. Shipping was a growth industry, while piracy and slavery were all but eradicated.

Wood had formally taken command of the entire Division of the Philippines on February 1, 1905. He believed at the time, and said in official correspondence, that the only remaining major Moro threat lay around an extinct volcano called Bud Dajo, where the remnants of the violent bands shredded in his earlier campaigns were known to be gathering. Bud Dajo would become Wood's most controversial battle. Questions concerning it would follow him for the remainder of his career.

Rising slightly more than two thousand feet above the jungle floor, the mountain provided an ideal fortress for the Moros. Although the lower elevations rise quite gradually, the slope approaches 60 degrees a few hundred feet from the summit and becomes almost vertical over the last 50 or so feet from the crater rim. The crater itself, fertile and with ample water, is about 100 feet deep and 500 feet across. The only access, other than by perilously grabbing roots and vines, were three trails cut into the side of the mountain.

Hundreds of the more hostile Moros, angry survivors of Wood's sweep through the island, were congregated there. As their numbers increased, so did their belligerency. Heavily armed, they entrenched and fortified the mountain and the crater rim. Some, although generally minor, depredations were alleged to have been launched from the Bud Dajo sanctuary.

Regarding Bud Dajo as a festering sore, Wood was determined to strike before the danger increased. Wood's direct role in the battle that followed is sometimes questioned. He was not officially the on-scene commander. That position was held by Colonel Joseph W. Duncan, who had been sent by Wood to deal with the insurgents at Bud Dajo. Many, however, assert that Wood was the driving force, planning the attack, insisting upon it, and then traveling to the site to witness or oversee the battle.

Wood had proposed a nighttime sneak attack by a small number of men who would first clear the crater rim and then fire from it into the interior. Surprise was lost, however, in a confusion of orders. Two of the three scout groups did not reach the summit.

Frustrated by the mix-up, Wood decided to go ahead. Field pieces were hauled up the mountain by block and tackle and positioned to fire into the crater floor. During the fight up the side of the mountain, the struggle for the crater rim, and the later battle inside the crater, the Americans lost 18 dead and 52 wounded. Casualties included army, navy, and Philippine Constabulary troops.

Moro dead numbered in the hundreds. Wood estimated six hundred, a figure that included both sexes and all age groups. Others put the figure as high as nine hundred. Guesses regarding the number of Moro survivors ranged from a low of seven to a high of one hundred. None attempted to escape. Toward the end of the battle, some essentially committed suicide by exposing themselves to fire.

Controversy immediately followed in some American newspapers. It was short-lived. Wood's explanation of events was generally accepted or at least tolerated by much of the American press and public. Wood met with leaders from nearby villages shortly after the battle. The *datos* fully understood the message of Bud Dajo and remained quiescent. Although Wood later dispatched troops to the island of Samar to put down a flare-up of raids on Christian communities by a pagan sect, the Moro provinces remained generally calm for the duration of Wood's stay in the Philippines.

Relative peace enabled Wood to again focus on administration: a bank to provide low-interest loans to farmers followed efforts to lower taxes and agricultural tariffs. He also found time to turn his attention to broader army matters, advocating a promotion system weighted more on performance and less on seniority. Wood attempted to turn Manila into a redoubt and saw the small island of Corregidor, situated in Manila

Bay, as the key to the city's defense. Wood fortified the island. A force of two thousand workers constructed massive gun emplacements, an electric railway, a water system, and power plant, so that, with adequately stockpiled supplies, Wood believed the island could withstand a siege of six to eight months.

Wood's statements and writings at the time reveal his prescient views regarding the region's future. He was one of only a handful of Americans who believed Japan would defeat Russia in the Russo-Japanese War (1904–5) and that the Japanese Empire would inevitably turn its attention to America's possessions in the Pacific. He thought it logical that any attempt on the Philippines would begin with landings at Lingayen Gulf. On December 22, 1941, the Japanese fulfilled that prophecy. Corregidor, strengthened in later years beyond Wood's beginning efforts, held out until May 6, 1942.

Wood left the Philippines on February 20, 1908. Few American military leaders have been as respected by their men. Wood's soldiers thought him to be concerned for their welfare, wary of unnecessary casualties, and more successful in battle than his contemporaries.

Jack McCallum, Wood's most noted biographer stated:

> Wood at his best was altruistic, intelligent, superbly self-confident, and indefatigable. As the architect of American twentieth-century nation building, he brought order out of chaos, overcame epidemics, established an equitable judiciary, opened schools, funded hospitals, built roads and eschewed personal wealth. Wood was also arrogant, intolerant, and autocratic. He did not believe the people he ruled were capable of self-government and never thought them his equal.... Convinced he knew more about the nation's military needs that the president, he sacrificed his career to his vision.... During his campaign [for the presidency] the public saw what was admirable in the general and would likely have elected him had professional politicians not focused on his flaws and combined parliamentary manipulation and bribery to derail his candidacy.

A FAMILIAR NAME IN A LESSER
KNOWN ROLE
JOHN J. PERSHING

Before fate took him to Europe and immortality as commander of the American Expeditionary Force during World War I, Pershing was acclaimed for his success in leading operations against Filipino insurgent forces.

Pershing is the towering American military figure of World War I. Indeed, for most Americans of recent generations, it is perhaps only his name that is recalled from among the hundreds of thousands who served in that conflict. Some may remember the feats of Captain Eddie Rickenbacker or Sergeant Alvin York, but those names are associated with individual achievements (Rickenbacker's 26 kills, making him the leading American air ace) or acts of heroism (York's Medal of Honor, awarded for single-handedly killing 28 Germans and capturing 132 others). Pershing, almost alone, is recollected for military leadership at the highest level.

Pershing's career was long and varied: he fought Natives in the closing era of Plains warfare, took American troops into Mexico on the Punitive Expedition, and in Europe led the largest American army yet assembled. Before fate took him to France and military immortality, he played an important but little known role in helping quell the Philippine Insurrection.

Pershing served three tours in the Philippines: the first from 1899 to 1903; the second, of only 20 months' duration, as commander of Fort McKinley on Luzon in 1907 and 1908; and the third from 1909 to 1913. On the first and last occasions, his duty took him to Mindanao and Jolo, the Moro heartland. It was his achievements in those settings that began to set him apart from his contemporaries.

Pershing was one of the small number of American officers who studied Moro culture and language and worked to gain the confidence of Moro chiefs. He kept the chiefs informed, visited their villages, and openly solicited their opinions and advice when planning projects. They came to trust him implicitly. In a letter home he said, "I have made many very strong personal friends among the Moros. Some of them will do anything for me. If I should say: 'Go kill this man or that' the next day they will appear in camp with his head." Pershing built roads and schools, buying supplies and paying Moro workers at slightly above the usual rates. His initiatives were regarded as particularly insightful and presaged the counterinsurgency techniques used by American forces in later wars.

On Mindanao and Jolo, Pershing rather quickly earned a reputation for being among the most successful of the American commanders.

However, not all Moros—particularly the *juramentados*, the fanatical Muslims who had sworn an oath to kill Christians—could be dissuaded from violence. In such instances, his opponents found Pershing to be an implacable foe—although he tended to be more patient, working harder and waiting longer while trying to achieve peaceful outcomes, than were most of his colleagues.

On October 1, 1902, after having built a road sufficient to transport artillery, Pershing confronted hundreds of belligerent Moros at Macia, a major fortified *cotta*. The presence of Pershing's massed artillery prompted about half of the Moros to foreswear their blood oaths and flee. Recognizing that body counts were not always the best measure of pacification, Pershing allowed them, and later others, to escape. At 3:00 the following morning, Pershing's riflemen tore apart an attack from inside the *cotta* before moving and burning the destroyed village.

Pershing's actions at Macia had an interesting side effect. At the nearby village of Bayan, an imam known for his ferocious hostility invited Pershing to his *cotta*. In front of other chiefs, he made Pershing an honorary *dato* and swore an oath of friendship to the Americans.

After Macia, one major fortification remained in the region. Bacoclod was the strongest and most threatening of the Moro strongholds. When attacks from the bastion persisted, Pershing received approval to eliminate the fortress.

In early April 1903, Pershing pushed his force of several hundred men through the jungle. Reaching the *cotta*, he placed his artillery and riflemen at locations that decimated the enormous village. Firing began in early morning and lasted until darkness fell. Over the next two days, the Moros refused two opportunities to surrender. By the afternoon of the second day, Pershing's artillery had turned Bacoclod into rubble. With the Moros pinned down by the shelling, Pershing moved his infantry close to the village walls and readied them for a final assault. When the attack came the following day, though the fighting was momentarily hand-to-hand, the Americans quickly carried the walls and stormed the destroyed village. Sixty Moro dead were counted inside and around the compound, and another 60 or so were thought to have died of wounds in the jungle.

Pershing followed with a two-week show-of-force march around the entire formerly hostile region of Lake Lanao. The successful trek, long remembered by Filipinos, marked the final campaign of Pershing's first tour in the Philippines. In the aftermath, he was lauded for having made more progress with less loss of blood than other commanders.

Pershing left Mindanao in the early summer of 1903. When he returned six years later, he found that much of the progress he had made had slipped away, lost in the intervening years by the less diligent and less effective commanders who had followed him.

Pershing came back to the Philippines for the third time on November 11, 1909. By now a brigadier general, he returned as military governor of Moro Province. Comprising Mindanao, Jolo, and hundreds of smaller islands, it was a region he knew well.

Pershing began with a listening tour, visiting local chiefs and learning their concerns. Years of inconsistently pursued pacification efforts had left conditions on the islands unsettled. Utilizing a technique that would anticipate later counterinsurgency doctrine, Pershing dispersed his troops in small packets around the countryside. In villages throughout the islands, his soldiers formed a visible presence providing security and teaching and training the Moros. In the coming months, he revitalized the rural economy in part by establishing trading stations and instituting well-attended local trading fairs. Pershing's staff experts reformed archaic laws and codes and forced decision-making downwards to the village level. Over the next four years, Pershing oversaw the construction of five hundred miles of roads, two hundred miles of telephone lines, and 37 medical stations.

While conditions significantly improved, instances of banditry and raids by *juramentado* terrorists continued to disrupt the progress. The *juramentados* were a particular concern, sometimes striking even the centers of major towns. To combat the threats, Pershing established flying columns—mobile, fast-moving strike forces to track down the insurgents and destroy their camps. What would now be called "PSYOPS" (psychological operations) were also employed. Some remain controversial to this day. To dissuade fanatical Muslims from engaging in attacks, Americans sometimes publicly buried the bodies of captured terrorists in graves with dead pigs. The technique was viewed as a deterrent because Muslims abhorred swine, and at least some believed the absence of a proper burial would prevent their entrance into heaven.

Eventually, Pershing decided on the ambitious step of disarming the entire Moro population. Although his proclamation, issued on September 8, 1911, met with scattered resistance across the province, there was general compliance except for two locations. On Jolo and in Lanao Province, disobedience continued, and soon after an attack on a U.S. camp resulted in American casualties.

At Taglibi on November 28, American entrenchments, barbed wire, and a two-hundred-yard free-fire zone cleared of jungle growth stopped a series of frenzied attacks by *juramentados*. When raids continued, Pershing sent five flying columns to the region of Bud Dajo—the crater that had been the scene of a major battle several years before—where hundreds of Moro warriors were known to be concentrating. Pershing's fast-moving forces converged from different directions and pinned the Moros inside their redoubt. Seeking to avoid the level of bloodshed that had occurred in the 1907 fight, Pershing offered the Moro leaders several opportunities to surrender. All were refused by the warriors, who had taken an oath to fight to the death.

Rather than attack immediately, Pershing placed the mountain fortress under siege, sealing off trails and planting outposts around the mountain. Each day Pershing pushed his lines closer to the fortress. Finally, after five ever-nearer lines of investment, his troops were only 30 yards from the Moro fortifications. Attempts by the Moros to break out were repulsed by close, heavy fire. Eventually groups of near-starving Moros began to surrender. A final large attack on Christmas Eve 1911, from Moros hidden in the jungle who thought Americans would leave the area of the now-abandoned *cotta*, was shattered. Forty-nine survivors, all that remained of the Moro forces, surrendered.

Within six months of the Battle of Bud Dajo, almost all Moro firearms had been collected. One glaring holdout remained. At Bud Bagsak, Moros led by a powerful chief had constructed an enormous fortification. Seeking to avoid bloodshed, Pershing negotiated the withdrawal of American troops in return for the Moros turning in their weapons.

When the Moros reneged on their bargain, Pershing planned a lightning assault, timed to strike when the women and children were working in the fields away from the complex of *cottas*.

In June 1913, Pershing, by a series of amphibious landings and overland marches, moved against Moro warriors numbering in the hundreds. Pershing's rapid advance took the outlying Moro posts by surprise, overwhelming them with few American losses. He then split his force, sending Major George Shaw to attack the nearby Pujagan *cotta*, which Shaw did successfully a day later.

By June 14, Pershing had moved his artillery into position at Bud Bagsak. At 9:00 the next morning, with Philippine Scouts (mostly Moros with U.S. commanders) in the van of the attackers, Pershing began his assault on the last stronghold in Moro Province. The ensuing battle was one of the fiercest of the entire war. For a time in early afternoon with casualties mounting and the advance stalled along the entire line and in danger of losing momentum, Pershing moved to the front, ordering other American officers to do the same. Pershing's example restored energy and direction to the assault. The fighting continued for nine hours. Not until 5:00 p.m. was the *cotta* declared secure.

Pershing's victory at Bud Bagsak was the last substantive battle of the Moro Rebellion. Pershing focused the following weeks on civic action projects—schools, roads, medical facilities, and agricultural enhancements—before departing the islands for the last time in August 1913. Pershing left the Philippines as a promising but junior one-star general. Five years later he was General of the Armies of the United States and, after President Woodrow Wilson, perhaps the world's most famous living American.

Pershing died in 1948 at age 87. He is buried at Arlington National Cemetery.

CHAPTER 3
WORLD WAR I

THE ROAD TO WAR

When the United States entered World War I on April 6, 1917, Europe had been at war for two and a half years. Precipitated by the assassination of Austrian archduke Franz Ferdinand in Sarajevo on June 28, 1914, systems of interlocking alliances fueled by territorial ambitions and age-old national animosities drew nation after nation toward the precipice. Like dominoes, mobilization followed mobilization and ultimatum followed ultimatum. By August, the continent was at war.

By the end of that month, entire graduating classes from some schools—students who had matriculated only a few weeks earlier during the glorious summer of 1914—had ceased to exist. Within weeks the war on the Western Front had become a stalemate. Opposing trench lines extended from the Swiss border to the coast of Belgium on the North Sea. Attempts to break the impasse led to slaughter on a scale previously unimagined. At the Somme on July 1, 1916, the British lost around 60,000 men in a single day. Ten months of carnage around Verdun in the same year resulted in 306,000 battlefield deaths and at least another half million wounded. Thousands pulverized by artillery fire—nearly *40 million* rounds were expended during the battle—would never be found.

When elected in November 1914, Woodrow Wilson had made clear his determination to keep the United States out of the war. There is such a thing, he said, as "being too proud to fight." Nonetheless, several events in the months ahead overwhelmed his attempts to maintain American neutrality.

On May 7, 1915, the German submarine *U-20* torpedoed the R.M.S. *Lusitania* off the coast of Ireland. The *Lusitania* sank with the loss of 1,196 lives, 128 of them American. German attempts to justify the attack, asserting among other arguments that the ship carried war matériel, were not accepted by the American government.

January 1917 witnessed a clumsy attempt by the German foreign minister, Arthur Zimmermann, to draw Mexico into the war as an ally of the Central Powers. In return, the Germans promised to help Mexico recover territories lost to the United States during the Mexican-American War of 1846–48. Famous as the Zimmermann Note, the coded telegram was intercepted by British intelligence and quickly passed to Washington. Its contents outraged the American public. Only days later the German government announced its intention to resume unrestricted submarine warfare effective February 1, 1917. When American protests failed, the die was cast. Congress declared war two months later.

When the war began on August 1914, the U.S. Army numbered less than 100,000 men. Moderately increased to about 127,000 at the time of America's entry into the conflict, the size remained negligible in comparison to the millions under arms for the belligerent powers. The army had not a single unit of division size. Armaments and aircraft industries were modest in scale. During the course of the war, most warplanes, tanks, and heavy weapons would be purchased from Allies. In the meantime, the army had to be built from scratch. It would take months to induct, train, equip, assemble, and organize an American Expeditionary Force (AEF) that eventually sent two million men to France, about a million and a quarter of whom saw combat before the war ended.

When the American war machine finally geared up, the flow of troops—eager, though raw and untrained as they were—increased dramatically. One hundred eighty-three thousand were in Europe in December 1917. By July 4, 1918, General Pershing announced the arrival of the millionth U.S. soldier. More were arriving at the rate of 10,000 a day.

More than a year would elapse before Americans in sizable numbers began taking their places in the trenches. Appeals for help from Allied nations desperately strained by years of conflict brought Americans into the fray during the Aisne Offense in May 1918 and along the Marne in June. During the 100 Day Offensive that closed the war, the AEF fought as an American army, winning difficult victories at Saint-Mihiel in September and at Meuse-Argonne in October.

Though its participation was relatively brief, the consequences of America's entry into the war and its contribution to the Allied victory cannot be minimized. Most of the nation's 53,402 combat deaths and

Newly arrived American troops prepare for action. The complex system of trenches extended from the North Sea to the Swiss border.

204,002 wounded occurred during four months of intense fighting prior to the November 11 armistice. (Another 63,114 U.S. servicemen died of disease during the war.) Total American losses numbered 320,518.

Many major histories of World War I devote not more than a line or two to American leaders other than General John J. Pershing. That circumstance reflects the fact that Pershing's role was transcendent in scope and importance and that America's participation in the war was relatively brief in duration. There were, however, American leaders other than Pershing who made significant contributions, although most are little remembered today.

HUNTER LIGGETT

America's foremost World War I soldier after John Pershing, Liggett trained and organized U.S. forces as they arrived in France and led combat commands at both the corps and army levels. He commanded the largest American component—over one million men—through difficult fighting that included the final offensive that destroyed German resistance west of the Meuse River.

Promoted to permanent lieutenant general after the war—a rank he held on a temporary basis during the conflict—Hunter Liggett was, after John Pershing, the U.S. Army's foremost senior soldier.

Liggett arrived in France with the 41st Division in February 1918 as the novice U.S. Army streamed onto the continent. He trained and organized the American force as it grew and took shape on French soil. Liggett would subsequently hold combat commands at both the corps and army levels and would lead the largest U.S. component, over one million men, through some of the war's most difficult fighting: the Marne, Saint-Mihiel, Argonne Forest, and the final offensive that destroyed German resistance west of the Meuse River.

As the Americans' strength increased month by month and major units were formed, Liggett was Pershing's choice to command I Corps and, later, the First Army, when those formations were activated. Liggett would take I Corps through the early battles at Cantigny and Belleau Wood and later through the massive July–August clashes along the Marne and at Saint-Mihiel.

As First Army commander, he directed the final stage of the Meuse-Argonne campaign and the destruction and pursuit of German forces along the Meuse River that was ongoing at the war's end. After the armistice, Liggett led the newly organized and designated U.S. Third Army—the Army of Occupation—that established the Allied presence on the bridgeheads of the Rhine River.

Liggett was commander of I Corps when one of its constituent elements, the 1st Division, commanded by General Robert L. Bullard, launched the first American offensive of World War I. Fought at Cantigny on May 28, 1918, the battle was small in comparison with those that would follow. However, the successful attack did much to inspire confidence in the previously untested U.S. Army.

Within two days of Cantigny, forces serving under Liggett were tested again, this time in a major way. At Belleau Wood from June 1 to June 26, the U.S. 2nd and 3rd Divisions, a brigade of U.S. Marines, and contingents from the French and British armies defeated a German attack, part of the massive 1918 Spring Offensive intended by Kaiser Wilhelm's government to win the war before American forces could intervene decisively.

CHATEAU-THIERRY OFFENSIVE
July 18–August 31, 1918

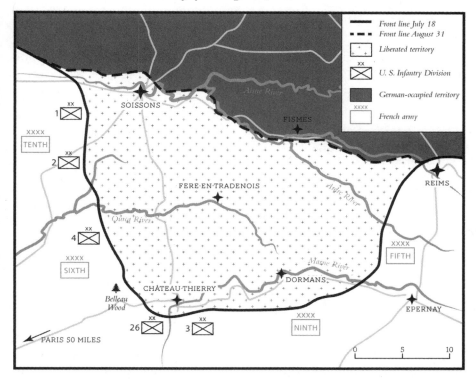

Seeking to strike a potentially war-winning blow before newly arriving American troops could be fully trained, German General Erich Ludendorff shifted troops from the Eastern Front following Russia's withdrawal from the war. The massive "Ludendorff Offensive" in the spring and summer of 1918 carried to the Marne River within 50 miles of Paris.

On July 15, German units struck U.S. forces newly in place at the front. The Allies countered on July 18 when French and American formations, in one of the first major actions involving U.S. troops, attacked on a 25-mile wide front with a portion of the U.S. assault focused on Chateau-Thierry.

The surprise assault, made without the usual preparatory artillery bombardment, was followed by precisely coordinated rolling barrages as the troops pushed forward. By the end of August, the offensive had carried 25–30 miles into formerly German-held territory, a precursor to the final Allied advances that ended the war.

With as many as 50 additional divisions newly available—freed by Russia's surrender on the Eastern Front—the German army began in March a series of major attacks aimed at ending the war. The first, in the north around the Somme, all but destroyed the British Fifth Army. Soon after, French forces near Soissons and Reims were forced to retreat.

Within days, the German army reached the Marne River at Château-Thierry. By May 27, they were only 40 miles from Paris.

A bit farther south, just north of the Paris-Metz highway, American forces held a 12-mile segment of the front along a line that traversed grain fields and hills cut intermittently by wooden areas. By pushing through Belleau Wood, one of the largest stands of timber in the area, the Germans aimed to cross the Marne and continue their advance toward Paris. The first few days of June were marked by heavy fighting as the Americans first plugged a gap in the French lines and then fought continuous German attacks to a standstill.

On the 6th of June, French and American forces launched a limited counterattack that included the capture by U.S. Marines of Hill 142, a key terrain feature. The advance brought the Americans near Belleau Wood. The battle that followed would become immortal in Marine Corps lore.

Commanded by U.S. Army general James Harbord, in the face of horrific casualties the Marines established a foothold in the timber. Over the next several days, attack followed counterattack as the opposing sides grappled in the shattered forest. On the 10th and 11th, Marine attacks from the north, west, and south pushed forward against trench lines and fire from interlocking machine-gun nests. Entire companies were shot to pieces before the southern-most German defenses were overcome. Bitter hand-to-hand combat and the use of mustard gas by the Germans would rage for 15 more days. Finally, on June 26, the Marines cleared the woods of German forces. Though worse would follow, the cost was high: 1,811 killed among nearly 10,000 total casualties.

Soon after, elements of Liggett's I Corps would be in action in a climactic struggle known in the present day as the Second Battle of the Marne. Fought during the period July 15 to August 5, 1918, a campaign the Germans projected as part of a war-winning offensive turned into a substantial Allied victory. Conceived by German field marshal Erich Ludendorff, the 40-division attack was aimed at splitting the French forces around the city of Reims. Held by the French Sixth Army supported by 85,000 Americans and portions of the British Expeditionary Force, a segment of the Allied line west of the city was initially driven back across the Marne. By July 17, the Germans were over the river in force, with a bridgehead nine miles long and four miles deep. The

U.S. Marines in action at Belleau Wood. Fought near the Marne River June 1–26, 1918, the battle took place during the German's spring offensive and became legendary in U.S. Marine Corps lore.

following day Marshal Ferdinand Foch, the Allied supreme commander, counterattacked the salient with 24 French divisions, supported by U.S. and British forces. Two days later the Germans began a retreat that by August 3 took them back to their original starting line. The Allied counterattack ended August 5 when lead elements came up against solidly reentrenched German units. Casualties were again extreme: 168,000 Germans, 95,000 French, 13,000 British, and 12,000 Americans fell during the three weeks of combat.

Among the several massive clashes that formed the Second Battle of the Marne, one of the most significant for the American army occurred at Château-Thierry on July 18, 1918. Three days after Ludendorff launched his massive offensive, Foch began counterattacking key German positions. For the green American units, a specific target of the German's push, Château-Thierry would provide a major proving ground. There, for one of the first times, large American formations contributed in a decisive way.

On a more than 20-mile, relatively quiet portion of the front, U.S., French, and Belgian forces launched an early-morning surprise attack. Made without the massive artillery bombardment that typically preceded major assaults, the well-coordinated assault was supported by rolling barrages that swept just ahead of the advancing troops. By nightfall, German opposition had been cleared, and Château-Thierry was in Allied hands.

Buttressed by growing numbers and increasing experience on the battlefield, Château-Thierry further primed the American army for its first large-scale independent offensive. That opportunity came soon, in mid-September.

Since September 1914, the Germans had held a long, protruding area south of Verdun near the town of Saint-Mihiel. Shaped like a triangle, the two-hundred-square mile Saint-Mihiel salient slashed 14 miles deep into Allied lines, a depth that hampered rail and other communications between Paris and eastern portions of the Allied front. Ironically, the Germans had made initial preparations to withdraw from the area and move back to the Hindenburg Line, an even more intensely fortified position farther to the rear.

The Germans had four years to fortify the salient. Their time was well spent. The Americans launched their attack through mud and rain against machine-gun nests, bunkers, barbed wire, and multiple lines of trenches. The American assault, conducted from September 12 to 16, took the Germans by surprise. Pershing committed to the attack 550,000 men— two full American corps, one of which was Liggett's I Corps—supported by four additional French divisions, three thousand artillery pieces, air attacks, and a contingent of French tanks. Sixty-five evacuation trains were lined up, and 26,000 hospital beds were made available to handle the anticipated casualties. Liggett's corps, comprising the 2nd, 5th, 40th, and 82nd U.S. divisions, struck the southeastern shoulder of the German salient. The corps's attack reached the first day's objectives by noon and the second day's by early evening of the following day.

Saint-Mihiel was the first American operation and first victory by an independent American army in World War I. The outcome effectively answered any remaining questions regarding the prowess of new American units. Two weeks later, in a massive undertaking, Foch shifted U.S. forces to the Argonne Forest. There, with more than a half million men in the assault units, they would play a major role in the Meuse-Argonne Offensive, which closed the war. During the course of the Meuse-Argonne battle, Hunter Liggett would take command of the American First Army.

Beginning on late September and fought over the remaining six weeks of the war, the Meuse-Argonne Offensive was the largest American battle of World War I. The objective of the campaign was Sedan, a vital hub whose rail network supported large portions of the German army in Occupied France and Flanders. The month and a half of fighting through hilly terrain held for years and laced with fortifications by the Germans would cost the Americans more than 26,000 killed and nearly 100,000 wounded.

Foch's realignment of forces brought much of the AEF from Saint-Mihiel to positions along a 30-mile section of the front line north and north-east of Verdun. The transfer involved a remarkable feat of logistics. The Americans shifted more than a million men with tanks, weapons, and supplies 40 to 50 miles undetected over poor roads and railways. The U.S. attack formed part of an Allied offensive that encompassed much of the Western Front. While the Americans struck towards Sedan, British and French forces attacked in the north, and British and Belgian units moved towards Ghent in Belgium. After a six-hour preparatory barrage by more than 2,500 guns, 600,000 men—three corps abreast (Liggett's I Corps along with the U.S. III and V Corps)—jumped off at 5:30 on the morning of September 26.

The U.S. troops faced a natural fortress, a 20-mile wide vortex bordered on one side by the Meuse River and on the other by the Argonne Forest. As at Saint-Mihiel, the Germans had used their four years of occupation to good advantage, saturating the already rugged landscape with blockhouses, wire, traps, and three major trench lines. During the initial days of bitter fighting, modest gains were interspersed with delays and setbacks. Liggett and other American commanders reshuffled and repositioned units to exploit opportunities or fill breeches created by German counterattacks. Underperforming units were replaced. The lack of roads through the rugged terrain created monumental traffic jams that slowed the flow of supplies and replacements to the assault units.

On October 3, near the western end of the American lines, the soon-to-be-famous Lost Battalion of the U.S. 77th Division was cut off and surrounded by German forces. Liggett launched a flanking attack by much of I Corps that relieved the battalion on October 8.

Soon after, with the further dispersal and growing numerical strength of the U.S. forces, Pershing reorganized the AEF. A newly created U.S. Second Army was given responsibility for the remnants of the salient around Saint-Mihiel. The U.S. First Army would operate along the Meuse-Argonne. With the AEF now comprising two active field armies, Pershing assumed the full-time role as overall commander of the AEF. Taking his place, effective October 16, 1918 as First Army commander was Hunter Liggett.

What happened next made Liggett well-known among American and Allied leaders. Liggett began by visiting corps and division headquarters and frontline units. He found them in deplorable shape. Some, after weeks of continuous combat, were at less than 25 percent of authorized strength. A lack of draft animals to pull artillery, essentially immobilizing much of his force's offensive punch, further added to the AEF's problems.

In the face of unrelenting pressure, Liggett ordered two weeks of down time to rest and refit. During that time, he remodeled the First Army. Selected units were specially trained to attack strongpoints. Infantry techniques were modified based on lessons learned. Artillery units were taught to provide better interdictory and counterbattery fire, with special emphasis on infantry support and suppression of enemy defenses.

Liggett's quickly reorganized forces first launched a series of smaller attacks that straightened out the American front and established suitable lines of departure for the major offensive yet to come. By the end of the month, the Argonne Forest and the fortified hills between it and the Meuse River were being cleared of German opposition.

Along the line, the offensive was spurred by the reconstructed American units and a French corps that contained three full U.S. divisions. All were supported by a newly constructed series of roads that funneled supplies and ammunition toward what soon became a fast-moving front. Lead elements of some American units advanced as much as six miles on the first day as German forces, surprised and overwhelmed, began to fall back. Advances over the next two days totaled another five miles, an almost unheard of figure given the experience of the previous four years when gains were often measured in yards and counted in numbers of thousands lost.

By the 3rd of November, lead elements of the American army forced a bridgehead over the Meuse River. On the 8th, American forces were on the hills overlooking Sedan. That day, the First Army boundary was shifted eastward to allow French forces the honor of capturing the city, held for four years by the Germans and the scene of a historic French defeat during the Franco–Prussian War in 1870.

The shift to the east allowed Liggett to reorient the First Army's route of advance. Units already east of the Meuse continued to strike north, while on November 10, amid signs of dissolution in some German formations, other forces began large-scale west-to-east crossings of the river. After rapid advances the following morning, Allied attacks all along the line were halted by news of the armistice, which reached most of the U.S. forward units by mid to late morning. The war was over.

Liggett's careful preparations had paid dividends for the Allied cause. The exceptional infantry-artillery coordination in American units was widely recognized. Liggett had his infantry push through or around German strongpoints while specially trained assault units reduced the most difficult fortifications. By the end of the campaign, the U.S. First Army had driven 43 German divisions back more than 30 miles over difficult terrain and some of the most heavily fortified positions on the Western Front.

Meuse-Argonne was Hunter Liggett's legacy to the U.S. Army. Under his tutelage, in a remarkably brief period of time, American units were transformed into a well-trained, well-organized, highly formidable fighting force.

Liggett remained in France after the armistice, serving as commander of the First Army until its deactivation in April 1919. It is indicative of Liggett's status among both American and Allied leaders that he was subsequently placed in command of the newly activated Third Army and led it during its occupation duty along the Rhine.

Before and After

Like that of Pershing and several other U.S. military leaders in World War I, Liggett's career stretched all the way back to warfare against Native tribes on America's Great Plains. Over the subsequent 42 years, the breadth of his assignments made Liggett one of the army's most experienced commanders.

A native of Pennsylvania, Liggett graduated from West Point in 1879. Initial postings took him primarily to the American West, where he participated in the final clashes of the Indian Wars. When the United States declared war on Spain in 1898, Liggett was sent to Cuba as adjutant general of the volunteer units. The following year he was assigned to the Philippines to command troops in the field as American forces struggled to put down the growing insurgency.

After returning from the Philippines, Liggett was assigned in 1907 to Fort Leavenworth, Kansas, as a battalion commander. In 1909, following his command tour, Liggett attended the Army War College, located at the time in Washington, DC. Liggett remained there after graduation, serving first as a faculty member and then as president from July 1913 to August 1914.

After his stint at the war college, Liggett served in command billets for the remainder of this career. The first, in Texas as commander of the 4th Brigade, 2nd Division, was followed by a series of key positions in the Philippines: brigade commander, commander of Fort William McKinley, and, for a year beginning in April 1916, commander of the Department of the Philippines. In April 1917, as America was gearing up for war, Liggett returned to the United States as commander of the Western Department in San Francisco. He served in that position only six months, until August 1917, when he was named commander of the 41st Division, the unit he would train and accompany to France.

During the closing months of the war as First Army commander, Liggett led more than one million soldiers. His tenure as commander of the Third Army, the Army of Occupation, was marked by further success. Liggett returned to the United States as commander of an Army corps based in San Francisco, serving in that duty until his retirement in 1921. Fort Hunter Liggett, an immense military training reservation near Monterey, California, now bears his name.

Liggett died in 1935 and is buried at San Francisco National Cemetery.

WILLIAM S. SIMS

Sims's signal contribution to the Allied cause was the role he played in combating the menace posed by German submarines that threatened to starve the European Allies into submission. Closely cooperating with the British navy, Sims instituted a convoy system, promoted new tactics, and successfully insisted on production of minesweepers, destroyers, and submarine chasers, which were then skillfully integrated into the antisubmarine effort.

When the United States declared war on Germany on April 6, 1917, the nation's military establishment faced two major problems. First, the country had almost no army to speak of. One would have to be built, quickly, from a miniscule foundation. The second problem, once an army had been created, was how to get it across the Atlantic without losing it on the way over.

The United States began the war as a first-class naval power. As would soon be apparent, however, it was not a navy well configured for the type of war the nation was about to enter. Like most navies of the world, the American version had emphasized the construction of capital ships, anticipating major fleet engagements that would destroy the enemy's opposing surface forces.

The reality turned out to be far different. During the course of World War I, the U.S. Navy would not sink a single surface combatant of the German navy and would lose only three themselves (one cruiser and two destroyers) to enemy action.

Still, the war could have been lost on the Atlantic. The menace came not from the surface but from beneath the sea. For a time, German submarines (known universally as U-boats, as derived from *unterseeboot*) preyed so successfully on merchant and transport ships that the flow of food and supplies to the Allies was threatened. In the months following the Germans' declaration of unrestricted submarine warfare in early 1917, the U-boat offensive came very close to tipping the balance.

When the United States entered the conflict, the Germans' strategic assessment was that American forces would not be able to influence the war for at least a year. In the meantime, increasing pressure on the Western Front and the U-boat campaign to starve the British of food and other supplies would defeat the Allies before the Americans' presence would be decisive.

Sinking 600,000 tons of Allied shipping per month, German military planners believed, would force Great Britain into submission. Accordingly, effective February 1, 1917, the Germans resumed unrestricted submarine warfare against noncombatant shipping in the war zone. Beginning initially with 105 submarines (about 46 were high-seas types), the offensive sank 500,000 tons in February and March,

800,000 in April, 600,000 in May, and 700,000 in June. Around the time America entered the fray, U-boats were sinking about 25 percent of all shipping bound for the United Kingdom. Even worse, perhaps, was that the devastation was inflicted at a cost of only nine submarines.

When Admiral William S. Sims first met his counterparts at the British Admiralty in the early days of the conflict, he was told that the war was being lost to U-boats. Sent first to London to serve as liaison with the British navy, Sims was soon after appointed commanding officer of U.S. Naval Forces in European Waters. He would remain in the post for the duration of the war.

An advocate of inter-Allied cooperation, Sims became a major figure in the Allied Naval Council, set up in 1917 to coordinate operations among the Allied navies. His ability to work with naval officials from other nations contributed notably to the group's effectiveness. His association—based on personal friendship as well as mutual interests— with British admiral Sir Lewis Bayly became especially close.

Sims's close working relationship with Admiralty officials would be mirrored by cooperation between the two navies on the high seas. Sims immediately urged the U.S. Department of the Navy to send all available antisubmarine craft to Europe. Over time, he attempted to make the U.S. Navy an effective extension of the Royal Navy's antisubmarine warfare operations. When the convoy system of escorting supply and transport ships was introduced, the two navies shared interchangeably in the task.

From the outset, Sims focused on winning the battle against the U-boats and providing support to the AEF. An early proponent of an expanded convoy system, Sims and his staff worked with the British to coordinate a program that shielded transports and merchant ships passing through the danger zone. During May and June 1917, an integrated convoy escort system was established that typically deployed six to eight destroyers or submarine chasers to screen 25 to 30 vessels. The presence of Allied warships, combined with a seemingly random zigzag pattern of movements (the slower-moving submarines of the era could not keep up when submerged) and instructions to destroyer captains to maintain an escort role rather than search for submarines, had an immediate impact.

Fewer merchant and transport vessels were lost, while submarine losses increased significantly. After July 1917, Allied tonnage lost to U-boats never again exceeded 500,000 tons per month. Although the total losses for 1917 totaled an enormous six million tons, by the end of the year the monthly losses were down to 300,000 tons.

The enhanced system had an impact on the numbers of U-boats sunk as well. From the beginning of the war in August 1914 up to February 1917, the Germans lost a total of only 48 U-boats. With the convoy system in effect for about half the year, 61 were sunk during the remainder of 1917.

The convoy system was only one of several measures Sims took to increase the striking power and coverage of his escort vessels. U.S. warships were deployed to Queenstown (now Cobh) and other locations along the Irish coast, extending the picket line farther west into the Atlantic. Inside the danger zone, U.S. destroyers were based at Ostend, Belgium, and other sites along the English Channel to further screen transports bound for Britain and France.

Aircraft and blimps—a first in antisubmarine warfare—were used in an innovative fashion. The long loiter time of Allied blimps was especially helpful in spotting U-boats on the surface and forcing them to dive, rendering them blind and far less mobile underwater. It is believed that during 1918 no convoy escorted by air patrol lost a ship to enemy action. Although the results were minimal, early attempts at aerial power projection were made with air strikes against German naval bases. Depth charges, first experimented with in 1910, were employed with varying degrees of effectiveness. The method of delivering the charges progressed from simply rolling them off the side of a ship to the use of rather sophisticated launchers at war's end.

Sims sent American vessels to help the British deploy and maintain what came to be known as the North Sea Mine Barrage, an immense mine field barrier positioned between Scotland and Norway. The barricades were intended to pin the German High Seas Fleet inside its Baltic Sea anchorages. In case the Germans attempted another sortie of their High Seas Fleet as at the Battle of Jutland, Sims sent five American capital ships to further improve the already formidable Allied advantage.

Admiral Sims co-located his London headquarters with those of his British counterparts. As with General Dwight Eisenhower during World War II, Sims's critics sometimes accused him of forming too close a relationship with the British and assigning higher priorities to Allied—as opposed to American—interests.

Sims, though, was anything but reticent. His occasional disputes with Secretary of the Navy Josephus Daniels were well aired in public. From the beginning, Sims pushed for increased production of submarine chasers, minesweepers, troop transport vessels, and merchant ships, while placing less emphasis on construction of capital ships. Secretary Daniels was initially reluctant to make drastic modifications to the production schedule, opposing Sims's view that development of antisubmarine vessels should receive near-exclusive priority. Fairly soon, however, construction of large ships was officially suspended and production shifted to destroyers, minesweepers, submarine chasers, and merchant vessels.

Sims and Daniels also disagreed over the allocation of vessels. Eventually, at Sims's urging, some of the newly produced destroyers and submarine chasers were sent to the Mediterranean to help Allied navies keep German and Austrian submarines bottled up in the Adriatic.

Perhaps because of the vantage point from his London headquarters, Sims was especially sensitive to the threat to British supplies posed by unrestricted submarine attacks. He was an advocate of the shipbuilding "crusade" that by mid-1918 saw American industry turning out enormous numbers of cargo vessels.

Before the war began, Sims's U.S. Army counterpart, General Leonard Wood, severely criticized the Wilson administration's lack of preparation in not having an American army ready to go to war. Sims voiced complaints about the Navy's preparation. Upset by lack of support from the Navy Department, he called attention to what he regarded as deficiencies in strategy, tactics, policies, and training.

Admiral Sims's signal contribution to the Allied cause was the role he played in helping defeat the U-boat threat. During the course of the war, German submarines sank more than 5,200 merchant ships—2,439 in 1917 alone. Losses of that magnitude could not be sustained. The convoy system and other measures introduced by Sims drastically reduced

Allied shipping losses. From 6,200,000 tons in 1917 (with a high month of 880,000 tons), losses fell to 2,660,000 tons in 1918 (with a high month of 343,000 tons). U-boat sinkings increased dramatically as well. By the close of the war, the Germans were losing five to 10 submarines per month, while convoy losses dropped from 25 percent to 1 percent. Most military historians regard the defeat of German U-boat warfare as the critical naval campaign of the war, crucial to the ultimate defeat of the Central Powers.

Admiral William S. Sims, a name little recalled today, contributed significantly to that victory.

Before and After

William Sowden Sims was born in 1858 to American parents living in Canada. He graduated in 1880 from the United States Naval Academy. Except for a year's sabbatical in Paris learning French and studying European navies, he spent the following decade and a half aboard the warships *Saratoga*, *Philadelphia*, and *Charleston*. From 1897 to 1900, he served as naval attaché in Paris, Madrid, and St. Petersburg. Further shipboard assignments followed on the USS *Kentucky* and the USS *Monterey* before staff duty with the commander in chief of the Asiatic Fleet, aboard the USS *Brooklyn*.

As a young officer, Sims worked to reform naval gunnery by introducing techniques to improve target practice and streamline the process of loading, aiming, and firing the navy's weapons. From his study of the British navy, Sims became an advocate of a technique called "continuous aim firing." When his suggestions were repeatedly ignored by his superiors, Sims—undeterred by his relatively low rank (he was a lieutenant commander at the time)—wrote directly to President Theodore Roosevelt. The president, a former assistant secretary of the navy, was intrigued by Sims's ideas. Soon after, when the Atlantic Fleet scored poorly on fleet gunnery exercises, Roosevelt appointed Sims inspector of target practice for the U.S. Navy. Sims held that post for the next six years (1902 to 1908) before being appointed naval aide to the president.

Sims' first shipboard command followed. From 1909 to 1911, he was commanding officer of the battleship USS *Minnesota*. Promoted to the rank of captain in 1911, he spent much of the next two years as a student, and for a time as faculty member, at the Naval War College, in Newport, Rhode Island. Further commands followed, first as commanding officer, Destroyer Flotilla, Atlantic Fleet, and then as commanding officer of the USS *Nevada*.

In early 1917, Sims was promoted to rear admiral and served briefly as president of the Naval War College and commandant of the Second Naval District. Sims was pulled from those duties and sent to Europe where he remained for the duration of the war.

In 1919, he resumed his duties as president of the Naval War College. Foreseeing the potential of carrier-borne aircraft, he introduced a program of aviation studies in the college's curriculum. Sims presided over the war college until his retirement in 1922. In 1925, he was temporarily returned to duty to serve on a variety of special boards.

Sims's book *Victory at Sea*, a thoughtful account of U.S. naval activities during the war, won the 1921 Pulitzer Prize for history. In 1930, he was promoted to full admiral on the retired list.

Sims died in 1936 and was buried at Arlington National Cemetery.

Deeper in the Shadows ...

JAMES G. HARBORD

As chief of services, Harbord brought order out of chaos in handling the thousands of American troops and mountains of matériel that arrived in France on a daily basis. Though a U.S. Army general, Harbord led Marine units during their fabled battle at Belleau Wood.

BELLEAU WOOD
June 25, 1918

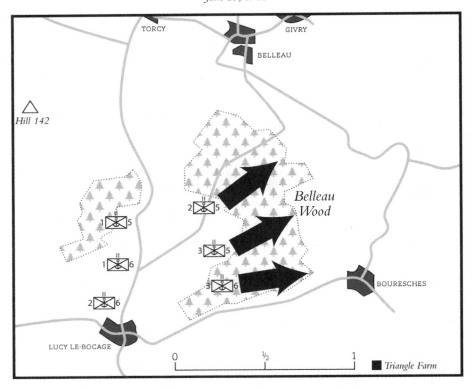

6 JUNE
Marines begin attack on Belleau Wood securing a foothold despite heavy casualties.

7–25 JUNE
The struggle turns into a series of attacks and counterattacks in fighting that featured massive artillery barrages, poison gas, and assaults against interlocking machine gun positions. Altogether the Marines launched six major attacks and fought off parts of five German divisions.

26 JUNE
Belleau Wood is reported cleared of German forces.

Brigadier General James Harbord began the war as General Pershing's chief of staff. Later in the war, with 10,000 American troops accompanied by thousands of tons of supplies and equipment pouring into France every day, Pershing assigned Harbord as chief of services and supplies in a generally successful attempt to bring order out of the chaos that was occurring behind the Allied lines. It was a task for which Harbord was well suited: a superb administrator, he would later become president and chairman of the board of RCA.

It is, however, a unique battlefield experience for which Harbord is most renowned. Though a U.S. Army general, Harbord commanded the U.S. Marine Corps units that waged their legendary battle at Belleau Wood. In the face of horrific losses, the Marines, assigned as part of the Army's 2nd Infantry Division, attacked six times and fought off parts of five German divisions before clearing the shattered woods. In a 1923 ceremony commemorating the battle, Harbord was made an honorary Marine.

Harbord grew up in Kansas. Commissioned from the ranks in 1891, he served on active duty until he retired in 1922 as a major general and deputy chief of staff of the U.S. Army. He was later advanced to lieutenant general on the retired list.

Harbord died in 1947 and is buried at Arlington.

ROBERT L. BULLARD

At Cantigny, Bullard led U.S. forces to the first significant American victory in World War I and then held his position in the face of repeated counterattacks. He later commanded the U.S. III Corps and, at war's end, the U.S. Second Army.

To Major General Robert L. Bullard went the honor of commanding the first sustained American offensive of World War I. At Cantigny, France, on May 28, 1918, Bullard, commander of the U.S. 1st Division, directed a regiment-sized attack against well-entrenched German positions.

Cantigny was situated at the tip of German salient that projected five kilometers deep into Allied lines. In addition to the military value, a U.S. victory there would instill confidence in the abilities of the still untested American army. Known as an aggressive commander, Bullard had proposed the attack after two earlier attempts by French forces had failed. At 6:45 a.m., after two hours of preparatory fire by 368 heavy guns, the U.S. 78th Regiment began moving behind a rolling barrage toward German lines. Supported by French tanks as well as artillery, trench mortars, flamethrowers, and air units from both nations, Bullard's forces took the village in a well-executed assault.

A greater difficulty now arose: holding Cantigny in the face of repeated German counterattacks. In the midst of the fighting, French artillery supporting Bullard's men was pulled away to defend against another nearby German offensive. When a weak spot developed in the American lines, Bullard sent reinforcements under the command of Theodore Roosevelt Jr. to bolster the defensive line.

Under constant pressure and despite the loss of much of their fire support, Bullard's men fought off six major counterattacks before the Germans finally withdrew. At the cost of two hundred killed and several hundred wounded, the Americans had taken and held Cantigny while pushing the American front line forward by about a mile.

In the months ahead, the four thousand "doughboys" who fought at Cantigny would be followed into the line by a million and a quarter others. The U.S. Army had taken its first small step.

Bullard advanced rapidly during the remainder of the war. As commander of the American III Corps, he led forces that saw major action during the Second Battle of the Marne and Meuse-Argonne Campaigns. In October 1918, when Pershing reorganized the AEF, Bullard became the first commander of the U.S. Second Army.

Bullard rendered valuable service in another area as well. Fluent in French, he often served in joint U.S.-French positions and was noted for his astute diplomatic skills.

Bullard died in 1947 at age 86. He is buried at the United States Military Academy.

Familiar Names in Lesser Known Roles

Many of the legendary names associated with World War II—Douglas MacArthur, George C. Marshall, George S. Patton—saw major action in World War I. Others, such as Billy Mitchell and John Lejeune, while most recalled for other aspects of their eventful lives, also made robust contributions to the Allied victory. To his considerable chagrin, Dwight Eisenhower, possibly the best-remembered of all, never got into combat. Like his friend Eisenhower, Omar Bradley never left the United States.

DWIGHT D. EISENHOWER

Through much of the war, Eisenhower directed training at Camp Colt, near Gettysburg, Pennsylvania. Though he never heard a shot fired in anger, his exceptional skills and organizational abilities were evident to colleagues and superiors.

Much to his discomfort, Eisenhower never witnessed a shot fired in anger during the course of the war. Although worried that his lack of combat experience might hamper his prospects for advancement, Eisenhower went on to become supreme Allied commander, leader of all Allied military forces in the European theater of operations (ETO) during World War II.

While not directly combat-related, Eisenhower's World War I role was significant nonetheless. Three years out of West Point, Eisenhower directed tank training at Camp Colt, a temporary installation established at Gettysburg, Pennsylvania. His exceptional abilities in handling that duty were duly noted by colleagues, however, and his later stellar performances in a variety of difficult positions eventually brought him to the attention of army chief of staff George Marshall. After he served 16 years as a major, the rapidity of Eisenhower's later promotions is indeed stunning: a colonel in October 1941, by December 1944 he was a five-star general.

After World War II, Eisenhower oversaw the army's demobilization as army chief of staff, left the service to become president of Columbia University, and then returned to the military as supreme Allied commander when the North Atlantic Treaty Organization (NATO) was formed. In 1955, he took office as the 34th president of the United States.

Eisenhower died in 1969. He is buried in a chapel on the grounds of the Eisenhower Presidential Library in Abilene, Kansas.

JOHN LEJEUNE

The Marine Corps's most legendary officer, Lejeune led the U.S. Army's 2nd Infantry Division through difficult fighting in the closing months of the war and remained with the unit through its occupation duty in Germany following the armistice.

One of the most legendary U.S. Marines, Lejeune arrived in France in June 1918. Lejeune was promoted to major general on July 28, 1918, and the same day took command of the U.S. Army's 2nd Infantry Division. Lejeune was only the second Marine officer to command an army division. (The first, Charles A. Doyen, held the position only a short time—October 25 to November 8, 1917—before relinquishing command because of illness.) Lejeune remained with the unit until it was disestablished in April 1919, having led it through the duration of the war and during its occupation duty in Germany.

Under Lejeune's command, the 2nd Division fought with particular success at Soissons, Mont Blanc Ridge, and during the Meuse-Argonne Offensive.

After the war, Lejeune served for a decade as Marine Corps commandant. He died in Baltimore in 1942 and is buried at Arlington National Cemetery.

DOUGLAS MACARTHUR

As chief of staff of the 42nd Division and later as commander of the 84th Infantry Brigade, MacArthur saw action during some of the most intense fighting of the war, earning seven Silver Stars, two Distinguished Service Crosses, and a host of honors from Allied nations.

Achievements of extraordinary number, scope, and magnitude mark Douglas MacArthur's status as one of America's great warriors. Indeed, there is almost a fictional quality associated with portions of his military career.

Nominated for the Medal of Honor for actions during the Meuse-Argonne Offensive (he would later receive the medal for his World War II service in the Philippines), he earned *seven* Silver Stars and two Distinguished Service Crosses during World War I, along with honors from several Allied nations. A 1903 graduate of West Point (first in his class), by June 1918 he was a brigadier general—the youngest in the AEF.

MacArthur went to France as chief of staff of the 42nd ("Rainbow") Division. He saw his first major action and won his first Silver Star in February 1918. Not long after, he was named commander of the division's 84th Infantry Brigade. Beginning at the Second Battle of the Marne, where the division first helped to stop the German offensive and then participated in the Allied counterattack, MacArthur and his unit were in combat for much of the rest of the war. After a brief respite following the battles along the Marne, the 42nd saw action at Saint-Mihiel and during the Meuse-Argonne Offensive.

After the armistice, MacArthur remained with the 42nd during its occupation of the Rhineland before returning with the division to the United States in April 1919.

MacArthur would go on to further renown as superintendent of the United States Military Academy, army chief of staff, and as a commander in the Pacific theater during World War II, where his "island-hopping" campaign helped stem the Japanese tide. Later still, in Korea, his amphibious landing at Inchon changed the complexion of that war as well.

Fired for insubordination by President Harry S. Truman in 1951, MacArthur returned to the United States for the first time since 1937, taking up residence at the Waldorf-Astoria in New York City. MacArthur died in 1964 and is interred in the MacArthur Memorial in Norfolk, Virginia.

GEORGE C. MARSHALL

Marshall's greatest achievement as a young colonel was his short-notice planning that, along with supplies, ammunition, and equipment, shifted 620,000 American and 200,000 French troops to positions 60 miles distant along the Marne River, positioning them for the offensives that brought the war to a conclusion.

George Marshall's participation in World War I is best remembered for his role in planning perhaps the most audacious logistical feat of the war. To fulfil a commitment made by Pershing to the French, the AEF conducted two major campaigns within 23 days. After prevailing at Saint-Mihiel, Marshall, then a young colonel and a member of Pershing's staff, shifted a sizable portion of the American army to locations as much as 60 miles distant. The move took the AEF to positions along the Meuse River near the Argonne Forest. From there, they contributed to the Allied offensive that brought the war to a close.

Marshall's plan involved the transfer of 820,000 soldiers—620,000 Americans moved into the line, while 200,000 French poilus were shifted elsewhere along the front. Support units, artillery, ammunition, and supplies accompanied the rotation of the more than half a million American soldiers. What makes the undertaking even more remarkable was that it was accomplished in three weeks, was done at night using three rather marginal roads, and complete security was maintained during the entire operation.

The accomplishment was unparalleled during the course of the war. Although Marshall also participated in planning the initial American offensive at Cantigny, the transfer of forces from Saint-Mihiel to the Meuse-Argonne Offensive remains his towering achievement of World War I.

Called "the organizer of victory" by Winston Churchill for his service during World War II, Marshall, as chief of staff of the U.S. Army, oversaw the largest expansion of the army in the nation's history while rendering invaluable service as military adviser to President Franklin D. Roosevelt. After the war he served President Truman as secretary of state and secretary of defense. He was awarded the Nobel Prize in 1953 for facilitating the economic recovery of Western Europe (the "Marshall Plan").

Marshall died in 1959 and is buried at Arlington National Cemetery.

WILLIAM "BILLY" MITCHELL

At Saint-Mihiel, Mitchell organized and led the largest force ever assembled for one air combat operation, nearly 1,500 aircraft flown by airmen from five Allied nations. His innovations across the full spectrum of air warfare operations, particularly regarding strategic bombardment, foreshadowed air operations in World War II.

Although he is best remembered in U.S. history as a critic of America's general lack of military preparedness and failure to modernize its small and obsolete air arm, Mitchell's innovations in World War I foreshadowed the integrated employment of airpower that characterized the nation's later conflicts.

In September 1918 at Saint-Mihiel, Mitchell organized and led the largest air force ever assembled for one combat operation. In support of the American offensive, Mitchell, commander of all American air combat units in France, directed the employment of 1,481 Allied aircraft—600 flown by Americans, the remainder piloted by British, French, Italian, and Portuguese airmen—against targets on the battlefield and in support cantonments. One of the first-ever coordinated air-ground offensives, it was easily the war's largest and most ambitious.

During the course of the conflict, Mitchell experimented across the full spectrum of air warfare operations: pursuit, reconnaissance, close air support of infantry attacks, and, most notably, mass bombardment of military formations and installations.

Regarded by some as the father of the U.S. Air Force, Mitchell remained a lifelong advocate of American airpower. Believing that command of the air would be decisive in future wars, he urged increased investment in aircraft research and development. But Mitchell's criticisms of the government's "almost treasonable administration of national defense" led to his 1925 court-martial. He resigned soon after.

Mitchell died in 1936. He is buried in Milwaukee, Wisconsin.

GEORGE S. PATTON

Patton's experience as a leader of armored forces began in World War I. In France he established a training school for tank warfare and later as a brigade commander led armored forces in combat at Saint-Mihiel and during the Meuse-Argonne Campaign.

Not widely known is the fact that George Patton's experience as a leader of armored forces began on the battlefields of France during World War I. Patton arrived early in France as a member of Pershing's staff. In November 1917, impressed by initial British and French operations with a new weapon—the tank—Pershing directed Patton to establish a tank training school for the AEF. The school received its first dedicated tanks (French Renaults) in March 1918. In August, Patton was named commander of a tank brigade and led armored forces in combat at Saint-Mihiel and during the Meuse-Argonne Campaign.

World War I saw the introduction of tank warfare. These Renault FT tanks operated by American crews were photographed on the road to Argonne, France. The small, light tanks with two-man crews were mass-produced by the French.

The leadership traits that would later make him famous were already much in evidence. Patton led from the front, reacting immediately to battlefield circumstances and exploiting the mobility of the new weapon. Near Jonville on September 13, he used his tanks in a cavalry-style sweep that disrupted German defenses and pushed through the main battle line. Patton was wounded in action on September 26, 1918, while leading an attack on German positions near Cheppy.

Known for his energy and boldness, as well as for his flamboyance, Patton would go on to become one of the U.S. Army's most successful, and controversial, World War II commanders.

Patton was injured in a road accident in Germany on December 9, 1945, and died 12 days later at a U.S. Army hospital in Heidelberg. He is buried at the Luxembourg American Cemetery near Luxembourg City.

OMAR BRADLEY

Of his colleagues, Bradley was the furthest removed from combat during World War I. Sent to guard copper mines in Montana, his unit's later deployment orders were cancelled when the war ended. Like his contemporary, Eisenhower, his talents were duly noted despite his lack of combat experience.

Of all of his contemporaries who later rose to prominence, Omar Bradley was the furthest removed from combat during World War I. Newly promoted to captain, he was sent to guard copper mines at Butte, Montana. When, in August 1918, he joined an infantry unit scheduled for deployment to the war zone, a flu epidemic and the November 11 armistice canceled the division's deployment orders.

Like his colleague Dwight Eisenhower, the absence of combat experience did not prevent Bradley's ascension to the highest levels in World War II. Beginning as a division commander in Tunisia in 1943, by the time the war ended he had led II Corps in Sicily, the First Army on D-Day and the subsequent breakout, and the 12th Army Group—four field armies and more than a million and a quarter men—through the end of the fighting in Europe.

After the war, he was appointed administrator of the Veterans Administration before becoming army chief of staff in 1948 and the first chairman of the newly created Joint Chiefs of Staff in 1949, serving in that capacity through the Korean War. Bradley eventually became an advocate for limiting the war, arguing that widening the conflict would involve the country "in the wrong war, at the wrong place, at the wrong time, and with the wrong enemy." In 1950, he was promoted to five-star general, the last officer to hold that rank.

The writer Ernie Pyle labeled Bradley the "GI's general," although the contention that he was regarded with special affection by front-line soldiers is disputed by some historians. General Marshall characterized him as "conspicuous for his ability to handle people."

Bradley died in New York City on April 8, 1981, aged 88. He is buried at Arlington National Cemetery.

CHAPTER 4
WORLD WAR II

THE ROAD TO WAR

The seeds of the world's deadliest conflict were sown decades before at the conclusion of World War I. Abnegating the lenient Fourteen Points proposal proffered by U.S. president Woodrow Wilson, the victorious Allies imposed draconian peace terms on the newly established German government. Exacerbating conditions of economic instability and widespread political unrest, the Treaty of Versailles assigned war guilt to the German people and imposed harsh monetary reparations, along with territorial adjustments and limitations on the nation's military forces.

In the unsettled times that followed, aggressive, nationalistic political movements—Fascists in Italy, Nazis in Germany, and militarists in Japan—rose to positions of power. During the turbulent 1930s, the League of Nations, a collective security organization established after World War I, proved ineffectual in maintaining peace. Japanese aggressions in Manchuria (1931) and China (1937) and Italy's invasion of Ethiopia (1935) were left unchecked. Later in the decade, the Spanish Civil War (1936–39) drew patron states in lineups that generally mirrored the competing alliances that would later oppose one another through much of the forthcoming global conflict.

In Germany, Hitler's rise to power in 1933 propelled a series of events that, viewed from the perspective of history, almost inexorably led the continent to war: remilitarizing the German state (1935), reoccupying the Rhineland (1936), annexing Austria (March 1938), and occupying the Sudetenland (October 1938). Britain and France did little to oppose these moves, and, although both nations had a military alliance with Czechoslovakia, the Munich Agreement gave formal sanction to Hitler's move into the Sudetenland.

When Hitler occupied the remaining portion of Czechoslovakia (March 1939) and made further threats in violation of his promise at Munich that the Sudetenland fulfilled his territorial ambitions, the Allies responded more forcefully. With Hitler's threat to move against Poland,

Britain and France formally aligned themselves with the Poles, making it clear that an attack on Poland would constitute a *casus belli*.

The attack came on September 1, 1939. War was officially declared two days later.

Meanwhile in the United States, confronted by a prevailing isolationist sentiment, the government of Franklin D. Roosevelt moved with caution. In September 1940, a conscription law passed Congress by a single vote. That same month, 50 aged destroyers were given to Great Britain in return for basing rights on British possessions. In March 1941, the Lend-Lease Act provided Allies with war matériel without committing U.S. troops. On the high seas, increasing threats from German U-boats prompted the government to arm merchant vessels and assign U.S. Navy ships to assist the Royal Navy in protecting sea lanes and escorting convoys.

In the Pacific, Japan's aggressive moves had begun in 1931 with the occupation of Manchuria, followed in 1937 by incursions deep into mainland China. Japan's militarist government sought to establish a Greater Southeast Asia Co-Prosperity Sphere, an economic and political zone dominated by Japan that would provide mineral resources, oil, rubber, and foodstuffs in support of the empire's expansionist policies while securing the nation's hegemony over the entirety of East Asia.

On September 27, 1940, Japan signed the Tripartite Pact with Germany and Italy. Though the treaty tied the three nations—the Axis Powers—in a loose general alliance, unlike with the Western Allies no formal mechanism was established to plan and coordinate military and political objectives.

Abetted by a sense of cultural superiority and a distorted view of the nation's industrial and economic strength, Japanese leaders—at least some of whom apparently held the view that the United States would not engage in a major conflict in the Pacific because to do so would enable Germany to triumph in Europe—set the empire's course towards war.

Militarily, Japan's intention was to create a defense perimeter midway through the Pacific that would safeguard its possessions and economic enterprises. Running from the Kuril Islands southward through several key island chains to Rabaul on New Britain and then westward to New Guinea, the line would encompass the many territories slated for invasion and occupation—Malaya, the Netherlands Indies, the Philippines, Wake Island, Guam, the Gilberts, Thailand, and Burma. Recognizing America's military weakness, Japan sought to deal a crippling blow, establish a strong defensive cordon, and aim for a negotiated peace before the United States could leverage its latent economic and military strength.

The intended killer strike was delivered at Pearl Harbor on Sunday morning, December 7, 1941. The United States declared war on the Japanese Empire the following day. Three days after that, Hitler, though not obligated by treaty to do so, declared war on the United States.

Two years and two months after the first shots were fired as German troops crossed the Polish border, the conflict had now truly become a world war. The European continent (including European Russia and the Balkans), the Mediterranean littoral, North Africa, mainland China, Southeast Asia, and heretofore little-known islands spread across the immense Pacific were, or soon would be, aflame.

U.S. battle deaths during World War II would number more than 405,000. Another 670,000 were wounded. Estimates of deaths worldwide vary considerably. A range of 60 to 80 million is often cited when fatalities from disease and famine are factored in. One major source estimates 22 to 25 million military deaths (including five million who died in captivity), about 38 million civilian casualties directly attributable to military actions, and another 19 to 25 million noncombatants who perished from war-related diseases or famine. Altogether, perhaps as much as 3 percent of the planet's prewar population may have died during a conflict that forever altered the world's political landscape.

TERRY DE LA MESA ALLEN

Allen trained and led two of the three divisions that were considered the best American units in the European theater. The 1st Infantry Division was an "old" division that Allen took into battle in North Africa and Sicily. The 104th was a new unit, only two years old when it came under fire for the first time. Allen led it from its inception and commanded it through 193 consecutive days of combat in Belgium, the Netherlands, and Germany until the end of the war. Both divisions were regarded by Allies and adversaries alike as the finest night fighters in the theater.

Terry de la Mesa Allen may be the most controversial of the officers whose stories are chronicled in these pages. He was once relieved of command under somewhat ambiguous circumstances; he was, at least at times, a heavy drinker; and—although dissenting opinions are plentiful—away from the battlefield the troops under his command had a reputation for rowdiness and lack of discipline.

Allen never commanded at the corps level. Thus, his responsibilities were more limited in scope than those carried by Patton, Bradley, Eisenhower, and others of his more well-known contemporaries. This level-of-duty consideration has caused come scholars to exclude him from ranking among the army's top World War II generals. Almost all, however, place him as one of its best soldiers.

During the course of World War II, three divisions—the 1st, the 9th, and the 104th—were rated as the finest American combat divisions in the ETO. The 1st and the 9th were old regular army divisions. The 104th was only two years old when it saw action for the first time. It was not by chance that Allen led two of the three—the old 1st and the new 104th, which he had trained and led almost from its inception.

Allen led the 1st Division—the "Big Red One"—through North Africa and Sicily. Indeed, when the Allies invaded Sicily, Patton insisted that the 1st under Allen's leadership be assigned the most difficult part of the invasion, the landings at Gela. In the closing days of the war, Allen's 104th raced through German territory to a junction with Soviet forces.

Almost alone among Allied commanders, Allen taught the 1st and the 104th to fight at night and featured that capability as a prominent part of the divisions' war-fighting repertoire. Both divisions came to be regarded by Allies and adversaries alike as the very best at the difficult business of nighttime combat.

Allen was the "soldier's general" who shared stories, hardships, cigarettes, and foxholes with infantrymen all along the front line. His concern for his enlisted troops bordered on legendary. By personality and example, Allen instilled in the 1st and 104th a unique camaraderie, a rare "all for one and one for all" spirit that permeated the organizations and made them perhaps the proudest, toughest, cockiest, and most confident outfits in the U.S. Army.

At the height of the war, the newspaper correspondent Quentin Reynolds wrote of Allen: "Never in my life have I seen a man so worshipped as Terry was.... As far as I am concerned, Terry Allen is the greatest leader of men and the greatest tactical genius of the war."

The wonderful prose of Ernie Pyle may have captured the man best of all:

> Major General Terry Allen was one of my favorite people. Partly because he didn't give a damn for hell or high water, partly because he was more colorful than most; and partly because he was the only general outside the Air Force I could call by his first name. If there was one thing in the world Allen lived and breathed for, it was to fight.... Allen's speech was picturesque. No writer could fully capture him on paper, because his talk was so wonderfully profane it couldn't be put down in black and white.

With the army gearing up for the war that loomed on the horizon, on October 1, 1940, Allen was promoted to brigadier general over nine hundred more senior officers, including all of those from the West Point class from which he had failed to graduate. He was one of only two brigadier generals appointed at the time. The other was George S. Patton. Allen never held the rank of colonel. In 1942, he took command of the 1st Infantry Division then at Fort Benning, Georgia, preparing for overseas deployment. Known for his foxhole visits and for sharing conversations and occasional bottles with enlisted men while on bivouac, he was quickly revered by the division's enlisted men. In June, he was promoted to major general, the highest rank he would hold.

Sent to Britain, the Big Red One underwent additional combat training and instruction on amphibious warfare. Allen's leadership— informal, aggressive, emphasizing military prowess rather than spit and polish—molded the division into a proud, cohesive force confident of its abilities and on occasion none too tolerant of outsiders.

Allen was 54 years old as he prepared his soldiers for America's first substantial World War II combat on ground washed by the Atlantic. He was described at the time as leathery in appearance, with a lantern jaw and bristly hair the color of gun metal. Two scars marked his cheeks, residue from his wounds in World War I. Allen was of medium height, athletic in appearance, and uncommonly strong.

The Big Red One saw its first action on November 8, 1942, with landings at Oran, Algeria, as part of Operation Torch, the Allied invasion of North Africa. Axis resistance around Oran was some of the fiercest of the initial stage of the campaign. After difficult fighting—the division sustained 418 casualties—the Axis force surrendered on November 16, capitulating to Allen in an impressive ceremony in the city center. Lessons were learned during the campaign. Allen's after-action assessment of the fighting reinforced his view of the importance of nighttime operations. As would occur later in Sicily and Germany, soldiers who had complained of the hard work and intensive training Allen had pushed them through became vocal in their praise for having been so well prepared.

After Oran, Allen's role over the next few months is difficult to assess. Much to his displeasure, parts of the division were split apart, assigned to other organizations, and placed under various Allied commanders. Allen and his headquarters element remained in Oran, but sizable formations were parceled out to the hard-pressed British V Corps in northern Algeria. Still others went to outfits in the Atlas Mountains of southern Tunisia, operating under Free French commanders or attached to any of several units employed by the U.S. II Corps. Allen complained personally, and bitterly, to Eisenhower about the fracturing of well-prepared units accustomed to working together. However, the division would not be completely reconstructed as an entity until shortly before victory was achieved in North Africa in 1943.

In the meantime, Allen did what he could with the units remaining to him and tried to observe and assist the formations that were assigned elsewhere, efforts that included setting up an advance detachment in Algiers. While those initiatives helped keep him in contact with his soldiers, Allen remained incensed at their dispersal. "A soldier," he said at the time, "doesn't fight to save suffering humanity or any other goddam nonsense. He fights to prove that his unit is the best in the Army and that he has as much guts as anybody else in the unit. Break up the unit and his incentive is gone." Ernie Pyle wrote that Allen believed he could have prevented some of the Allied defeats had he been allowed to command his unit intact. Eventually Allen's persistent requests to get into the fray alienated Major General Walter Bedell Smith, a choleric personality who served as Eisenhower's black-hat chief of staff. Smith would become one of Allen's harshest critics.

Allen's opportunity to demonstrate the capabilities of the 1st Division (more precisely, the partial formation left under his command), occurred when the Germans threatened a major breakthrough near the Kasserine Pass. The Germans' initial attack, begun on February 14, 1943, shattered the U.S. II Corps units posted in the area. Allen, under the overall command of a Free French general, rushed his truncated division into the void. Arriving on the night of February 19, Allen's mortars and artillery bolstered a dogged defense that first slowed and then halted the German advance. Though Field Marshal Erwin Rommel threw his vaunted 10th and 21st Panzer Divisions into the fight, desperate, costly resistance bled away the momentum of their assault. Eventually, pinned inside the narrow valley with little room to maneuver, the panzers were decimated by Allen's artillery and waves of Allied airpower. Stunned by a counterattack that came at them from three sides, the Germans' tactical withdrawal was turned into a rout when Allen struck the retreating columns with fast-moving infantry. Fierce fighting continued to rage for a time at points all around the pass. The German surge was stopped, however, and, by February 22, Rommel abandoned the Kasserine offensive completely.

Even after that success, for a time other parts of the 1st Division were split off and sent farther north in Tunisia to assist the British First Army. Finally, weeks later, the entire division was returned to Allen's command. At Morsott, Tunisia, he instituted a training program that was noted both for its enlightenment and its severity. In a school for incoming replacements, newcomers were taught by combat-seasoned officers and noncommissioned officers (NCOs). All underwent intensive physical conditioning and exhaustive weapons and tactics training. As always with Allen, night combat received special emphasis. In accordance with his strong belief in unit cohesion and loyalty, all newcomers were instructed on the Big Red One's history and traditions.

When the Allies resumed the offensive aimed at trapping the Axis forces in northern Tunisia, the 1st Division—operating as part of the U.S. II Corps, now led by George S. Patton—drew the southernmost portion of the advance. The unit's immediate objective was a road and railway complex at Gafsa, about 50 miles south of the Kasserine Pass battlefield. In the campaign that followed, the 1st won victories at Gafsa, Fériana, and El Guettar. The latter, where the Big Red One again faced the now-replenished 10th Panzer Division, was the largest and most significant. El Guettar was notable in another way as well: it was Patton's spotlight opportunity—a final chance to show his prowess as commander, II Corps. Even Omar Bradley noted that "El Guettar was the first solid, indisputable defeat the U.S. inflicted on the German Army in the war." Patton pushed Allen and other division commanders incessantly. Their conversations, at least on Allen's part, were not always well or politely received. "The air would turn blue as the two friends cursed each other in the most obscene terms. Patton may have outranked Allen, but in all their public exchanges, Allen cursed his friend and superior as an equal."

In mid-April, after a brief period of rest and refitting, the 1st Division saw action again, this time on the northern flank of the British First Army. In the face of often bitter resistance fought inside a miles-long complex of hills well suited to defense, the 1st drove against German defenders west of the Tine Valley, seeking a breakthrough that would clear the path and permit a decisive thrust by the division's armor. Although a confused setback along the Tine River on May 5 delayed the inevitable, by this time the Germans had been forced into a final stand inside a shrunken area near Tunis. Soon after, on May 13, German forces surrendered. The war in North Africa was over.

The end came none too soon for Allen and his division. Over the last 17 days of the campaign, the unit had sustained more than two thousand casualties. Allen, though visibly tired, exulted in the 1st Division's triumph. When the battle was over, Allen met with small groups of the division's officers and men and, without mentioning his own role, spoke to them of his pride in their courage and performance and of his privilege to have been their commander. One officer remarked that Allen's words had "captured every man in the audience."

The interregnum between North Africa and the invasion of Sicily saw "Terrible Terry" again in hot water. In a performance that was quintessential Allen, he personally flew to Algiers and lambasted the staff from Eisenhower down for not approving battlefield promotions he had ordered (which was within his prerogative to do) and medals such as the Silver Star and Distinguished Service Cross (which was not). His heated remarks and disdain for rear-echelon staff members did little to enhance a reputation already in tatters among key players such as Walter Bedell Smith.

Nor did the conduct of some Big Red One troops improve the division's, or its leader's, credit with Eisenhower, Smith, and Bradley. Given liberty in Oran, some of the 1st Division troops "trashed clubs constructed for rear echelon personnel, celebrated too enthusiastically in wine bars, and ran afoul of military police who were assigned not only to keep order but to enforce dress code regulations and other army niceties. The disorder grew large enough to require an infusion of soldiers to restore tranquility and even an order from Eisenhower to Allen to remove all 1st Division men from the city."

Three conditions fueled the division's outrage. First, only limited time was given the unit's members for travel from the bivouac area to the city before the bars closed. Second, 1st Division personnel were still wearing woolen, olive drab uniforms visibly tattered after weeks of frontline duty. Almost every other GI in the crowded city was clothed in fresh, newly issued khakis. Third, many of the rear-echelon troops were sporting campaign ribbons that the soldiers of the Big Red One had never seen. Many of the ribbons were ripped off the shirts of the clerks and support staffers.

Allen took the hits for the Oran episode and others like it. There were contradictory views regarding his attitude toward discipline. Bradley believed him to be unconcerned about enforcement. Others, though, including the noted writer/historian Carlo D'Este, insist that after Oran, Allen was relentless in rooting out and disciplining the offenders. On another occasion, a two-star investigating officer sent by Eisenhower to check out an additional infraction allegedly perpetrated by 1st Division personnel—the destruction of an olive grove—exonerated unit members and reported that the division's discipline and military courtesy were the best he had observed. Another of Eisenhower's coterie, though,

disparaged the unit's lack of military courtesy in terms of proper reporting and saluting.

Disciplinary problems or not, no one questioned the Big Red One's
fighting ability. When initial plans for the Sicily campaign called for
other formations to handle the key landings at Gela, Patton insisted that
the job go to Terry Allen and the 1st Division.

Behind the scenes, Allen was a team player. In late December an
incident involving one of the 1st Division's units—the 18th Regiment—
threatened to disrupt Allied unity. In the Battle of Backstop Hill, British
Coldstream Guards occupied a portion of the hill. The plan called for
the Guards to be relieved at night—always a tricky operation—by the
1st Battalion of the 18th Regiment, newly arrived on scene. In the first
of a long series of snafus, British guides took the Americans to the wrong
positions. When the British withdrew from the hill, they advised the
advanced American echelon that few if any Germans remained on the
heights. In fact, on Backstop Hill, which really consisted of five hills,
large parts of two of the heights were laden with top-notch German
troops. The Coldstream Guards evacuated the area before the Americans
arrived in strength to set up a defense, eat, and site their artillery—a
lapse exploited by veteran German units that quickly counterattacked.
Despite the circumstances, the Americans succeeded in taking one of
the objectives. The other, though—Hill 4—was the scene of horrific
fighting laced with repeated attacks and counterattacks during which
the heights changed hands several times. Assaulted by Coldstream Guard
units called back into the fray and by the 18th's mortars and machine
guns, the hill was regained again for a time, only to be subjected to a
yet another massive German attack. The assault drove British and Free
French units off the hill. Left in an untenable position, the newly arrived
American units were forced to withdraw with heavy losses—nine officers
and 347 enlisted men. British reports of the action publicly placed the
blame on American troops: "incompetent" was a word reported to
Smith and Eisenhower.

Allen investigated thoroughly, his inquiry corroborating information
provided by American troops. After preparing a report that laid out the
events of the night in great detail, he quietly went behind the scenes to

talk with the responsible British commanders. When the British officers, chagrined, asked what Allen intended to do with the document, Allen tore it up in front of them—after stating that he would expect better handling of American troops under British commanders in the future and that he would have treated British troops under his command more professionally. Allen's low-key approach ingratiated him with the British hierarchy, who came to regard him as the U.S. Army's premier division commander.

As plans for the invasion of Sicily progressed, Patton demanded that the landings at Gela, judged to be the most difficult of the initial operations, be assigned to Allen and the Big Red One. Eisenhower yielded to Patton's insistence, though perhaps not without some misgivings. While expressing admiration for the 1st's legendary fighting qualities, because of its bawdy, ill-disciplined reputation both Eisenhower and Bradley held a somewhat jaundiced view of the division. Eisenhower no doubt recalled a memo he had written while the division was training in England. Eisenhower's communication noted that of all the American soldiers arrested in Britain during the previous month, two-thirds were Allen's men. Nonetheless, Patton's view prevailed, and the unit was given the task of taking Gela, securing the beachhead, and moving inland. As events would play out, after difficult fighting it succeeded in achieving each of its objectives.

The landings took place in the early morning hours of July 10, 1943, after a six-mile run-in to the beach made especially difficult by violent winds and high seas. At the outset, the issue was for a time in doubt as the Germans aggressively counterattacked the landings with a veteran unit—the Hermann Göring Division—and a large column of tanks that very nearly penetrated to the beach. As the fighting at times raged almost down to the water line, the 1st Division, aided by effective naval gunfire, held on. Finally, after two days of intense combat, Gela was secure. Even Bradley noted that perhaps only the tough and experienced 1st Division could have saved the landings. Late in the evening of July 11, with the beachhead still under enormous pressure, seeking to strike the Germans hard and preempt another counterattack, Allen ordered a night attack. The move achieved almost complete surprise. Within hours the

1st Division broke out of the beachhead and began rolling through the countryside.

Notable struggles along the Salso River, at Mazzarino, and Barrafranca followed. At Petralia another surprise night attack brought the 1st Division to within 15 miles of the north coast of Sicily. Ten days after landing at Gela, the division had driven 70 miles and fulfilled Patton's objective of cutting the island in half.

As Patton drove toward Palermo, the 1st Division shifted eastward toward Nicosia to cover the left flank of General Bernard Law Montgomery's stymied British Eighth Army. Victories at Enna on July 20 and Calscibetta on July 21 brought elements of the division to the approaches of Nicosia. They were confronted there by some of the most difficult fighting of the Sicilian campaign. Rugged hills, embedded artillery, mines by the hundreds if not thousands, and increasingly large formations of German armor confronted Allen's soldiers. Seeing that straight-ahead attacks would be suicidal, Allen struck at the flanks of the Axis defenses. Moving at night, regiments of the Big Red One pushed ahead. After fighting off heavy counterattacks, on July 27 yet another of Allen's nighttime assaults brought the division to the gates of the city, which fell to Allen after a concerted artillery barrage the following day. With the capture of Nicosia, the panzer grenadier formations facing the 1st Division moved out of the area, retreating toward Troina.

An episode at Troina would provide a pretext for Bradley to remove Allen from command. Asserting that the 1st Division had failed in its initial assault, Bradley received approval from Eisenhower to reassign Allen. In reality, the attack was conducted by a regiment of the 9th Infantry Division that had been temporarily attached to the Big Red One only a few days before the battle. Events during the run-up to Troina likely sowed Bradley's discontent. To be sure, he was already angry at the 1st Division. At Nicosia, in Allen's absence and without this knowledge, a subordinate had reshuffled a unit without his (Bradley's) permission. A problem then arose in coordinating with Canadian army units moving to the right of the 1st Division. Troina itself posed a difficult challenge. Perched on the spur of a mountaintop, its height afforded excellent firing placements for Axis artillery. Still, the attack began satisfactorily on July

31 with the capture of a village about eight miles away. Soon after, things began to go awry. Poor intelligence—German forces assessed to have mostly vacated the area had in fact returned in substantial numbers—faulty maps, and improper tactical dispositions delayed the capture of the city by about a week. For Bradley, that was enough.

The roots of Bradley's antagonism toward Allen and the 1st Division were apparently long-standing. Both officers were exceptionally competent, dedicated, and highly respected. Their personalities, though, differed considerably. Bradley, a straightlaced teetotaler, chafed at Allen's cocky, freewheeling command style, and the path of destruction left by the division while it was on rest and rehabilitation. Bradley publicly bemoaned the lack of court-martials within the 1st Division. There were indeed very few. Allen believed that infractions were best handled internally by the division's NCOs rather than by formal proceedings (which he regarded as a crutch used by less competent commanders).

While Bradley acknowledged that Allen was unsurpassed as a leader of troops in combat, he was uncomfortable that the soldiers of the 1st Division tied their loyalty to the unit and not to the army as a whole. He apparently regarded the general attitude of the Big Red One as being disrespectful and thought that the insouciance of its soldiers mirrored Allen's cavalier conduct. Bradley also believed, at least at times with some apparent justification, that Allen or his staff had not always kept him informed.

Patton cast Allen's reassignment in a different light, labeling it as a standard rotation of frontline commanders who warranted breaks from the demands of lengthy combat. Patton believed the transfer had been planned even before the invasion of Sicily and that it was his insistence that Allen and the 1st Division lead the attacks that influenced the timing. It is uncertain if Patton's words were an attempt to massage Allen's ego, though it would seem that Bradley had for quite some time been of a mind to replace Allen. Bradley surely remembered an incident along the Tine River in the closing days of the North African campaign when the 1st Division launched an attack—unsuccessful—without securing his approval. Patton stated that on occasion he had defended Allen when Eisenhower spoke of the Big Red One's disciplinary problems. That may well be. It does seem clear that Patton was concerned that his friend had been under enormous strain for an extended period of time.

The leadership styles of both men had much in common. Each was an aggressive commander who believed in speed, mobility, and continuous assault. Allen had a magnetic personality that drew people to him. The most obvious difference in the minds of some scholars and officers close to them was that Allen was visibly more concerned about the welfare of those who served under him and with the lives of those he sent into combat. In a guarded sort of way, soldiers perhaps tolerated George Patton. They loved Terry Allen.

Whatever the factors leading up to it, Troina served as justification for Allen's transfer, which was effected on August 6, 1943. Before leaving he met with his replacement, Major General Clarence R. Huebner, gave him a complete tour of the division, and introduced him personally to every battalion commander. It was a gesture that Huebner never forgot.

Allen reported initially to Eisenhower at his headquarters in Algiers. Eisenhower was gracious in his comments, saying that Allen "had the longest, most arduous and most successful combat record of any general officer in this war." Patton had insisted that Allen's relief be without prejudice, and Eisenhower stipulated that Allen must receive an equivalent command when he rotated back to the States.

After a 30-day leave spent with his family in El Paso, Allen received his new assignment. The 104th Infantry Division had been activated in September 1942. Called the "Timberwolves," the division was posted at Camp Adair, Oregon. The unit was green, composed almost entirely of new enlistees and untried officers. In October, 1943, the 104th would begin to learn to fight: its new commander was Terry de la Mesa Allen.

Anticipating that the unit would see action rather quickly, Allen set a furious pace. Discipline, military courtesy, and saluting were hammered home. Sloppiness in appearance and conduct were not tolerated. Field training took place during a grueling 13-week period at Camp Horn, Arizona. As always, Allen taught the troops how to wage war at night. Maneuvers in California followed. There, Allen engaged the entire 104th in night exercises against a division-sized opposing force.

From the Arizona desert and California plateau, the 104th went to Camp Carson, Colorado, where its night-fighting prowess was further fine-tuned along with map reading, patrolling, and firing practice. There Allen wrote a well-regarded training manual emphasizing night operations and discussing lessons learned in North Africa and Sicily. A memorable discourse, *Combat Leadership*, soon followed. The publication stressed the importance of leadership example, unit pride, and teamwork. *Directive for Offensive Combat* was the third, and final, volume written at Camp Carson. In clear, easy-to-follow prose, Allen set forth his war-fighting concepts. Training regimens were built around the precepts of his "little red books." As newcomers filtered into the unit, many remarked in later years how quickly they were welcomed and felt themselves part of the 104th as a result of Allen's orientation program. Allen's publications and his orientation program were complemented by another asset that added to the war-fighting capabilities of the units touched by his leadership: Allen became known throughout the Army for the brevity and clarity of his field orders.

On September 7, 1944, the 104th landed at Cherbourg, the first American unit during the war to be sent directly from New York City to France. As usual, Allen chafed about delays in getting his unit into the fight. In late October, the division moved from France to Belgium. A few days later, Terry Allen was back in combat.

The next six months would see the division in almost constant action. The 104th's engagements read like an overview of the war in the north-central region of the ETO. Beginning soon after its arrival in Belgium, the division saw 195 consecutive days of combat, a period that extended to the end of the war. The time under fire for the Timberwolves began with major actions in both Belgium and the Netherlands assisting the Canadian First Army in the reduction of Antwerp. The 104th fought through the Siegfried Line, advanced to the Rhine, crossed it and the Inde River beyond, and in March 1945 took Cologne in house-to-house fighting. A month later, Halle fell to the Timberwolves as well. As the war drew down, the 104th assisted in closing the Ruhr Pocket and raced deep into Germany, eventually linking up with Soviet army forces near Torgau on the Elbe River on April 26, 1945.

American GIs cross the Siegfried Line, early 1945.

Ironically, when the 104th shifted from actions along the Scheldt Estuary in Belgium to take over an eight-mile section of the front near Aachen, Germany, the unit the Timberwolves replaced was the 1st Infantry Division, Allen's former command. The unit's first assignment in that sector was a difficult one: to take the well-defended city of Stolberg. After three days of intense combat, often house to house and sometimes hand to hand, the city fell to the 104th on November 19. Allen had initiated the attack with a nighttime assault.

Three days later it was the turn of Eschweiler, a heavily fortified city to the northwest on the banks of the Inde River. Night operations again played a major role in the capture of the city, and the 104th began to gain a well-earned notoriety as the ETO's foremost night-fighting specialists.

Luchterberg, a small village across the Inde, was next in line. It fell to Allen's men after a masterful employment of artillery and an infantry assault across the icy, waist-deep river. By mid-December, the capture of Pier, Merken, and Schophoven by Allen's fast-moving soldiers—often with Allen in the lead—brought the 104th to the banks of the Roer River.

Allen quickly sent patrols across the stream as the division, along with other Allied forces, prepared to push on to the Rhine. Plans for additional advances were brought to a halt as elsewhere on the front the Germans mounted a massive surprise counterstroke that eventually carried 60 miles deep into Allied lines. Undetected by Allied intelligence officers or dismissed as improbable by them, the blow struck thinly held sectors of the American front in the Ardennes Forest. Launched on December 16, 1944, the attack rolled forward creating a "bulge" that threatened to split the Allied defenses and carry all the way to Antwerp—which indeed was the German high command's objective.

The 104th was quickly moved to the relief of two ground-up U.S. divisions along a nine-mile sector of front bordering the Roer, as the Allies went onto the defensive. The Timberwolves remained at that location through much of February until the assault was blunted and the original front restored.

While the 104th stood in place during the Battle of the Bulge, Allen used the time to provide additional training for newly arrived replacements. As with the "school" he had operated as commander of the 1st Division, he personally met with each group of replacements and had unit veterans conduct a two-week war-fighting course for the newcomers. By the end of the war, more than three thousand replacements had received what amounted to an advanced degree in combat operations.

One of the characteristics that marked Allen's leadership was his sense of anticipation. As always, his preparations were thorough and insightful. Assuming that the 104th would eventually be called upon to jump across the Roer, he conducted assault-boat training and practiced river crossings using the Inde as the venue. By the time the Timberwolves were called upon to move, small-boat operations had been perfected and communications had been thoroughly nailed down.

Throughout one of the most bitter winters in decades, Allen put constant pressure on subordinates to provide warm clothing, shoes, and socks to his frontline troops. Soldiers on patrol, guarding outposts, and on duty in frontline foxholes were to receive hot coffee and a warm, secure place to change out of wet clothes. Allen's training regimen and solicitous concern for his soldiers' welfare were rewarded with success on the battlefield. During the course of the war his unit accomplished all of its objectives and suffered numerically fewer casualties than those sustained by companion units.

At three o'clock on the morning of February 23, 1945, the 104th crossed the Roer. Preceded by an artillery and mortar barrage, Allen's small boats, with ten soldiers and two engineers in each, crossed the river near Düren and pressed on, leaping the Erft Canal and moving to the outskirts of Cologne. The complex crossing of the Roer—Marshall likened it to the cross-channel assault—blew aside the Siegfried Line and opened the path into Germany.

At Cologne, the 104th, joined by the 8th Infantry Division and the 3rd Armored Division, took the city—one treacherous house at a time. By March 6, the Americans were in full control of it. At mid-month the Timberwolves were across the Rhine, transported by a truck convoy over pontoon causeways. Once over the river, the 104th, along with the 3rd Armored, set about enlarging the bridgehead on the eastern bank of the river.

Months of near-continuous fighting had drained the 104th and other infantry divisions of foot soldiers. In some units, shortages of riflemen became critical. The U.S. Army was segregated at the time. Calls for volunteers went out to black quartermasters and rear-service organizations where the majority of black soldiers were assigned. About five thousand volunteered and underwent training. Black soldiers assigned to the 104th received the same battle course training given to all Timberwolf replacements. About three platoons were eventually assigned to the division. Allen met with all of them and personally handed them their. Timberwolf patches.

With the Rhine bridgehead secured, the 104th and other Allied units exploded eastwards across Germany, taking thousands of prisoners and gobbling up miles of the Fatherland. At Paderborn, SS recruits put up a fanatical resistance but were overwhelmed by 104th troops who rode into the battle atop 3rd Armored Division tanks.

River barriers posed some of the most difficult obstacles in the path of Allen's soldiers. The Weser was yet another major waterway bisecting the route into central Germany. The 104th jumped across it in an early morning attack and continued driving toward the Harz Mountains, the last natural barrier before reaching the plains of northern Germany.

On April 12, elements of the division reached the Nordhausen concentration camp. Visions of the decaying bodies, walking dead, and crematoria would remain with the soldiers who saw them for the rest of their days. Lots of 104th GIs did see them—Allen made sure they did, sending all who could be spared to see the camp. "Terrible Terry" intended Nordhausen to serve as a reminder to his soldiers of what they were fighting for. The more the better; all could serve as witnesses to the civilized world. Able-bodied German civilians from nearby towns were sent to bury the dead and clear up the site. They, too, would learn from and remember the lessons of Nordhausen.

Halle, one of Germany's largest cities, was 50 miles farther east. Guarded by a large, well-equipped garrison, the city presented a formidable obstacle in the last stage of the war. Four days of house-to-house fighting took a 104th task force into the city. An agreement between Allen and a German official seeking to prevent total destruction of the metropolitan sector led to a German withdrawal from major areas and confined fighting to roughly the southern third of the town. Three days later, the 104th completed the capture of the holdout section and took the remainder of the garrison prisoner.

A short distance farther east of Halle lay first the Mulde and then the Elbe Rivers. Orders soon arrived halting the division slightly west of the Mulde. In the meantime, Soviet forces advancing from the east reached the Elbe. On April 25, advance scouts linked up with the Red Army. On the 28th, Allen met with the commander of a Soviet infantry division. In a memorable evening of celebration and drinking—Allen was alleged to have more than held his own with the Soviets—Soviet marshal Ivan Konev awarded a medal to Allen.

A few days later the war in Europe was over.

But the war was perhaps not entirely over for the 104th. On May 12, the division was alerted that it would be among the first American units deployed to the Pacific. Plans called for the 104th to be shipped back to the United States in early June. After a 30-day leave, they would be reconstituted and prepared for transportation to the Pacific.

By the time the division sailed from France, Allen had devised a training regimen that would prepare them for combat in the Pacific. The eight-week session would consist of discipline, drill, military conduct, physical conditioning, distance marches, hand-to-hand combat, bayonet drill, obstacle courses, weapons firing, precautions against booby traps, and much more. It would be an intensive course, and, as always, there would be considerable emphasis on fighting at night.

Allen's ambitious training program was never to take place. As the division's 30-day furlough ended and its members began reporting to their base at San Luis Obispo, California, atomic bombs dropped on Hiroshima and Nagasaki forced the Japanese to surrender. The division's soldiers performed a final review for Allen on September 15. The unit was officially demobilized on December 20. By then, all the Timberwolf soldiers were gone, leaving for a time only Allen and a small caretaker staff.

Before and After

Allen was born on April Fool's Day, 1888, at Fort Douglas, Utah. The son and grandson of U.S. Army officers, he grew up on military posts throughout the United States. It seems unlikely that he ever seriously considered any career other than a military one. Although his academic credentials were not strong, he received an appointment to West Point in 1907.

Dark-haired, of medium height and weight, Allen was a natural storyteller. Gregarious and easy-going, he was well liked by a wide circle of his academy classmates. From the start, however, he struggled with his course work, his difficulties exacerbated by an occasional stutter that afflicted him at the time. At the end of his second year, he was held back a class after failing mathematics. In his final year, he did not pass a required ordnance and gunnery course and failed to graduate.

Determined to become an officer, he enrolled in the Catholic University of America in Washington, DC, and received a bachelor of arts degree in 1912. Immediately afterwards, he passed the army's officer qualification examination and in November of that year received his commission as a second lieutenant of cavalry.

Allen was briefly posted at Fort Myer, Virginia, before being sent to Eagle Pass, Texas. Over the next four-plus years, he and his 14th Cavalry troopers chased smugglers along the Mexican border.

Allen made captain a month after the United States entered World War I. Sent to France, he was assigned initially to command an ammunition train. Wary that the job would keep him from seeing action, through bluff and bluster Allen finagled a diploma from an infantry officer training school. Made a temporary major, he was assigned to the 3rd Battalion, 358th Infantry Regiment, of the 90th Division and led the unit through the heavy fighting at Saint-Mihiel and Aincreville.

In mid-September, Allen and his unit were in action on the Saint-Mihiel salient. In the midst of a heavy fight, Allen was knocked unconscious by a shell. Taken to an evacuation station, he regained consciousness, tore off his medical evacuation tag, and set out to rejoin the battalion, organizing stragglers and other strays picked up along the way. He led his improvised unit into the fight, engaging a series of machine-gun nests that were holding up the advance of two full battalions of the 358th Infantry. Allen's makeshift detachment took on the machine-gun nests and destroyed them in fighting so close and intense that at one point Allen used his fists to get at the enemy. In late morning, he was shot through the jaw and mouth and taken to a field hospital. He left the hospital the next day, riding a motorcycle to rejoin his unit. The following day he was evacuated by direct order of the regimental surgeon. After a month's recuperation and a new set of teeth, he returned to action. Interestingly, after the facial wound he never stuttered again.

At Aincreville, it was Allen's plan that led to the town's capture. Allen personally reconnoitered the objective and led the first wave of the attack—not usual roles for a battalion commander. Typical of his pugnaciousness is that on one occasion his battalion took an objective originally assigned to another unit that had failed in the attempt and retreated from the battlefield. Allen's men sent the other unit a note telling them that the battalion had taken the ground and would leave some people there to hold it for them until they felt comfortable enough to return.

Allen's actions during his convalescence also spoke much about his character and determination. As soon as he was able, he resumed jogging, a longtime exercise for him. Rather quickly he was logging ten miles per day in the area near the hospital. Decades before the activity became fashionable, Allen made it a standard part of his fitness routine and incorporated it into his unit's training regimen.

The emphasis on physical conditioning would remain a featured part of Allen's leadership. In place of drill and ceremonies, he introduced realistic training exercises, expanded weapons firing, and introduced walking/hiking activities, which he sometimes personally led. Early in his career he developed an affinity for nighttime assaults, believing that it was a form of warfare whose advantages—including, he believed, fewer casualties—were not fully exploited. Allen saw night operations as potential "game changers" and drilled his units incessantly in night exercises.

After the armistice, Allen remained with his battalion on occupation duty in Germany before finally returning to the United States in September 1920.

The years between the wars were not without personal advantages and notoriety for Allen. Known throughout the army as a superb horseman, he was so adept as a polo player that when duties allowed he competed in national and international matches. In January 1922, he entered an unusual competition. Texas promoters sponsored a challenge that would match a former cowboy against a U.S. cavalryman in a 300-mile race, each using a single horse. Riding a huge black mount that was a combination of quarter horse and Thoroughbred, Allen won by seven hours. Later at Fort Riley he wrote a well-regarded treatise on the use of cavalry in reconnaissance.

The interwar years saw Allen cycled through a series of command positions interspersed with school assignments that drew increasing notice to his professional competence. After postings at Camp Travis and Fort McIntosh in Texas, he was assigned for a time to the 61st Cavalry in New York City before attending another series of professional development courses: an advanced cavalry session at Fort Riley, Kansas; the Command and General Staff School at Fort Leavenworth, Kansas; the Infantry School at Fort Benning, Georgia; and the Army War College in Washington, DC, as well as additional infantry-related command courses.

Understandably, Allen was reluctant to see the demise of the horse cavalry. Nonetheless, his performance at the Infantry School at Fort Benning had so impressed Lieutenant Colonel George Marshall, the assistant director of the school, that Marshall included him in his famous "black book," earmarking him for leadership positions in wartime. Although by some accounts Marshall remained concerned about Allen's drinking and casual manner, so exceptional was Allen's grasp of strategy and so extraordinary was his leadership during major exercises at Fort Benning that Marshall began grooming him for key infantry command duties. Clear to Marshall was that Allen's past academic issues at West Point did not reflect his potential to lead American troops in combat.

Allen's performance during World War II confirmed Marshall's high regard for his capabilities. Before Allen left Europe, even Bradley, no great admirer, told Allen that the 104th was indeed one of the best American divisions on the continent. Precise numbers are somewhat uncertain, but it would appear that the Timberwolves had "cleared 8,000 square miles of Europe, captured 51,724 prisoners, and inflicted an estimated 18,000 casualties." The 104th casualties were 1,447 killed, 4,778 wounded, and 76 missing.

When World War II ended and with no further conflicts on the horizon Allen, the consummate warrior, retired from the army at age 58 on August 31, 1946. He returned to El Paso and for a number of years worked for various insurance companies, while maintaining an active involvement in veterans' organizations and community affairs. His acquaintances commented that he never looked "quite right" in civilian clothes.

Over the years, Allen's legacy continued to be memorialized in gatherings of 1st Division and 104th Division veterans. Tributes to his leadership from peers, historians, and dogfaces are notable for their depth and conviction:

- Writer/historian Gerald Astor: "The 1st Division under Allen's leadership was recognized by his peers as the best foot soldier outfit in the North African campaign."
- Ernie Pyle: "As far as I know, Terry Allen was the only general in Tunisia who slept on the ground. All others carried folding cots (or slept in houses, villas, or hotels). General Allen didn't allow any of his staff to sleep on a cot. He said if everybody in his headquarters did it would take several extra trucks to carry them and he could use his trucks for better purposes."
- General Omar Bradley, one of Allen's harshest critics: "Among the division commanders, none excelled the unpredictable Terry Allen in his leadership of troops."
- Writer/historian John C. McManus: "In combat, he was the embodiment of the inspirational commander—courageous, relentless, and energetic—the sort of general who circulated easily from the lowest-ranking private to staff officers."
- Combat journal of the 26th Infantry: "It meant something to the sweating, tired, bone-weary men to see the general walking around when the action got hot and heavy."
- British General Sir Harold Alexander, who had no particular fondness for American troops: "The finest division commander [I] encountered during two wars."

Terry Allen's son, Terry de la Mesa Allen Jr., an infantry officer like his father, was killed in Vietnam on October 17, 1967, while serving with the 1st Infantry Division. Allen died on September 12, 1969, in El Paso. He is buried next to his son at the Fort Bliss National Cemetery.

RAYMOND A. SPRUANCE

Spruance was a last-minute replacement whose superb leadership guided an outmanned and outgunned fleet to the victory at Midway that changed the course of the war in the Pacific. Later he led naval forces in campaigns throughout the Central Pacific and, as commander of the Fifth Fleet, led the largest American naval force ever assembled. His achievements led naval historian Samuel Eliot Morrison to rate him as one of the greatest admirals in U.S. naval history.

Admiral Raymond A. Spruance is probably the "least in the shadows" of the military leaders discussed in this section. Nonetheless, the names Nimitz, Halsey, and King are far more likely to be conjured up when the American public recalls World War II naval leaders.

Quiet and modest to a fault, Spruance shunned publicity and avoided the notoriety associated with many of his army and navy contemporaries. Cool, calm, and intellectual, he was cut from a different mold than many of his more renowned colleagues. He was a nonsmoker, seldom drank, and enjoyed symphonic music. He is remembered for vigorously exercising on deck while at sea. On shore, he walked eight to ten miles a day. While at sea, he insisted on an undisturbed night's sleep when his force was not in combat. In command, his ships operated under a "quiet bridge," with no idle chatter and orders renowned for being transmitted with clarity and conciseness. He began each day with a cup of hot chocolate, which he brewed himself.

At the time of the Battle of Midway, an action that many historians regard as the turning point of the war in the Pacific, Spruance was somewhat of an unknown quantity. He was a last-minute replacement for Vice Admiral William F. Halsey Jr., who was sick at the time. As the opposing fleets converged, Rear Admiral Frank Jack Fletcher, senior in rank, transferred operational command of the battle to Spruance when his own ship, the carrier *Yorktown*, was put out of action while sailing separately toward Midway. That Spruance was a junior admiral at the time and a nonflier adds more luster to his accomplishment. It was at Midway that his legendary coolness in action was first demonstrated to a fleet-wide audience. His actions during that battle and those that would follow in the Philippine Sea, at Okinawa and other sites across the Pacific, led naval historian Samuel Eliot Morrison to rate Spruance as one of the greatest admirals in U.S. naval history.

On December 7, 1941, Spruance was at sea, two thousand miles west of Oahu, accompanying Halsey's carrier *Enterprise*, which had just delivered 12 fighter planes to Wake Island. Spruance's name first surfaced, albeit in a minor way on April 8 1942, when he commanded the cruiser screen that shielded Halsey's carrier *Hornet* during Lieutenant Colonel James Doolittle's raid on Tokyo. Although little known to the

THE BATTLE OF MIDWAY
June 4, 1942

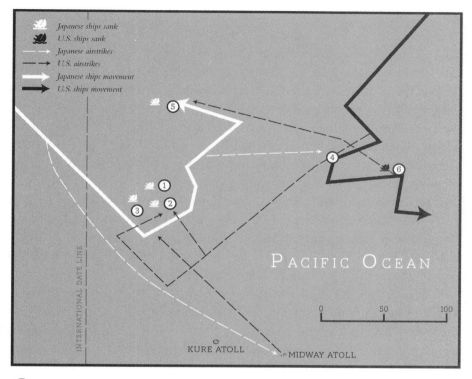

Japanese ships sank
U.S. ships sank
Japanese airstrikes
U.S. airstrikes
Japanese ships movement
U.S. ships movement

PACIFIC OCEAN

0   50   100

INTERNATIONAL DATE LINE

KURE ATOLL   MIDWAY ATOLL

(1) **SORYU · JUNE 4 1020 ·** Soryu *struck by three 1000lb bombs from USS* Yorktown *aircraft. Abandoned at 1020. Scuttled; sank at 1515.*

(2) **KAGA · JUNE 4 1022 ·** Kaga *struck by one 1000lb and three 500lb bombs from USS* Enterprise *aircraft. Scuttled, sank at 1925.*

(3) **AGAKI · JUNE 4 1026 ·** Agaki *struck by dive bombers from USS* Enterprise. *Dead in water at 1350. Scuttled; sank June 5 at 0450.*

(4) **USS YORKTOWN · JUNE 4 1400 ·** *Hit by three bombs from VAL aircraft from the Hiryu. Temporarily dead in the water at 14:40. Prepared to get underway again at 1540. Struck by two torpedoes at 1640. Dead in water. Later abandoned. Still afloat the following day; efforts were underway to save the ship when at 1536 she was struck again by two torpedoes fired from Japanese submarine I-168.*

(5) **HIRYU · JUNE 4 1701 ·** Hiryu *struck by four 1000lb bombs from Douglass Dauntless aircraft. Abandoned at 0315 June 5. Scuttled at 0510. Sank at 0912.*

(6) **USS YORKTOWN · JUNE 7 0701 ·** *Sank.*

American public, Spruance had a well-established reputation among his naval contemporaries as a thoughtful, publicity-shy officer—a leader, not a driver.

On January 8 1942, Spruance, along with Halsey and other senior officers attended a meeting at Pearl Harbor convened by Admiral Chester W. Nimitz, newly appointed as Commander in Chief, Pacific (CINCPAC). Urged by the Chief of Naval Operations (CNO), Admiral Ernest J. King, Nimitz proposed a series of early retaliatory strikes against Japanese installations on the so-called Pacific Mandate Islands—island chains ceded to Japan by Germany at the end of World War I. Faced at the time with a paucity of men, ships, and matériel, participants at the meeting realized that a defensive perimeter that ran from the Aleutians through Midway Island, Samoa, and Fiji to Australia had to be held at all costs. Thus the raids posed a considerable risk: there could be no immediate replacements for potential losses in men and ships.

Beginning on February 1, a series of raids conducted under Halsey's overall command hit Wotje, Maleolap, and Eniwetok Atolls. Spruance, with his flag on the USS *Northampton*, led the cruiser force that struck Wotje. Though small in scale by later standards, the successful attacks represented America's first significant offensive actions in the Pacific. As would be his custom throughout the war, Spruance remained visible on the bridge during the encounters, believing that commander should demonstrate a disregard for personal danger.

Meanwhile, events were brewing that would bring opposing forces together in a titanic clash that would change the course of the war. Admiral Isoroko Yamamoto, commander of Japan's Combined Fleet, believed that Japan must force a decisive naval victory in 1942 to bring about a negotiated peace before the United States could mobilize its immense latent industrial base. Seeking a crushing triumph that would shatter the U.S. defensive perimeter, Yamamoto assembled an enormous armada and moved toward Midway Island. Within his huge flotilla were a carrier striking force with four carriers and a Midway occupation force consisting of a close-support group and transport ships carrying the five thousand troops who would assault the island. The main battle fleet was under his personal command aboard the giant battleship *Yamato*. Meanwhile, he sent a northern strike force with two carriers, a heavy cruiser, and transports to the Aleutians in an attempt to confuse American planners and divert U.S. forces from the main objective: Midway Island.

The U.S. Navy faced the forthcoming battle with a shortage of aircraft carriers. The *Saratoga* had been damaged in earlier fighting and was in port at San Diego for repair and aircrew training. The new carrier *Wasp* was sailing from Gibraltar on a thousands-of-miles journey to the Pacific war zone. The *Yorktown*, severely battered during the Battle of the Coral Sea, was on its way back to Pearl Harbor. The ship reached Pearl on May 27 and was met by 1,400 shipyard personnel who labored around the clock, some even continuing their work as the ship put to sea a few days later. Making the *Yorktown* battle-ready was an epic achievement: the damage had been extensive, and most experts—including the Japanese—believed it would take weeks if not months to repair. The *Enterprise* and the *Hornet*, having missed the Coral Sea combat because of the Tokyo Raid, were berthed at Pearl Harbor to provision for the anticipated action.

As the ships were being readied, a last-minute change occurred in the fleet's senior leadership. Halsey, in command of the forces that included the *Enterprise* and the *Hornet*, was hospitalized with a painful skin disease. Spruance was named as his replacement. Though Spruance was recommended by Halsey and highly regarded by Nimitz, he was a non–aviator, so his selection for command of the carrier task force came as a surprise. For the United States, the choice would be fortuitous indeed.

Spruance was respected throughout the higher echelons of the navy for his brilliant mind and cool judgment. Even the abrasive, egotistical CNO, Ernest J. King, was known to have said that (except for himself) "Spruance is the smartest officer in the Navy."

With U.S. strength so limited, many scholars believe that Spruance's operational orders contained the implicit caution not to lose the carriers or at least not to risk them unduly. Thus, the forthcoming battle would call for a leader with the instincts of a warrior but one also able to calculate coolly in the midst of a struggle whose outcome might shape the future of the war in the Pacific. Nimitz saw those qualities in Spruance.

Interestingly, those traits were decidedly not part of Halsey's makeup. Though they were the closest of friends, in many ways Spruance and Halsey were polar opposites in temperament. Halsey was aggressive, sometimes to a fault, imprudent, and prone to risk-taking that could have invited catastrophe at Midway, which by now had been identified as the likely target of Yamamoto's armada.

As the American ships left Pearl Harbor, Spruance, with the *Enterprise* and the *Hornet*, was nominally under the command of the more senior Admiral Frank Jack Fletcher, who would sail later aboard the heroically repaired *Yorktown*. As events unfolded, however, Spruance would assume independent command from his flagship, the *Enterprise*.

By late May the opposing fleets were converging in mid-Pacific. On June 3, an American Catalina flying boat spotted Japanese warships about seven hundred miles southwest of Midway. Spruance responded by positioning his carriers two hundred miles northeast of the island, putting him in a position to outflank incoming enemy vessels. Anticipating a June 4 attack on Midway, as suggested by intelligence intercepts, intensive search efforts were conducted by Catalinas and carrier aircraft. Eventually, a Catalina sighted Japanese vessels and identified them as carriers.

The battle began later that day with a Japanese air attack on the island. Then, in one of the key decisions of the war, Spruance decided to launch strikes against the Japanese fleet, although the enemy vessels were at maximum range for his own aircraft. Believing from his own assessment and initial lessons learned elsewhere in the war that in carrier warfare the advantage went to the side that struck first, Spruance turned his ships into the wind and ordered his planes to launch.

Spruance clearly wanted a coordinated attack: torpedo planes to strike first, flying fast and low, and dive-bombers striking from overhead, while fighter aircraft provided protective cover. Amid the "fog of war," however, nothing like a coordinated attack took place. Despite initial staff confusion—Spruance was not well served by the aides he inherited from Halsey—Spruance persisted in his determination to strike the Japanese as quickly as possible. He calmly watched the confusion and ordered available aircraft to proceed without waiting to assemble for a fully coordinated strike.

American torpedo squadrons flying old and slow Devastator air-craft were the first to close with the Japanese fleet. The obsolescent Devastators were no match for the firepower confronting them and from the Zero fighters that swarmed on them as they made their long, sluggish, straight-in torpedo runs. The first squadron lost all 15 planes. The second lost 10 of 14, and the third lost 7. None inflicted material damage on the Japanese carriers. Their sacrifice—only 6 of 41 torpedo planes returned safely to U.S. carriers—was not in vain, however. Their attacks forced the action to the surface level, causing Zeros to dive from providing protective cover over the carriers to take part in action occurring not much above the water line. For the Japanese navy, the results of that action were catastrophic.

As the Japanese fighters left to handle the threat posed down low by U.S. torpedo planes, the overhead defense of the fleet was left unat-tended. Swarms of navy dive-bombers struck while the Zeroes were otherwise occupied. Within perhaps as few as six fatal minutes, three of the four Japanese carriers—the *Akagi*, the *Kaga*, and the *Sōryū*—were sunk. American aircraft returned with minimum fuel, landing on the first available carrier or ditching in the sea close by. The fourth Japanese carrier, the *Hiryū*, separated slightly from the other three, survived the initial attacks, and launched an all-out retaliatory strike on the U.S carriers. A few Japanese dive-bombers got through to the *Yorktown*, initially hitting the just-repaired vessel while it was refueling planes and severely damaging it. A second strike devastated the ship and caused it to be abandoned.

Admiral Fletcher, having transferred his flag from the *Yorktown*, informed Spruance to assume full tactical command of the battle. Spruance waited until the location of the *Hiryū* was confirmed and then ordered strikes against it from the *Enterprise* and the *Hornet*. By the end of the day, the *Hiryū* was also sunk. The final totals from the Battle of Midway included four main Japanese carriers and 250 frontline aircraft—enormous losses that blunted the forward thrust of the Japanese Empire.

Spruance was left to make one more decision with particularly momentous implications. Although the Japanese carriers had been destroyed, danger still lurked from the immense force under the direct command of Admiral Yamamoto. With his powerful flotilla of battleships and cruisers, Yamamoto planned a night battle—for which the Japanese fleet was at the time much better trained and proficient—against the U.S. carrier force. Sensing the danger, Spruance pulled away to the east, not willing to further risk his two remaining carriers. Yamamoto sailed back to Japan.

Spruance was sometimes criticized—though not by King or Nimitz— for not staying in place or aggressively moving west to seek out the remainder of the Japanese fleet. His choice to withdraw was a decision that many of his contemporaries—Halsey likely among them—would probably not have made. However, as Spruance recognized, at the time the navy was woefully unprepared to fight at night. Then, too, the remainder of the Japanese fleet had not been located, and the presence of additional Japanese carriers was uncertain.

Spruance's decision was later vindicated by intercepts of Japanese transmissions indicating that had Spruance not slipped away, the American fleet would have been directly in Yamamoto's path for a night battle— which, indeed, might have altered the outcome at Midway.

The naval historian Samuel Eliot Morrison wrote: "Now that we have ample data of Japanese ship movements, it is clear that Spruance's judgement was sound and his decision correct—if *Enterprise* and *Hornet* had steamed westward instead of eastward ... they would have run smack into a heavy enemy concentration shortly after midnight which is exactly what the Japanese wanted."

The struggle at Midway also revealed another side of Spruance's character. He was willing to back whomever he thought was right regardless of considerations of rank. On the second day, Spruance overruled the plans of his chief of staff, who proposed arming his dive-bombers with thousand-pound bombs. When pilots advised Spruance that the heavy bomb load combined with the great distance of the targets made it uncertain whether the planes would have enough fuel to get back to the carriers, Spruance ordered a revision to the plan. The planes flew that day with five-hundred-pound bombs, and Spruance delayed their launch to reduce the distance.

With his ships needing replenishment and now vulnerable to attack by land-based Japanese aircraft on Wake Island, Spruance moved this force back to Pearl Harbor. The Battle of Midway was over. For the first time in three hundred years, the Japanese fleet had suffered defeat. The tide of war in the Pacific had turned. Morrison said of Spruance's actions at Midway that "Raymond Spruance emerged from the battle as one of the greatest fighting admirals and thinkers in American naval history."

A new assignment awaited Spruance at Pearl Harbor: he was named chief of staff to CINCPAC Nimitz. In his new role, Spruance quickly took on a problem of low morale among the carrier aircrews who saw their future in bleak terms—flying mission after mission until their luck ran out. Spruance persuaded Nimitz to institute a rotation policy that after a period of combat time allowed aviators to return to the States for instructor duty before going to sea again. The policy lasted for the duration of the war and was eventually applied to submariners as well.

In his duties as chief of staff, Spruance proved to be a no-nonsense, businesslike administrator. His personal office featured a standup desk and no chairs for visitors, so callers would not loiter. He worked best with an exceptionally small staff with which he discussed issues, made plans and decisions, and, as required, issued orders that were models for brevity and clarity. On May 30 1943, he was promoted to vice admiral. Soon after, Nimitz decided it was time for him to return to action.

On August 5, Spruance was named commander, Central Pacific Force, and placed in charge of the next Pacific operation: Tarawa Atoll in the Gilbert Islands. Spruance put his flag on the USS *Indianapolis*, a fast ship that could maneuver quickly from one formation to another. The vessel was not an essential component of any fire-support mission, allowing Spruance the freedom to move quickly to looming hot spots. The quarters on the ship were of minimal size, well suited to Spruance's working style, since they allowed room for only a limited number of staff members.

By this time, the U.S. Navy had come a considerable way since Pearl Harbor and Midway. Spruance now commanded a sizable fleet: six fast carriers, five light carriers, seven escort carriers, 12 battleships, 15 cruisers, 65 destroyers, 33 amphibious transports, 29 tank landing ships, 28 miscellaneous support ships, 90 army bombers, 66 land-based navy bombers, and about 200 additional Marine Corps aircraft.

U.S. Marines storm Tarawa Atoll, Gilbert Islands, November 20–23, 1943. In campaigns on islands such as Tarawa, Makin, Peleliu, and Guadalcanal, Marines faced well-emplaced foes who fought to the death.

On November 20, Marines waded ashore on "Bloody Tarawa." The surrounding reefs were hazardous, and the tides—low and unpredictable, ebbing and flowing several times a day at seemingly random moments—caused landing craft to hang up on the coral. Some Marines had to walk five hundred yards under fire. Smoke obscured the island, inhibiting navy gunners. Communication broke down between on- and offshore parties, spotters, and senior officers.

For a considerable time, Spruance and his commanders could not get reliable information on what was taking place on the landing beaches. As was his style, Spruance remained unflappable, trusting his subordinates to make the proper decisions and prosecute the battle until conditions got sorted out. Reinforcements were sent in, and the next day brought a higher tide, enabling landing craft to sail over the reefs directly to the beach. Finally, after 76 hours of desperate combat, the atoll's airstrips were taken, and Tarawa was secured.

The cost had been high, and Spruance launched an aggressive after-action assessment that would provide operational models for the remainder of the war. His recommendations included longer preliminary bombardments—days, not hours; improved landing craft; probes for underwater obstacles; better intelligence on beach gradients (which led to the development of underwater demolition teams); and transitioning some carrier aircrews to night-fighter operations. Spruance also recommended safer bomb-storage compartments on light escort carriers, one of which, the *Liscome Bay*, had been struck by a Japanese torpedo and exploded with great loss of life. Last, he urged the development of special amphibious-support ships designed specifically to assure communication between commanders and staffs at all levels, onshore and offshore. In one historian's view, the Gilbert Islands provided the navy with the "seedbed for victory."

After the Gilberts, Spruance developed what came to be known as his principles for Pacific warfare. He saw the remainder of the war as a series of amphibious operations; achieving success in those venues was the key to victory. He believed it essential to strike with quick, overwhelming force. The invasion locale should be isolated by achieving superiority above it and in the surrounding waters. Finally, secure communications were necessary to link commanders with invasion forces.

Teamwork, he later wrote, was a decisive factor in winning battles. In his view, teamwork was derived from training, close association, and indoctrination. In the rapid flow of combat operations, teamwork was vital; on-scene judgments were best left to the discretions of capable subordinates placed in positions of responsibility by virtue of their demonstrated competence.

Spruance would soon be in a position to apply his thesis. Looming up for his next objective was Kwajalein, the world's largest coral atoll. The plan approved by Spruance called for three attacking forces and included strikes on outlying islands. D-day for Kwajalein was set for January 31, 1944. The invasion began with an attack by the 4th Marine Division on Roi Island, while the army's 7th Infantry Division assaulted its companion islet, Namur, each connected by a small causeway. By February 7, the whole of Kwajalein Atoll was in American hands.

The Kwajalein operation was one of the most complex of the war. Altogether, landings took place on nearly 30 small islands, with combat occurring on 10 of them. Casualties were extremely light: 372 soldiers and Marines killed. No ships were lost. The lessons of Tarawa had been well learned. Cooperation between the services involved—army, navy, and Marine Corps—was seldom better than at Kwajalein.

Further action quickly followed. With Nimitz's approval, Spruance detached an expeditionary force to assault Eniwetok Atoll. Though it was not handled as crisply as the assault on Kwajalein, army and Marine forces under the overall command of Rear Admiral Henry W. Hill completed the capture of the atoll's final island on February 23.

As Hill's forces were steaming toward Eniwetok, Spruance led a major assault on Truk, a major Japanese base in the Caroline Islands. Long a key bastion in the Japanese line of defense, Truk served as headquarters of the Japanese Combined Fleet. Ringed by small islets and sharp volcanic cones towering more than a thousand feet, the central lagoon formed one of the best fleet anchorages in the Central Pacific. Truk had been the subject of long and intense debate by American planners: whether to bypass and isolate the atoll or directly assault its formidable defenses.

Beginning at dawn on February 17, Spruance, operating from the new battleship *New Jersey*, directed a series of combined air and sea attacks. Officially anointed as commander of the Fifth Fleet, Spruance launched swarms of aircraft from five carriers that bombed and strafed airfields and support facilities. When Spruance's raids were over, his aircrews had destroyed 265 of the 365 Japanese aircraft on the island. Japanese ships anchored in the central lagoon were struck repeatedly in day and night attacks that sank more than 200,000 tons of Japanese shipping. While those attacks were under way, Spruance personally led a sweep around the island to catch enemy ships attempting to escape, sinking four more vessels in a series of running battles.

Truk was a debacle for the Japanese. After Spruance's raid, they never again used the lagoon as a fleet anchorage. The atoll was removed from the list of possible targets requiring invasion.

The triumph at Truk had other important consequences: it sealed the conquest of the Marshall Islands and opened the way for an American drive through the Central Pacific. The Marianas—which included Saipan, Tinian, and Guam—would be next in line.

As planning was under way, Spruance was promoted to four-star admiral. For the fighting that loomed ahead, his Fifth Fleet would consist of Fast Carrier Force 58, a joint expeditionary force, and forward-based aircraft. The fast carrier force alone consisted of 17 big carriers, seven fast battleships, 21 cruisers, and 69 destroyers. The expeditionary force comprised 535 ships carrying assault troops.

Events were now moving quickly. Preceded by aircraft and naval bombardment, Marines waded ashore at Saipan on June 15. As the Marianas campaign was gearing up, advance planners had become concerned about the movement of large segments of the Japanese fleet sighted moving eastward by U.S. submarines. Ominously for the Fifth Fleet, portions of the Japanese task force seemed to be steering toward the Marianas and, perhaps, the Marine beachheads on Saipan.

For Spruance, back about the *Indianapolis*, the circumstance posed a dilemma and provoked another lingering controversy. Submarine sightings left open the possibility that there might be at least two major Japanese forces at sea. Spruance's fleet had been given two primary (and, as events would play out, partially competing) objectives: protect the Marine beachheads on Saipan and seek out the Japanese fleet. Spruance gave priority to safeguarding the Marine landings. Concerned that the Japanese fleet might outflank him and destroy the valuable transport vessels, he kept his force close by rather than venturing away in the direction from which the Japanese were thought to be approaching.

Spruance was criticized for not sailing out in an attempt to bring on an early battle. He chose not to do so, reasoning that Japanese tactics typically called for separating their units and attacking from several directions. Then, too, naval intelligence had not identified the location of the Japanese task force with any degree of certainty. Japanese scout planes had greater range than their U.S. counterparts, another factor that weighed in Spruance's decision: the Japanese might first detect any sortie away from Saipan before he could locate and stop their attack. All things considered, he chose not to risk the beachheads on Saipan or the Marines fighting there.

In the days ahead, Spruance ordered early-morning attacks on Japanese airfields on Guam and Rota that disrupted enemy plans to use land-based aircraft for shuttle bombing attacks on the U.S. fleet.

On June 19, the massive Japanese fleet—nine carriers, a battleship, 12 heavy cruisers, and 23 destroyers—materialized in the waters off Saipan. U.S. carriers cleared their decks and launched every available fighter plane to confront the swarms of aircraft approaching the American fleet. One of the largest air battles of the Pacific war ensued as Hellcat fighters took on Japanese fighters, bombers, and torpedo planes in dogfights that filled the sky from wave-top height to high altitude. During the long and desperate day of fighting, four massive air raids were launched against ships of the Fifth Fleet.

By the time darkness fell, the Japanese fleet was radically depleted as a fighting force. For the Japanese navy and the Japanese Empire, the day—soon labeled the "Marianas Turkey Shoot"—was an unmitigated disaster. Forty-two of 69 Japanese aircraft had been shot down during the first attack, 97 of 128 in the second, 7 of 47 in a weakly prosecuted third strike, and 73 out of 83 in the fourth and final raid in which American pilots followed Japanese planes back to Guam and destroyed several after they landed. Other scattered attacks cost the Japanese additional numbers of aircraft. Not a single American carrier had been hit, although some were damaged by near misses. The most severe damage occurred to the battleship *South Dakota*, which had been struck by a bomb that took the lives of 27 sailors. Meanwhile, the Japanese carriers *Shōkaku* and *Taihō* had been sunk by U.S. submarines.

The previous few days had been catastrophic for the Japanese war effort. On June 18, the empire had 435 combat-capable carrier aircraft. By the end of the day on June 20, only 35 remained.

Japanese plane shot down as it attempted to attack the USS Kitkin Bay. *The action took place near the Marianas Islands in June 1944.*

It was not until that day—June 20—that the location of the main Japanese fleet was finally identified. Spruance sent six fast carriers and five light carriers under Admiral Marc Mitscher, who pursued the Japanese and struck them as they fled out of range. Mitscher's chase was well handled, but by that time the distance was great; although Mitscher's force sank an oiler and another carrier and shot down 80 more Japanese planes, the remainder of the Japanese ships escaped. Including Mitscher's tally, some authoritative naval historians place the total number of Japanese aircraft lost in actions associated with Saipan as 476, a figure that included the loss of at least 450 aviators.

Admiral King fully supported Spruance's decisions regarding operations around Saipan: "As the primary objective of American forces in the area was to capture the Marianas, the Saipan amphibious action had to be protected at all costs. Spruance was rightly guided by his obligation."

Tinian followed Saipan in the invasion sequence. Spruance had to personally intervene to settle a dispute between the admiral in overall command of the operation (Richmond Kelly Turner) and the Marine general (H. M. "Howlin' Mad" Smith) responsible for the landings. Spruance called a gathering of his senior navy and Marine officers and subsequently chose the beach favored by the Marines, whose 2nd and 4th Divisions captured the island after a week of fighting.

As fighting in the Pacific wore on, Admiral Nimitz devised a unique rotational scheme for his senior commanders. Spruance and Halsey and their staffs would periodically swap positions, alternating command at sea with time back at Pearl Harbor planning the next operation. While the ships would remain the same, the seagoing force would be known as the Fifth Fleet when Spruance was in command and the Third Fleet when Halsey was aboard. Accordingly, in November and December 1944, Spruance was in Hawaii, engaged with others in planning the invasion of Iwo Jima, slated for early 1945.

Three Marine divisions, the 1st, 3rd, and 4th, formed the landing force that went ashore on D-day, February 19. Despite the heaviest bombardment of the war, murderous combat lasted until March 16, when fanatical resistance by veteran Japanese soldiers fighting from hundreds of almost impregnable underground shelters was at last overcome. Iwo Jima also saw the recurrence on a sizable scale of another form of warfare: the kamikaze (literally "divine wind"). In waters around the island, suicide aerial raids severely damaged the *Saratoga*, destroying 42 planes, and struck the escort carrier *Bismarck Sea*. Still, the raids would be nothing like those the navy would soon be confronted with.

Okinawa was next.

In late March, an enormous fleet sailing from Ulithi, Manus, Hawaii, and Saipan converged on the island. Altogether 48 flag officers plus an additional five in a British carrier force were on board. They led an array of carriers, battleships, cruisers, amphibious ships, minesweepers, and service vessels, altogether 3,800 ships—the largest naval force ever to sail under an American flag. All were commanded by Raymond Spruance.

In the last few days of March, the armada began a five-day bombard-ment, hurling thousands of shells at Japanese defensive positions. On April 1, the Marine III Corps landed halfway up the west side of the island and struck for Yontan airfield, its initial objective. Marines were to split the island in half and then head north. The army XXIV Corps landed farther south. The army's role was also to move west to east across Okinawa, then turn south, isolating and then capturing the most populated part of the island.

The Marines moved quickly, severing the island by April 4. In a week of heavy fighting after turning north, they reduced a heavily fortified area situated in rugged terrain on Motobu Peninsula. The Marines then wheeled to assist army units engaged in bitter fighting near the southern end of the island in terrain ideal for defense.

Although the first month after the landings was characterized by fierce fighting, operations seemed to be progressing generally as planned. Then, on May 4, the Japanese launched a major counterstroke. Heavy combat raged across the island before the Japanese attack was repelled.

On May 23, the 6th Marine Division captured Naha, the island's cap-ital. In late June the island was finally secured. The cost was enormous: 7,613 Americans killed or missing and another 31,807 wounded—the highest casualty toll of any battle in the Pacific war. Indeed, such severe losses may have been an influence in the later decision to employ atomic weapons against Japan rather than invade territory likely to be defended with equal or more fanaticism and where casualties on both sides could only be assumed to be appalling.

As if the casualties sustained by army and Marine forces in capturing Okinawa were not sufficiently daunting, for Admiral Spruance and his sailors the battles in the waters offshore were among the bloodiest in the history of the U.S. Navy. Even before troops began landing on the island, kamikaze attacks numbering in the hundreds began strik-ing the invasion fleet. On March 18, the *Yorktown* and the *Hornet* were hit, resulting in loss of life on both carriers. The next day, the *Wasp* suffered heavy damage, forcing its eventual departure for repairs. The same day, the *Franklin* was nearly gutted by explosions and fire. More than 700 crewmen were killed or missing and 205 more were wounded, many horrifically burned. For a time dead in the water and nearly abandoned, the *Franklin* was later able to proceed under its own power.

Although carriers were the obvious targets of the kamikaze raids, destroyers—many of them isolated on radar-picket duty guarding the rest of the fleet—suffered most heavily. During the battle for Okinawa, 34 destroyers and smaller craft were sunk and many more were damaged, some severely.

Japanese zeal to get after American carriers and other capital ships intensified during the battle as ships in position off Okinawa conducted heavy raids on the Japanese homeland, striking ports and airfields up and down the coastline. In early August, a last-gasp sortie by the powerful remainder of the Japanese fleet sailed from the home islands seeking to strike the Allied armada operating against Okinawa. Included in the attacking force was the *Yamato*, the world's largest battleship, sporting 18-inch main guns. Spotted by American submarines and scout planes, the Japanese flotilla was attacked by planes from two carrier groups. After a desperate two hours of combat, the *Yamato*—a threat to U.S. forces since the days of Midway—was sunk, as were four destroyers. Four more destroyers were damaged and left the battle.

The Japanese surface navy was now essentially destroyed. The threat from kamikazes, however, remained as deadly as ever. Vengeance for the *Yamato* was not long in coming. One raid struck the carriers *Hancock*, *Enterprise*, and *Essex* and the battleship *Missouri*. All sustained considerable damage but remained in action.

April 11 and the days after marked a particularly intense period of kamikaze attacks on Spruance's Fifth Fleet. On the 11th, 185 kamikazes along with an additional 145 fighters and 45 torpedo planes struck the fleet, sinking a destroyer and putting a minesweeper out of action. The battleship *Tennessee* was also severely hit, sustaining nearly 150 casualties, and three destroyer escorts sustained varying degrees of damage.

For a time later in the struggle, kamikaze strikes specifically targeted destroyers on radar-picket duty. A 165-plane attack on April 16 exploded one destroyer and caused extensive damage to four others and the near destruction of a minesweeper. Losses on some of the ships numbered more than a hundred killed or wounded.

After a brief respite from almost constant attacks, heavy raids resumed again on April 27. Four destroyers were damaged as was a Canadian communications ship. On the evening of the 28th, a kamikaze hit the hospital ship *Comfort*, causing heavy loss of life. On May 3, one destroyer was sunk and a second so severely damaged the ship was withdrawn from the battle.

The focus of the Japanese attacks then shifted again to capital ships. On the morning of May 11, the carrier *Bunker Hill*, Admiral Mitscher's flagship, was struck with catastrophic results. Two kamikazes hit the big ship within minutes of each other, killing nearly 400 and wounding 260 more. Mitscher transferred his flag from the burning ship to the *Enterprise*. Mitscher transferred again the following day, this time to the *Randolph*, after the *Enterprise* was severely damaged. Although the *Bunker Hill* managed to stay afloat and limp back to Pearl Harbor, the ship was through for the remainder of the war.

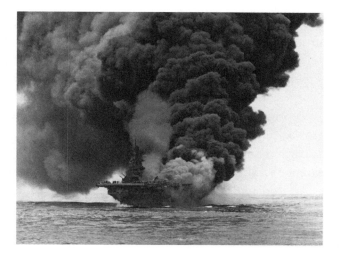

The American aircraft carrier USS Bunker Hill *ablaze after a Japanese kamikaze strike near Okinawa on May 11, 1945. Kamikaze attacks posed significant threats to American vessels in the latter stages of the war.*

Spruance, aboard the *Indianapolis*, was also in the midst of heavy action. Just prior to the invasion, the *Indianapolis* was shelling Japanese positions on the island when a kamikaze struck the ship's stern, killing or wounding nearly 30 sailors. The damage affected the vessel's steering, forcing Spruance to transfer his flag to the battleship *New Mexico*. A few days later, in the early evening hours of May 12, the *New Mexico* was also heavily damaged when a suicide plane cratered the ship's bridge, killing 54, wounding 119, and barely missing Spruance. Fearing for his safety, his staff searched the vessel and found him manning a fire hose along with other members of the crew.

In late May, with the end of the Okinawa campaign reasonably in sight, Nimitz pulled Spruance and his staff back to Pearl Harbor to begin planning for the anticipated invasion of Japan. Spruance was at Pearl Harbor when the war ended.

Ironically, even though Spruance had been in the forefront of actions in the Pacific from the earliest days of the war, he was not well known to the American public. That was as he preferred, believing that in war personal publicity could be detrimental because it could influence the commander's thinking: having been in the headlines, the officer might be more attentive to doing what his reputation would seem to call for than doing what was best to respond to the action at hand.

Averse to personal publicity, cool and unruffled, Spruance commanded the largest naval force ever put to sea by the United States. He chose exceptionally gifted subordinates—most notable among them Richmond Kelly Turner, his amphibious commander, and Marc Mitscher, his carrier force commander—and trusted them to do their jobs. As Spruance's biographers have noted, he had an unusual gift: the ability, associated with only the most gifted commanders, to make fast, accurate decisions in fluid situations under the pressure of heavy combat.

Before and After

Raymond Ames Spruance was born in Baltimore, Maryland, on July 3, 1886. After attending high school in New Jersey and Indiana, he entered the United States Naval Academy in 1903 at age 17, graduating 26th in the class of 1907. After graduation, he served first on the battleship

Iowa and then joined the *Minnesota* on the fleet's world cruise, After attending an electrical engineering course at General Electric's plant in Schenectady, New York, Spruance returned to sea duties first as engineering officer on the USS *Connecticut* and then on the USS *Cincinnati*. In March 1913, he received his first command billet as skipper of the destroyer *Bainbridge*. The following year he was assigned as assistant to the inspector of machinery at the Newport News, Virginia, shipbuilding and drydock facility. In 1916, Spruance began a tour on the newly commissioned USS *Pennsylvania*. In November 1917, he was posted as assistant engineering officer at the Brooklyn Navy Yard, with collateral duties in London and Edinburgh.

After the war, Spruance served on the USS *Agamemnon*, transporting American troops back to the United States from Europe. Command billets on the *Aaron Ward* and the *Osborne* followed, bracketed around a Bureau of Engineering tour in Washington, DC.

By June 1926, he was ready for the senior course—a program to prepare selected commanders and captains for higher responsibilities as senior captains or flag officers—at the Naval War College in Newport, Rhode Island. A tour with the Office of Naval Intelligence followed before he went back to sea as executive officer on the USS *Mississippi*.

June 1931 brought a return to the Naval War College for a two-year tour as instructor. The position would be the first of two assignments to the war college faculty; from March 1935 to August 1938, he would be posted as head of the tactics section. Between the faculty tours, he was chief of staff and aide to the commander of the Destroyer and Scouting Fleet. From the war college, he returned to the *Mississippi*, this time as commander—a post he held for two years. In February 1940, orders took him to San Juan, Puerto Rico, as commander of the Tenth Naval District, with additional assigned duty as commander of the Caribbean Sea Frontier. On September 17, 1941, Spruance was sent to the Pacific as commander of Cruiser Division Five and was in those duties when the United States entered the war. For a short time after the war, Spruance replaced Nimitz as commander of the U.S. Pacific Fleet. In February 1946, he returned to Newport, Rhode Island as president of the Naval War College. He served in that role for two years before retiring from the navy on July 1, 1948.

In retirement, Spruance moved to Pebble Beach, California. In January 1952, President Harry S. Truman appointed him ambassador to the Philippines, a post that he held until March 1955. Spruance then returned to Pebble Beach, living there quietly for the remainder of his long life. He died on December 13, 1969.

Spruance is buried at Golden Gate Cemetery, overlooking San Francisco Bay. He is interred alongside his colleagues Chester Nimitz, Richmond Kelly Turner, and Charles Lockwood in fulfillment of a pact arranged years before by the longtime friends.

ELWOOD R. "PETE" QUESADA

Building on lessons learned in North Africa, Quesada created a close-air-support capability for infantry and armored forces that was unmatched by any military in the world. Quesada developed a near-legendary rapport with ground commanders, pioneering the use of radar to vector aircraft to targets, placing forward air controllers with infantry and armored units, and providing on-call cover to units on the move. During the Battle of the Bulge, in an unprecedented move, all Allied tactical aircraft were placed under his control as the Allies sought to turn back the German attack.

During World War II, close-air-support missions to help defend a position or assist an advancing unit were available within minutes to American ground and armored forces. It was a capability that no other military in the world possessed at the time and proved to be a decisive factor in the war in Europe. The United States and its allies owed this extraordinary war-fighting advantage primarily to Lieutenant General "Pete" Quesada.

Quesada pioneered the use of radar to vector aircraft to targets in real time, placed pilots as forward air controllers in tanks equipped with VHF radios so units engaged or on the move could talk directly with aircraft overhead, and posted airmen with armored and infantry units to provide direct liaison with frontline troops. Quesada's squadrons covered Allied operations in the ETO from the D-Day landings through to Germany's surrender. Quesada's radar-equipped aircraft contributed to Allied success in the Battle of the Bulge, as horrific weather brought a halt to normal air operations. When the weather eventually cleared, Quesada's air units along with the Royal Air Force (RAF) annihilated German supply convoys and swept the Luftwaffe from the skies. It was but a harbinger of things to come as Quesada's legions helped tear open the path into Germany. Although Quesada was already known within the small army establishment for his exploits during the early days of the fledgling air service, it would be early 1943 before he became directly involved in combat operations. When the war began, he was commander of a fighter group at Mitchell Field, New York. Responsibility for air defense operations in the Philadelphia region followed in July 1942, and soon after he was officially designated as commander of the 1st Air Defense Wing. More critical to what would soon follow, with General George C. Marshall's intervention Quesada was jumped three grades as the army grew exponentially in size and geared up for combat on a worldwide scale.

Early in 1943, Quesada took his wing to North Africa, where Allied forces had landed the previous November. In the days that followed, he was given command of the 12th Fighter Command and named deputy commander of the Northwest African Coastal Air Force. The North African Campaign would prove to be a training ground for American air units.

Quesada and other air commanders used it to iron out procedures and improve tactics in preparation for the invasion of the European mainland.

There were indeed many lessons to learn. The US Army Air Corps, like the entire army, was raw and inexperienced. There were further complications as well. Pre-war emphasis in the service's professional schools had focused heavily on strategic bombardment. Mobile warfare and the trackless wastes of North Africa created an entirely new problem set. Difficulties extended far beyond tactics. Maintenance crews, for example, found the desert environment was destructive of planes and equipment at a level never previously anticipated.

During the outset of the North African Campaign, air assets were parceled out in small numbers to individual field commanders. Inefficient, ineffective, and easily overwhelmed by Luftwaffe attackers, these penny-packet small units served no one well. Quesada and his colleagues argued for, and eventually attained, central control of air assets, an enormous advantage that allowed Allied planners and combatants to fully exploit the inherent strengths and flexibility of airpower. Central control of airpower was subsequently enshrined in army doctrine (per the US Army Air Force field regulations *Command and Employment of Air Power*, July 1943), a watershed decision that changed the army's traditional approach to, and relationship with, the air arm.

Quesada was a hard charger who was not initially well liked by his British contemporaries or his aircrews. Brash and assertive at the outset, he ratcheted down his approach somewhat in the days that followed— although "mellow" would never be a quality associated with his name. As the war progressed and his competence became evident to all, he became a valued favorite of his Allied colleagues and the officers and men who served under him.

Operations in Tunisia, the invasion of Sicily, and landings in Italy followed. Quesada was not a behind-the-lines commander. To the occasional chagrin of his superiors, beginning in North Africa he led operational flights during each of those operations. Later in the war on one occasion, he flew Supreme Allied Commander General Dwight D. Eisenhower in a two-seat P-51 fighter on a reconnaissance mission over enemy lines.

Quesada's planes helped shut off the flow of supplies to Axis forces in North Africa, reducing the 69,000 tons-per-month minimum level for sustainment to 14,000 tons as the campaign drew to a close. After Axis forces surrendered in Tunisia, Quesada flew missions with the aerial armada that struck the island of Pantelleria, abetting the garrison's June 11 surrender after the most complete air assault the world had seen at that time: 4,973 sorties and eight million pounds of bombs. Soon after, with Quesada again in the air with them, his squadrons did laudable work in covering the invasion fleet transporting Allied troops to the landing beaches in Sicily.

For Quesada, the importance of signal communications and radar in tactical operations were among the most important lessons learned in Sicily. Allied gunners had shot down several C-47s carrying American and British paratroopers, many planes missed their drop zones by miles, and Quesada's radar operators had stepped in to vector many lost aircraft to safety.

On September 3, Quesada flew above the Allied convoy that left Oran bound for Salerno and the invasion of the Italian mainland. He was in the air again four days later when American forces hit the beach and walked into an ambush. As the infantry struggled to maintain a tenuous hold, Allied air forces flew cover for the 200,000 troops, 150,000 tons of supplies, and 30,000 vehicles that went ashore in Operation Avalanche. Altogether, more than 24,500 sorties were flown by both strategic and tactical air units that dropped full loads on German emplacements. Unlike in Sicily, close air support came more quickly and with greater effect, and in a series of night drops C-47s delivered their paratroopers with exceptional precision.

In mid-October 1943, Quesada was sent to England to assist planners in preparations for the D-Day landings. There, he would be given command of what would eventually be designed the IX Tactical Air Command (TAC), part of the Ninth Air Force. He carried with him staff and command experience gained in North Africa, Sicily, Italy, and 21 operational missions, as well as a reputation as a flying general.

Quesada faced a daunting task. As commander of the newly created IX TAC and its major subordinate units, he would control the fighter planes designated for close air support of American ground troops. Thousands of aircrew members were arriving each month, along with planes and support equipment. By D-Day, the Ninth Air Force would be the largest air force in the world, bigger even than its more famous contemporary, the Eighth Air Force. As Operation Overlord drew ever nearer, Quesada ruthlessly weeded out officers who did not measure up to his exacting standards. He trained his force relentlessly, emphasizing dive-bombing as a vital tool in close-air-support operations. Early in 1944, his units escorted heavy bombers in the operations known as "Big Week," intended to reduce the staying power of the Luftwaffe prior to the Allied invasion of the continent.

May 15 was a red letter day for Pete Quesada. On that morning, in front of an entire auditorium full of Allied leaders—including King George VI, Churchill, Eisenhower, Montgomery, Bradley, Patton, the British chiefs of staff, and a host of other senior British, Canadian, and American generals—Quesada briefed the final tactical airpower plan for Operation Overlord.

Operations aimed at isolating the battlefield continued throughout the pre-invasion period. In the two weeks prior to D-Day, Allied fighter-bombers claimed 445 locomotives destroyed and rail lines cut in 150 places. By D-Day, not a single railroad bridge across the Seine would be left standing.

As the sun rose over Western Europe on June 6, 1944, Allied armies waded ashore at five beaches on the northern coast of France. At one of the American beaches, code-named Omaha, the issue remained in doubt for much of the day. As German units moved toward the beach to throw back the battered landing force, Quesada's flyers pitched into the advancing armor and troops with decisive effect. In mid-afternoon, 15 of his P-47s struck the German 6th Parachute Regiment three miles from the beachhead and stopped all but a small portion from moving farther. Air strikes in the days ahead made movement during daylight hours almost impossible for German formations. So fierce and pervasive were the fighter attacks that German field marshal Gerd von Rundstedt, commander of Army Group West, declared the German area near the front lines a "traffic desert."

"The Longest Day." U.S. troops landing on the northern coast of France, June 6, 1944.

Quesada's direct involvement in operations and his close ties with infantry units became quickly evident: by D-Day plus one, he had established an advance headquarters on a Normandy beachhead. Operations during the landings and the breakout established the pattern of close air support and air cover for ground troops that would characterize the remainder of the campaign in Europe. By June 10, more than six thousand men of the Ninth Air Force and a thousand of their graders and ground-support vehicles were on foreign soil. Combat operations from airfields quickly built near Utah and Omaha Beaches began almost immediately. By the end of June 7, the second day of the invasion, Quesada's crews had already flown 3,303 sorties. As the war expanded across the European continent, Ninth Air Force engineers would eventually build 241 airfields in France, Belgium, Holland, and Luxembourg. Quesada placed them as close to the front lines as soil, geography, and supply considerations would allow. By June 18, 13,000 sorties had been flown in close-air-support and interdiction operations. Rails had been cut in 170 places; 38 bridges and tunnels, 17 ammunitions dumps, and 53 marshalling yards had been damaged or destroyed. By mid-month five runways had been built in France, enabling planes to refuel and rearm without returning to Britain.

In the first days after Allied landings, the Ninth's aircraft focused on targets in the Cotentin Peninsula, then shifted to support Operation Cobra, the breakout from Normandy. Later they would strike targets in the Falaise-Argentan Gap. Target sets included tanks, motorized vehicles, and troop concentrations. Targets of opportunity were hammered by Quesada's aggressive, far-ranging P-47s, while P-51s, P-38s, and British Spitfires cleared the skies of Luftwaffe defenders.

Omaha Beach shortly after D-Day. Among other factors, plunging fire from adjoining bluffs made "Bloody Omaha" the costliest of the five invasion beaches.

Frustrated by a period of horrible weather in June and July and a stale-mated battlefield around Saint-Lô, Quesada used the period of reduced activity to begin experimenting with, and subsequently installing, radios in tanks that could communicate with aircraft overhead. He followed by putting forward air controllers (often pilots) in tanks and began regular four-plane flights over armored columns. At about the same time, he worked to connect his microwave early warning (MEW) radar in ways that would enhance blind-bombing efforts and revector flights to pop-up targets of opportunity.

In mid-July, rockets were attached to the suite of weapons on Quesada's P-47s, making it the world's most heavily armed fighter. The Thunderbolt's payload now consisted of two rockets under each wing, two five-hundred-pound bombs, and six thousand rounds of 50 mm ammunition. Called "Jabos" by the Germans, and the "Jug" by the Americans, the P-47 became one of the most feared weapons in the Allies' arsenal.

Not long after, napalm bombs were added to the P-47s' repertoire. Learning of its successful use on battlefields in the Pacific, Quesada insisted on feasibility tests in the ETO. Napalm proved especially effect-ive against supply dumps and targets obscured in wooded areas—and it produced abject terror among those subjected to its attacks.

On July 24, seven hundred of Quesada's fighter-bombers flew the opening sorties of Operation Cobra, General Omar Bradley's plan to break out of the stalemate near the beachheads by blasting a gap through the hedgerows so skillfully used by the Germans for defense. Bradley's hope was that a breach could be torn open in the German lines that would allow Allied armor to pour through and reach open ground more conducive to fast-moving mobile warfare. The fighter-bombers strike was generally effective, but the massive saturation bombing by 1,586 heavy bombers was much less so. Both strikes suffered from "short-bombing" friendly fire incidents, and there was considerable confusion in route planning for the bombers.

The attacks were repeated the following day with devastating effects that were not immediately known or appreciated. In reality, the vaunted Panzer Lehr Division, holding defensive positions around Saint-Lô, had been essentially destroyed. Eventually almost alone among Allied commanders, General J. Lawton Collins, commander of VII Corps, sensed that the German defenses had been devastated and what remained was a thin shell that could be cracked open. Quesada readily agreed with Collins and designed close-air-support packages to help propel Collins's attack, positioning flights of fighter-bombers over the tank columns leading the advance. The breakout, when it came, was explosive. Advances of as many as five to six miles a day at long last took Allied armor out of the dreaded hedgerows and into open country.

The days that followed were the highlight of mobile warfare in Europe. Quesada sent swarms of P-47s, P-51s, and P-38s to attack fleeing, disorganized columns of German troops. In the last week of July, Quesada's 17 fighter groups flew nine thousand close-air-support missions and claimed nearly four hundred tanks, more than two thousand trucks and vehicles, and scores of artillery pieces destroyed. Bradley was effusive in his praise for Quesada's efforts, writing General Marshall that "I simply can't imagine any other officer that would have given us as much ... help as Pete. He was willing to try anything."

On August 1, a new American army, the Third (commanded by George S. Patton) was activated on the continent. American air units were reorganized to accommodate the change. Henceforth, Quesada's IX TAC would support General Courtney Hodges's First Army, while XIX TAC under O. P. Weyland would accompany Patton.

Five days later, the Germans used a short breather in Allied offensive action to launch a nighttime counterattack near Mortain. The strike made initial progress, threatening a breakthrough and a severing of supply lines that could cut off Patton's Third Army. Quesada sent his aircraft on raids that shielded American defenders in isolated pockets and supported countermoves by U.S. armored formations. Beginning with attacks in the early morning hours of August 7, Quesada's pilots tore into the advancing German units. By the end of the day, they had destroyed nearly 20 percent of the German force—including 28 tanks, 10 halftracks, and numerous 88mm artillery pieces—that had been battering its way toward Avranches in an attempt to split the seam between the American First and Third Armies. The following two days added to the score. In 980 sorties, 76 tanks and 1,000 transport vehicles were destroyed, most by aircraft assigned as cover over U.S. armored columns.

By August 10, the Germans' thrust had been blunted, leaving their forces in an extended position vulnerable to a sweeping Allied counterstroke. British and Canadian forces moved from the north, while U.S. units primarily under Patton circled from the south to surround and trap thousands of German troops along with their accompanying armor, transports, and other support vehicles. Coordinating with British Spitfires, Quesada's airmen struck at German formations in what became known as the Falaise Pocket.

Trapped inside the closing cauldron, German columns often miles long provided a target-rich environment for Allied aircrews. While sizable numbers of infantry eventually escaped the Allied ring, much of their supporting armor, vehicles, and artillery was destroyed or left behind starved of fuel. In addition to 10,000 dead and 50,000 captured, German losses in the pocket included two hundred tanks, nearly a thousand heavy weapons, and five thousand trucks and vehicles. As the Germans fled, fighter-bombers blew up fuel dumps and made daylight travel on the area's road network a lethal hazard.

August 1944 turned out to be an extraordinary month for Quesada's fighter command. His airmen flew nearly nine thousand sorties, dropped more than 21,000 tons of bombs, destroyed 684 tanks, and shot down 26 enemy planes. His units continued to improve their capabilities in conducting radar-controlled flights. Enhancements, aided by 10,000 miles of telephone wire, facilitated operations in marginal weather conditions and aided the vectoring of missions to assist units in distress.

Fall 1944 brought difficulties to American air units beyond those associated with combat. Shortages of bombs and fuel plagued Quesada's units. In September, none of his nine fighter-bomber groups had sufficient amounts of oil, fuel, or bombs. In five groups, shortages were severe enough to force eleven days of stand-down.

When conditions improved, Quesada sought permission to assist Collins's VII Corps attempt to take the ancient city of Aachen. Sheltered in heavily protected bunkers and pillboxes, immune from all but direct hits or repeated attack, the Germans resisted fiercely. Nearly six weeks

U.S. troops of the 28th Infantry Division march down the Champs Élysées, August 29, 1944.

of desperate fighting followed before Aachen fell on October 21. When the struggle finally ended, 13,000 Germans had been taken prisoner. Quesada's airmen had dropped about nine thousand tons of bombs in 10,000 sorties. Quesada's losses, though, were among the most severe in his squadrons' experience: 79 planes and 58 pilots were lost in actions around the city.

November saw Quesada's squadrons in support of the First Army's attempt to shatter German lines near Cologne. Despite the Operation Cobra–like saturation bombing by B-17s and B-24s of the Eighth Air Force, repeated attacks resulted in little forward movement.

December brought the Battle of the Bulge. For the first and only time, tactical airpower was used in a reactive, largely unplanned manner, hurled at enemy forces that were tearing gaping holes in Allied lines. Their actions in the Bulge would show that tactical airpower could be as valuable for defense as it was on the offensive operations that had generally characterized the American effort up to that time.

For the first several days, abominable weather aided the German spearheads, shielding them from attack. As the penetrations became more alarming, with Liège and even Antwerp apparently at risk, Quesada asked his veteran crews to do the unthinkable. He sent P-47s and P-51s down through pea-soup overcasts with ceilings almost nonexistent in an attempt to locate and attack the rapidly advancing German armor. Feeling their way along, dodging hills, trees, and terrain features nearly invisible in the fog, somehow avoiding collisions, they did so. Often breaking out only a few feet above the ground, Quesada's planes hammered at the lead units, causing considerable disruption and delaying the advance of panzer units surprised by the strikes. Still, the horrific weather—the worst in Europe in years—prevailed from December 18–22, inhibiting air operations.

On December 21, in a nearly unprecedented gesture, British air vice marshal Arthur Coningham, commander of the British Second Tactical Air Force, placed all of his fighter-bombers under Quesada's control—an action that allowed the American general to plan, coordinate, and control the air battle. Finally, on the morning of December 23, clouds began to clear. Quesada sent units from bases in England, France, and Belgium swarming to the attack, concentrating on close-air-support missions and destroying supply lines in the northern and central sections of the Bulge. Attacks continued unabated the following day. Near Saint-Vith, P-47s found a massive German column in the open and rained catastrophe on it, wrecking five hundred motor transports and dozens of tanks and armored vehicles. So intense were the attacks that the German column could not advance for the remainder of the day.

Indeed, by the following day—Christmas Eve—momentum had clearly begun to shift in favor of the Allies. Heroic resistance by American infantry, armor, and airborne units at places such as Bastogne had channelized German armor into narrow rural lanes. The effect was to increase its vulnerability to air strikes. Quesada's airmen developed the technique of destroying lead vehicles, thus blocking entire columns unable to get around them in the constricted roadway.

On Christmas Day, General J. Lawton Collins's VII Corps found the main portion of the German 2nd Panzer Division just five miles from the Meuse River. Working together, Quesada and Collins quickly devised a coordinated assault combining infantry, armor, and artillery attacks along with massive air strikes from IX TAC fighter-bombers. Hundreds of German armored vehicles were trapped and destroyed. The battle stopped the Germans' most westerly advance. Afterward Collins was effusive in his praise of Quesada's aircrews.

Altogether, Allied tactical air units ruined five hundred vehicles, destroyed 90 gun positions, and attacked dozens of strongpoints. By December 26, Patton's troops reached the besieged city of Bastogne. The tide had clearly turned.

As weather permitted, intense air strikes continued on the following days. On January 22 and 23, hundreds of additional German vehicles were destroyed. By this time, enemy supply routes were almost nonexistent, having been devastated by repeated strikes from scores of Allied fighter-bombers. When the Battle of the Bulge was officially over, British and American aircraft claimed 290 gun positions, 751 tanks and armored vehicles, and six thousand motor transports destroyed, as well as locomotive and rail segments too numerous to count. Speaking later of the struggle in the Ardennes, Luftwaffe fighter commander Adolf Galland said, "The American fighter-bombers destroyed us."

As the war wound down, Quesada tasked his staff to compile data, perform tests, and create a reference document detailing operating procedures for the close air support of troops. Part history, part legacy, the resulting work documented the role of tactical airpower in World War II. For the airmen of Quesada's IX TAC and other tactical air units, the war in Europe had indeed been a formative experience. Despite the overarching emphasis on strategic bombing by airpower advocates before the war, less than a quarter of the army's air combat effort was allocated to strategic bombardment by the time of Germany's surrender. Much of the rest was committed to tactical air operations.

In late April 1945, more than a week after American troops made initial contact with the Soviets at Torgau on the Elbe River, the U.S. Army and IX TAC stopped offensive operations. Finally, it was over.

Quesada's innovations had been ongoing throughout the course of the war in Europe. His units designed the signals systems used for close air support and developed standard practices for bomb selection and fuse lengths. His airmen were the first to use small spotter planes on scouting missions along the front lines. Quesada's squadrons expanded and improved dive-bombing training as new crews were fed into the air units, creating a capability appreciated by Allied foot soldiers and feared by German infantry and armor.

Under Quesada's leadership, the Ninth Air Force became the world's premier air-ground unit. Close-air-support capabilities reached new levels of effectiveness, new systems were introduced, and precision bombing advanced in terms of accuracy, timeliness, and lethality. Quesada worked tirelessly to mold air and ground officers into a seamless, unified fighting unit. He cultivated close personal relationships with Patton, Bradley, Collins, Hodges, and other infantrymen that became the model for harmony and integrated operations. Perhaps no other non-infantryman did as much to assist America's foot soldiers as did Pete Quesada.

As his units steadily increased in effectiveness, Quesada's relationship with senior ground commanders was solidified. Bradley said there was "nothing conventional about Quesada, when he talks power he means everything but the kitchen sink." After observing Quesada's operations shortly after D-Day, he reported that "Quesada has a fine reputation among field soldiers and he does more than anyone else to bring air and ground closer together." Bradley spoke for other commanders of infantry and armored units when he told Army Air Forces chief General Henry H. "Hap" Arnold that "this man Quesada is a jewel." After the war, he wrote that "unlike most airmen who viewed ground support as a bothersome diversion ... Quesada approached it as vast new frontier waiting to be explored."

By the time the shooting ended, Quesada had been selected for reassignment. On April 13, his command held a combined birthday (his 41st) and farewell party for him. The event was attended by Eisenhower, Bradley, Patton, Montgomery, and a host of other senior Allied air and ground leaders. One officer noted that "I have never seen such affection between air and ground officers as I saw last night when General Quesada left us."

It was time for Pete Quesada to go home.

Soon after V-E Day, Quesada returned to the United States. Assigned to Washington, Quesada served as assistant chief of the Air Staff for intelligence and was in that position when the Japanese surrendered.

Before and After

Pete Quesada was a legendary airman even before gaining further renown as an innovative genius in providing air support for American ground forces. In 1929, along with Air Corps notables Ira Eaker and Carl "Tooey" Spaatz, he flew the legendary aircraft *Question Mark* in a flight demonstration that, through pioneering aerial refueling techniques, kept it aloft for six days.

Born April 13, 1904, in Washington, DC, Quesada was the son of a Spanish father and Irish American mother. He attended Wyoming Seminary in Kingston, Pennsylvania, the University of Maryland, and Georgetown University before enlisting as a flying cadet in 1924. After earning his wings and receiving a regular commission a year later, he reverted to inactive status for the following year and a half. A gifted athlete, Quesada played professional baseball in the St. Louis Cardinals organization while he awaited a call to return to active duty. (For a time in his retirement years, he would be part owner of a major league franchise.)

Quesada returned to active duty in 1927 as an engineering officer at Bolling Field in Washington, DC. His multiple talents were quickly recognized, and the following summer he became aide-de-camp to Air Corps chief Major General James Fechet.

Much to his satisfaction, 1929 brought a return to flying duties and with it the epic *Question Mark* flight. With a crew of five that included Spaatz and Eaker, the *Question Mark*, a Fokker Trimotor, stayed aloft for six days orbiting Los Angeles. The saga entailed 43 aerial refuelings in a pioneering bucket-and-line operation, some of which were conducted at night. The *Question Mark* flight demonstrated the feasibility of long-range, long-duration refueling. It was a forerunner, planting the seeds for the present-day U.S. Air Force capability that is without equal by the air arms of any other nation.

A fluent Spanish speaker, Quesada was next posted as assistant military attaché to Cuba, serving there from October 1930 until April 1932. A second aide-de-camp tour followed, this time serving the assistant secretary for air, F. Trubee Davison. The assignment was highlighted by a flight piloted by Quesada, who also served as Davison's personal pilot, that touched down in several African nations.

During the 1934 interregnum when the Air Corps assumed responsibility for flying the nation's airmail, Quesada served as chief pilot on the New York–Cleveland route. A series of rapid moves then ensued over the next four years: his first command billet at Langley Field, Virginia; further executive support duties culminating with service as aide-de-camp to the secretary of war, George Dern; attendance at the Army Command and General Staff College at Fort Leavenworth, Kansas; and finally as a flight commander with the 1st Bomb Squadron at Mitchell Field, New York. At a time when ground and air commanders were bitterly divided about the proper role of airpower, Quesada's observations at the Command and Staff College were particularly prescient. Almost alone among his contemporaries, he was of the opinion that "future wars will require all sorts of arrangements between the air and ground, and the two will have to work closer than a lot of people think or want."

A lengthy two-and-a-half year assignment as adviser to the Argentine air force followed in June 1938. October 1940 found Quesada back in Washington as an intelligence officer in the Air Corps office. For a time, Air Chief General Henry H. "Hap" Arnold used him as the Air Corps liaison to foreign embassies in Washington. Nine months later he was back at Mitchell Field, this time as commander of the 33rd Fighter Group, his position when the United States entered World War II.

When the war in Europe ended, Quesada returned to Washington as assistant chief of Air Staff for intelligence. He served in those duties for nine months before being posted to Tampa, Florida, as commander of the Third Air Force.

The Third Air Force rather quickly morphed into TAC, with Quesada as its first commander. A short time later, Quesada moved TAC headquarters to Langley AFB, Virginia, a location close to army ground force leaders. As the U.S. Air Force's most notable proponent of tactical airpower, Quesada objected to the primacy accorded at the time to strategic aircraft funding, requirements, and doctrine. Reassigned at his request in November 1948, Quesada began a series of air staff and joint staff postings, eventually serving as special assistant for reserve forces, later as commander of the Joint Technical Planning Committee, and finally as commander of Joint Task Force 3.

Disenchanted with the air force's policy of subjugating tactical air, Quesada requested retirement in the fall of 1948. Air force leaders were reluctant to let him go, and three years elapsed before approval was finally given. Quesada retired from the Air Force as a lieutenant general on October 31, 1951. He remained active in aircraft industry–related positions during his retirement years, serving in executive roles with several companies, including Lockheed Aircraft and American Airlines. Most notable, perhaps, was his service as President Eisenhower's special adviser for aviation and later as the first director of the newly established Federal Aviation Agency (FAA).

As FAA administrator, Quesada established the agency's basic organizational structure and immediately launched an intensive campaign to improve safety, replace outdated equipment, update standards, prescribe maintenance procedures, and institute physical and proficiency requirements for aircrews. Some of Quesada's new rules and procedures, such as putting FAA inspectors on flights, were not always well received by pilots but by and large were supported by the public, who saw visible evidence that flying was becoming safer. Typical of Quesada, he was undeterred by criticism: "The public acts in faith, faith in the system, and we'll see to backing up that faith. I'm here to represent the public and dammit, the public will be represented." During his tenure at the FAA, *Time* magazine characterized Quesada as "a rare bird: a military man with a lively and uncluttered mind."

After leaving the FAA, Quesada became part owner of a major league baseball franchise and participated in several projects to enhance the beauty of Washington DC. The legacy of Quesada's military service is unique in that it is for the most part not tied to specific battles or a distinct series of operations. Rather, it is reflective of the air-ground war-fighting concept that he developed. By the end of the war, Allied air capabilities in support of ground operations were unmatched. Quesada was one of a small group of airmen who recognized early on the enormous benefits dedicated close air support could provide to ground combat units. During his tenure at the Army Command and General Staff College, he foresaw, and began working on, the interconnections between air and ground units necessary to tie them together as a cohesive fighting apparatus. His early work would come to full fruition over the skies of Europe.

His role in developing the *Command and Employment of Air Power* regulations recognized the role of air superiority in facilitating successful ground operations. To exploit the full advantages of airpower, the new doctrine established centralized command and control of air assets and institutionalized the equal status of ground and air commanders

Quesada took enormous pride in his airmen and was effusive in giving public credit for their accomplishments. More than most other senior American leaders, Quesada was highly respected by his junior officers and enlisted men. Many a P-38, P-47, or P-51 mechanic kept as a most treasured memory of World War II a photo of himself alongside Pete Quesada.

One of the measures of a leader is what other knowledgeable contemporaries said and thought about him.

To Dwight Eisenhower, Quesada was "a dashing, cooperative leader."

Fellow senior airman General John Cannon saw Quesada as an "officer of engaging personality, self-confident, and capable of taking a definite stand."

Omar Bradley, whose army group was directly supported for many months by Quesada's airmen during some of the most difficult days in Europe, developed an especially close relationship with Quesada and wrote often of his contributions. It was Bradley's assessment that "although Quesada could have passed for a prototype of the hot pilot with his shiny green trousers, broad easy smile, and crumpled but jaunty hat, he was a brilliant, hard, and daring commander.... He had come into the war as a young and imaginative man unencumbered by the prejudice and theories of so many of his seniors on the employment of tactical air. To Quesada the fighter was a little-known weapon with vast unexplored potentialities in support of ground troops. He conceived it as his duty to learn what they were."

In Bradley's view, other airmen "suffered by comparison to General Pete Q, who is the doughboy's champion and the doughboy's idea of a very great airman."

Pete Quesada oversaw the birth of a new military tactic that continues to serve his nation well. Perhaps the greatest compliment to Quesada's abilities came soon after the war when Eisenhower asked Bradley to rank the 30 most important American generals who had contributed to the victory in Europe. Bradley ranked Pete Quesada fourth. Only Smith (Eisenhower's chief of staff), Spaatz (commander, U.S. Strategic Air Forces in Europe), and Hodges (commander, U.S. First Army) ranked ahead of him. Bradley's placement put Quesada ahead of Patton (sixth) and all other ground and air force commanders in Europe, including his airmen contemporaries Doolittle (17th), Eaker (26th), and Hoyt S. Vandenberg (28th).

Quesada died on February 9, 1993. He is buried at Arlington National Cemetery.

J. LAWTON COLLINS

Regarded by many as one of the best American corps commanders, "Lightning Joe" was one of the few American leaders who commanded major forces in both the Pacific and European Theaters. In the Pacific, Collins led the 25th Infantry Division during the battle for Guadalcanal. In Europe, Collins led VII Corps in the storming of Utah Beach and later spearheaded the Operation Cobra breakout from the hedgerow impasse in Normandy. As the war progressed, Collins's units captured Aachen, led the counterattack on the northern shoulder of the Bulge, took Cologne, and played a major role in closing the Ruhr Pocket, trapping large numbers of German soldiers.

Joseph Lawton ("Lightning Joe") Collins was one of the few American generals who led major forces in both the Pacific and European theaters. In the Pacific, Collins commanded the 25th Infantry Division in actions on Guadalcanal and New Georgia. In Europe, he led VII Corps from Utah Beach through major engagements across the continent: Cherbourg, the Operation Cobra breakout at Saint-Lô, Mortain, Falaise, the Bulge, Aachen, the Ruhr Pocket, and closing actions along the Elbe.

The division commanders who worked for him—including Terry de la Mesa Allen, the best of the lot—lauded Collins's leadership. His boss, General Omar Bradley, regarded Collins as the ablest American corps commander. Bradley wrote, "Had we created another ETO Army, despite his youth and lack of seniority, Collins certainly would have been named commander."

Perhaps the surest testimony to Collins's abilities came from those who opposed him on the battlefield. German generals ranked Collins (along with General Troy Middleton) as the best American corps commanders in Europe.

Nine days after the attack on Pearl Harbor, Collins transferred from his position as chief of staff, VII Corps, where for several months in 1941 he had helped plan and conduct a series of maneuvers aimed at preparing the army for war. Collins, a colonel, was initially posted to Honolulu and assigned to the Hawaiian Department, again in a chief of staff billet. Quick promotions followed: in February 1942 to brigadier general followed two months later to major general. The two-star rank came coincident with a new posting as commander of the 25th Infantry Division. The 25th (nicknamed "Tropic Lightning") had a relatively poor reputation in army circles. Collins drilled his unit without letup for nearly six months on Oahu and nearby islands. Late that year, the 25th was sent to Guadalcanal to relieve the 1st Marine Division, which had assaulted the island in August.

The 25th first saw significant action in January 1943 as part of a three-division assault on key Japanese positions at Kokumbona and Mt. Austen. A month later Japanese resistance ended with fighting around Cape Esperance led by a 25th Division regiment.

July–October of that year saw the 25th Division in action again in operations that resulted in the capture of Munda on New Georgia Island. Along with other army units, the Collins-led 25th secured the island and its airstrip for use against the Japanese bastion on nearby Rabaul, New Guinea. Rest and rehabilitation in New Zealand followed in November.

Collins's aggressive, quick-striking operations earned him his "Lightning Joe" nickname. For Collins, New Zealand brought an end to his duties in the Pacific. His exemplary performance led Army Chief of Staff General George C. Marshall to appoint him as commander of VII Corps, which by then was training in Great Britain in preparation for the invasion of Europe. Collins arrived in England on February 12, 1944, and for the next three months at locations across Britain oversaw VII Corps intensive training as the unit rehearsed plans for the cross-channel assault on the European continent.

VII Corps's objective on D-Day was Utah Beach. Thinking that flooded areas close to the beach would dissuade a major landing there, the Germans initially offered only light resistance. Taking advantage of the unexpected opportunity, Collins's divisions pushed quickly inland. Collins himself was ashore on D+1. In a pattern that would persist for the duration of the war, he began making daily visits to the units in contact, establishing his reputation as a general who led from the front. Later he would use a Piper Cub scout plane for daily face-to-face contact with his frontline divisions as they battled their way across the continent.

By this time, having made his acquaintance in England, Collins had formed a close bond with Major General "Pete" Quesada, commander of IX TAC. In his own words, Collins was "a tremendous believer in doing everything we could in the combined arms."

Collins's experience in the Pacific had led him to believe that winning on the battlefield required "a coordinated attack and that means infantry, artillery, air, and engineers." In Quesada, Collins found a kindred spirit. Both were smart, energetic, independent thinkers. Each was highly aggressive in moving toward the sound of the guns, and both were comfortable with the nuts of bolts of operational planning.

After securing the beachhead, Collins sent his divisions toward the western coast of the Cotentin Peninsula, his assigned objective. He reached it on June 18 and captured Cherbourg, his follow-on objective, on the 27th. The battle for the port city was a weeklong struggle, the intensity and viciousness of which would be reflective of many more battles in many more towns as the Allies pushed towards Germany. The Wehrmacht's soldiers fought street by street, house by house, eventually holding out in isolated pockets until organized resistance mercifully ended.

Elsewhere, though, Allied forces were being fought to a standstill after pushing inland only a few miles from the invasion beaches. Six weeks after the landings, the key city of Caen had still not been captured, although British general Bernard Law Montgomery had announced that he would take it on D-Day. Across the tenuously held front, Allied troops were pinned down by tenacious German defenders operating in the *bocage*—the hedgerow country—that made maneuver warfare impossible.

As the battle for Cherbourg was winding down, Collins turned his VII Corps southward to assist in General Omar Bradley's plan to break the impasse. Called Operation *Cobra*, Bradley's plan was to blast through the hedgerow barriers and reach open French countryside where Allied armor could be unleashed in a war of movement.

Despite high hopes, initial attacks on July 25 were unsuccessful, stymied by determined resistance and friendly-fire bombings of frontline troops by American heavy bombers. By nightfall, only meager advances had been made, although the pre-attack saturation bombing had been the most intense of the war.

The disappointing results caused senior Allied leaders to consider canceling or delaying further attempts or shifting the focus of other parts of the front. Closer to the front and with a much better feel for the battle, Collins—initially alone among Allied commanders—sensed that the Germans were cracking. Noting that Axis counterstrikes had evidenced a more than usual lack of coordination and flair, Collins believed that the Germans' command structure and communications had been damaged more than initial assessments indicated. He decided that the attack should be pressed. The Germans should be allowed no time to recover. Instead, Collins would hurl at them the full weight of VII Corps, plus his armored reserve.

Aided by carpet bombing from American heavy and medium bombers and by Quesada's fighter-bombers strafing and bombing in the van of the attack, at 7:00 a.m. on July 26, Collins sent his 1st Division—the Big Red One—bulked up with additional tanks, and the entire 2nd Armored Division against the battered German line. Eventually four infantry and two armored divisions would quickly assault the German positions.

By July 28, two days later, to the profound relief of Allied leaders from Eisenhower down, substantial resistance no longer faced the American advance. The Allies were free of the hedgerows and moving in open country. Collins described the actions that followed as "some of the wildest melees of the war." Panzer Lehr, the crack German division that faced Collins's lead units, was utterly destroyed. The division's commander, General Fritz Bayerlein, after escaping with nothing but the clothes on his back, eventually got a report through to his headquarters advising that there was nothing left of the division—its armor was decimated, its soldiers killed, wounded, or captured, and its equipment, supplies, and staff were irretrievably lost. The weight of the attack was such that, as Baylerlein later recalled, "after an hour I had no communication with anybody, even by radio. By noon nothing was visible but dust and smoke. My front lines looked like the face of the moon and at least 70 percent of my troops were knocked out—dead, wounded, crazed, or numbed."

Before Collins's attacks, gains along the front were typically measured in yards per day. Now, free of the hedgerows and with resistance withering, advances of five or more miles became commonplace. By the end of the month, with Allied armor running free, the momentum of the attacks increased even more.

With the doorway to France being blown open by Operation *Cobra*, propelled by the aggressiveness of commanders such as Collins and Patton (whose Third Army had been activated on August 1), Allied armies swept east and north into France, eventually trapping large German formations in what became known as the Falaise Pocket. Allied armor, though, was spread thin in the aftermath of the rapid advance. The Germans resisted fiercely, launching a massive counterstrike from

Mortain in the direction of Avranches that threatened to sever Patton's 12 divisions from their supply line.

Collins's VII Corps, already tired by heavy fighting following the Cobra breakout, bore the brunt of the assault. The attack came as Collins was swapping out the exhausted 1st Division, replacing it with the 13th, a fresher unit. Somehow Collins's units held on. Aided by a battalion that managed to hold a key position on Hill 317 as the attack flowed around it, Collins cabled together a makeshift defense that tied his outposts together. As the Germans advanced, Collins sent the 2nd Armored Division to hammer at the assault's expanding flanks. Accompanied by devastating attacks by Pete Quesada's P-47 Thunderbolts and RAF Typhoons, which struck along and behind the lines, the 2nd Armored's tanks tore into the Axis pincers. By August 7, the intensity of the German attack began to wane, and the threat was fully contained by the 10th. Collins had put together a masterful response and gave ample credit to U.S. and British air units in after-action reports.

After Mortain, Collins sent his corps against the southwestern flank of the Falaise Pocket. The Allied advance then continued, leading some to hope that the war in Europe might be over by the end of the year. As later events would show, that hope was premature.

By early September, the Allies' eastward push brought Collins's VII Corps to the western border of Germany. With American supply lines stretched to the breaking point, his soldiers closed up against the powerful Siegfried Line. Collins's boss, General Courtney Hodges, committed VII Corps against Aachen—the first major German city faced by an Allied force along the German frontier. Strategically important almost from the dawn of European history, Aachen was a vital transportation and communications center. The extensive network of roads that flowed from the city presented the Allies with a gateway to the interior of Germany. Aachen's importance was obvious to friend and foe alike; it would be defended by elite troops, including I SS Panzer Corps.

After first targeting several forts that ringed the city, on September 12, Hodges ordered Collins to strike directly toward Aachen. Collins began the attack the next day, moving forward with three divisions, the 1st and 9th Infantry Divisions and the 3rd Armored. Bitter fighting ensued in the small villages west of the city. Days of desperate combat with heavy casualties brought Collins's force up against the outer reaches of the Siegfried Line, an immense fortification laden with gun emplacements sheltered behind and under seven feet of reinforced concrete, all surrounded by thick forest. The Germans had drawn VII Corps into a killing zone.

A week of combat with significant losses resulted in gains of only three to five miles. Collins adjusted his plans, requesting and securing additional air support from Quesada's IX TAC fighter-bombers in an attempt to penetrate the defensive perimeter surrounding the city. The attacks, which dropped enormous tonnage on the German fortifications, were only marginally successful. The majority of pillboxes, strongpoints, and gun emplacements were nearly impervious even to direct hits by five-hundred-pound bombs. Of 43 strongpoints struck on September 23, only seven suffered major damage, and only four or five were captured in the next two days.

Nonetheless, taking the city was essential. Collins believed the defenses were weakened by the continuous pressure, and he and Quesada continued to hammer the German positions, seeking to break through at any spot that cracked open. The Germans defended tenaciously. In a two-week period from late September until early October, two Wehrmacht corps and I SS Panzer Corps were brought into the battle for the city. Faced with 50,000 veteran defenders determined to hold on, Hodges committed an additional corps and brought in even more air support. With the American XIX Corps circling in from the west and north and Collins's VII Corps moving from the east and south, the Allies sought to ring the city, choke it off from outside support, and force it into submission. The struggle turned into an infantry battle as terrain and heavy forest precluded the effective use of armored formations. Quesada's fighter-bombers struck ahead of the American assault lines, lashing at heavily defended, hidden German emplacements.

Still, the going was tough. In some of the most desperate combat of the war, gains sometimes averaged less than a thousand yards a day. Increasingly, though, the pincers formed by XIX Corps and VII Corps came together, closing the city within them. Finally, on October 16, the jaws of the trap came together. Thinly closed at first, within two days further linkups sealed Aachen in an impenetrable ring. On October 21, organized resistance in the city ended. Brutal fighting around Aachen in the Hürtgen Forest provided further indication of the Wehrmacht's determination to defend the German homeland. Collins called it "the toughest fighting since the *bocage* days in Normandy."

Any remaining hopes for an early end to the war inspired by the rapid advances and freewheeling warfare of midsummer and fall were about to be shattered on dozens of frozen battlefields scattered across Belgium and Luxembourg. On December 16, amidst bitter cold and driving snow, Hitler launched his last great roll of the dice.

The massive rolling assault struck weakly held American positions in the Ardennes. Horrific weather conditions persisted for days, grounding Allied aircraft and enabling German armor and infantry, unthreatened from the skies, to move unchecked across the countryside. For a few agonizing days, Hitler's goal of reaching Antwerp and splitting the Allied armies seemed within reach. Then, with advancing German formations already approaching the Meuse River, Allied forces reshuffled and pulled together from distant locations, struck back.

When the German attack occurred, Collins and his VII Corps were a considerable distance away, near Aachen along the Siegfried Line. As the size and severity of the Bulge attack became evident, Collins disengaged from his position on the eastern edge of the Allied advance and turned his divisions south to confront the growing threat. Hurrying his corps to the attack, Collins struck the northern shoulder of the Bulge while Patton's force moved in from the south. On December 24, VII Corps came up against the major portion of the 2nd Panzer Division just five miles from the Meuse River near the town of Celles.

On Christmas Day, the weather cleared, and Collins ordered his corps to strike the Germans in a coordinated attack with Pete Quesada, who sent waves of fighter-bombers at the German columns. For the Wehrmacht, the results were catastrophic—hundreds of armored vehicles were destroyed. Collins's troops moved into Celles in late afternoon.

In the aftermath, the battle assumed considerable historical import-ance. For the Wehrmacht, Celles was the high-water mark of the Battle

BATTLE OF THE BULGE
December 16 1944–January 16, 1945

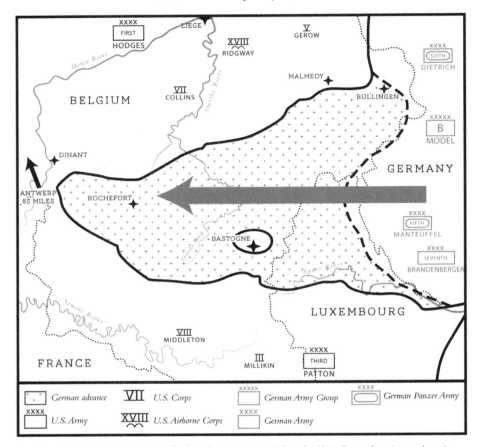

In what was to be the largest engagement ever fought by the U.S. Army, on 16 December 1944, German formations struck a quiet, lightly defended sector in the Ardennes front used by the Allies to acclimate and train replacement troops. The attack aimed at splitting Allied forces and, optimally, seizing the port of Antwerp. At the minimum, German leaders hoped to buy time to allow them to deal with Russian advances in the east.

The German attack, employing 250,000 men, 1,900 artillery pieces, 970 tanks, and 2,000 aircraft, eventually created a "bulge" 50 miles wide and 70 miles deep. For several days at the outset, inclement weather conditions inhibited Allied air intervention. As the scope of the attack became apparent, the U.S. 101st Airborne Division was sent to Bastogne, arriving there by truck at midnight 18 December. Surrounded by German forces, the 101st's stand from 19–26 December at the key crossroads town played a decisive role in the battle.

Throughout the campaign, pockets of determined resistence slowed the German advance. As the weather changed, a thaw disrupted the movement of Panzer forces and clearing skies allowed Allied aircraft to inflict heavy losses, particularly on German armor. Meanwhile, units of the U.S. First and Third Armies began hammering at the shoulders of the bulge. Losses were extremely heavy on both sides. German losses — 100,000 men, 700 tanks, 1,600 aircraft — were irreplaceable. The battle depleted Germany's remaining reserves of men, tanks, aircraft, guns, ammunition, and fuel. By late January, the Germans were forced back to the original start lines.

of the Bulge: the battle in and around the city would be the farthest
westward advance of the German forces. Collins's VII Corps, aided
admirably by Quesada's IX TAC, stopped the most extensive penetration
of the massive attack that only a few days before had seemed to be
sweeping irreversibly toward Antwerp.

Still, the Wehrmacht was not quite finished. Collins's forces had
trapped large numbers of German infantry and armor inside what became
known as the "Celles Pocket." Desperate to free their vital panzers from
encirclement, at mid-day on December 26 the Germans launched a strong
counterattack, hoping to achieve a breakout. Shifting units to meet the
assault, Collins's defenders, assisted this time by British Typhoons, lashed
at the German formations. The struggle was over by nightfall, with the
remnants of the German attackers in full retreat. As the struggle evolved,
Collins continued to batter the northern shoulder of the Bulge, blocking
German transportation routes through the Belgian town of Saint-Vith.
By mid-January, the battle was over. Battered and reeling, the Wehrmacht
pulled out, leaving behind hundreds of irreplaceable vehicles either destroyed or starved of fuel. Hitler had lost his great gamble.

The front having been restored, Collins resumed the offensive,
capturing Cologne on March 11, 1945. On March 28, in a lightning
raid, Collins's 3rd Armored Division rolled into Marburg, an important
medical and cultural center, taking the town completely by surprise and
capturing hundreds of convalescing soldiers.

Pushing farther eastward, Collins's units provided the main thrust in
Omar Bradley's attempt to encircle the Ruhr industrial area, joining his
First Army with William Simpson's Ninth Army to trap the German
army's entire Army Group B. As the operation developed, VII Corps
set off for the Kassel-Paderborn area to close the ring.

Led by fast-moving armored divisions in columns sometimes separated by three to five miles, VII Corps swept east toward the area of the
Remagen Bridge and north toward Paderborn.

As Collins drove his forces toward the converging Ninth Army, Field
Marshal Walter Model, commander of Army Group B, saw the trap
about to spring shut. Desperate to save his group, he committed LIII
Corps, his only remaining reserve. The corps, commanded by General

Fritz Bayerlein, launched an attack from Winterberg, a town south of Paderborn. Collins, helped by reports from recently captured German prisoners, anticipated Model's move and shifted his 9th and 104th Infantry Divisions to meet Bayerlein's assault. Though thinly spread, the American divisions beat back the German attempt, further narrowing the potential escape corridor for Model's formations. A lane still remained open, however, north of the Ruhr and west of Paderborn. Seeing it, Collins urged General William Simpson, operating at the time under Field Marshal Montgomery, to strike for Paderborn. Meanwhile, Collins would send a combat command from the 3rd Armored Division racing to meet them at Lippstadt. On Easter Sunday, the junction came together. The Ruhr Pocket was closed. Trapped inside were more than 300,000 *soldaten* of Army Group B. Trapped also was Field Marshal Model, who committed suicide.

Collins's leadership during operations around the Ruhr Pocket was of the highest caliber. Moving from unit to unit, skillfully coordinating maneuvers, shifting forces to exploit breakthroughs, Collins masterfully handled five infantry divisions and an entire armored cavalry group strung out in a 175-mile arc from Remagen to the outskirts of Paderborn. His leadership contributed greatly to the Allied triumph in the Ruhr Pocket, a victory that sealed the fate of one of the last powerful formations in the Wehrmacht.

VII Corps's work was not quite done. After assisting in the closure of the Ruhr Pocket, Collins shifted his forces to the south on a sweep around the edge of the Harz Mountains. By mid-April, VII Corps was on the Elbe River. On April 22, resistance on his section of the front came to a halt.

Two days before the shooting ended, Collins learned he had been promoted to lieutenant general. As was perhaps fitting, he was with VII Corps when the war ended.

Before and After

Joseph Lawton Collins was born May 1, 1896, in the Algiers section of New Orleans, Louisiana. After receiving a fortuitous appointment to

West Point when the anointed selectee failed to qualify, Collins graduated 35th of 139 cadets in the class of 1917.

A significant portion of Collins's first two decades in the military was spent in training courses, professional schools, and instructor duties:

- 1921–25: Instructor of chemistry at West Point.
- 1926: Company Officer Training Course, Infantry School, Fort Benning.
- 1927: Field Artillery School, Fort Sill, Oklahoma.
- 1927–31: Instructor of weapons and tactics, Fort Benning.
- 1931–33: Command and General Staff College, Fort Leavenworth.
- 1937: Army Industrial College, Washington, DC.
- 1938: Army War College, Carlisle, Pennsylvania.
- 1938–40: Instructor, War Plans Division, Army War College.

This unusual career pattern gave Collins a broad background and understanding across the spectrum of modern conflict, capabilities he would later exploit fully as his VII Corps powered its way across Europe. An insightful student of warfare, Collins appreciated the advantages offered by individual weapon systems and was adept at combining their features. He would be one of the first major commanders to extensively interject dedicated close air support into his operations.

With war having been declared on April 6, 1917, graduation for that year's West Point class was accelerated, and Collins and his classmates received their commissions two weeks later. As a newly commissioned junior officer, Collins served in company commander duties at posts in the North-west as America geared up for combat. In September of the following year, he was given a battalion command in the 22nd Infantry. Two months later, the war ended before Collins's unit was deployed overseas. The following spring, however, he was sent to Europe, serving initially in the headquarters echelon of the American forces in Germany. Brief battalion commands followed before he was posted as assistant chief of staff for operations at the headquarters of American occupation forces in the Rhineland, a position he held for much of his time in Germany. In 1921, Collins returned to the United States to begin a teaching assignment at West Point.

In 1934, after an extended, near-continuous 13-year period of instructor duty and professional schooling, the army sent Collins to Fort William McKinley in Manila to serve as brigade executive officer and assistant chief of staff for intelligence in the Philippine Division. After three years in the Pacific, he returned to the States and spent three more years as a student and instructor. Collins was teaching at the Army War College in June 1940 when classes were suspended as the army shifted toward a wartime establishment.

In January 1941, after brief headquarters-related duties in Washington, Collins was assigned as chief of staff of VII Corps (Second Army). There was irony in his assignment. Three years later he would return to VII Corps as commander and lead it through the duration of World War II.

With war looming on the horizon, the remainder of 1941 brought a flurry of activity as the army—woefully unprepared and ill-equipped— struggled to transform itself into a combat ready force capable of waging modern warfare. With simulated tanks, artillery, and machine guns, the fledgling army geared up to face experienced veteran armies well-practiced in the art of war. (By this time, Germany had been at war for two years and Japan for nearly four.) As VII Corps chief of staff, Collins helped plan and conduct the series of maneuvers executed by the army during that busy year: the Tennessee Maneuvers (June), the Arkansas Maneuvers (August), and, most famous of all, the Louisiana Maneuvers (September). He was in those duties when the United States entered the war. Nine days later he was on his way to the Pacific.

Collins's postwar career was noted for the scope and significance of the positions he held and the special assignments he was given. In the years immediately following the war, he climbed rapidly up the army's ladder: deputy commanding general and chief of staff of army ground forces, director of information, and deputy chief of staff of the U.S. Army (initially under Eisenhower and subsequently under Bradley). In 1948, he received his fourth star and was appointed vice chief of staff. On April 16, 1949, President Truman named him to succeed Bradley as chief of staff of the U.S. Army.

Collins served in that role through August 1953, leading the army through the conflict in Korea and the turbulence surrounding President Truman's firing of General Douglas MacArthur. Collins supported the decision to relieve MacArthur and, by virtue of his position in the organizational chain, served as the official intermediary between Washington and the general.

Matters other than combat and MacArthur's removal confronted Collins, whose extended service in Washington was marked by particularly momentous events. Collins dealt with desegregation issues (President Truman integrated the armed forces in 1948), the development and "stand up" of NATO, and President Truman's seizure of American railroads when a major labor strike threatened to shut down the flow of essential matériel to combat forces in Korea. With general support from both labor and management, the army supervised railway operations until a settlement was reached. Perhaps with premonition of things to come, in 1952 Collins introduced the first Special Forces group into the army establishment.

At President Eisenhower's personal request, Collins's tour as chief of staff was followed by an especially prestigious posting as U.S. ambassador to NATO's Military Committee. His NATO tour was interrupted by an eight-month period (October 1954 to May 1955) when he served as a special envoy with ambassadorial rank to the government of South Vietnam. Collins was wary of the war and its prospects and called for reevaluation of plans for aid to South Vietnam.

Collins retired from the army in 1956 after 43 years of service. A year later he became vice chairman of Pfizer's international division, a position he held for 12 years. His retirement years were notable for his leadership in a variety of charitable and humanitarian organizations, including Hungarian Refugee Relief, the Foreign Student Service Council, the Institute of International Education, and the Society for the Prevention of Blindness. He was particularly recalled by acquaintances for his affection for animals and for his love of music. In 1984, Collins served as President Ronald Reagan's personal representative at ceremonies commemorating the 40th anniversary of D-Day.

"Lightning Joe" Collins died September 12, 1987, at age 91. He is buried at Arlington National Cemetery.

Collins's nephew, Michael Collins, was the command module pilot on the Apollo 11 spaceflight, which landed the first astronauts on the moon.

CHARLES A. LOCKWOOD

When Lockwood commanded the American submarine force in the Pacific, his crews, consisting of less than 2 percent of the total navy establishment, accounted for 55 percent of Japan's shipping losses, sinking numerous major warships of the Japanese navy and more than half of Japan's merchant fleet, starving the military of essential fuel and matériel. Acting on his own initiative in the opening months of the war, Lockwood uncovered major flaws in the design of the torpedoes used in American submarines.

Though not intentional by any means, one of the well-kept secrets of America's victory in the Pacific is the extent of the contributions made by the American submarine fleet to the defeat of the Japanese navy. While history is replete with descriptions of the great surface battles at places such as Midway, the Philippine Sea, and the waters off Okinawa, public accountings of the equally important triumphs of the "Silent Service" have been far more muted. In fact, the undersea campaign constituted "a little known war: the U.S. submarine offensive against Japan mauled shipping and naval forces. A mere handful of submarines, taking a small force of boats on 1,600-odd war patrols, sank more than 1,000 Japanese merchant ships and a significant portion of the Japanese Navy, including one battleship, eight aircraft carriers, three heavy cruisers, and eight light cruisers."

All told, during the course of the war, American submarines sank half of Japan's merchant fleet. For an island nation dependent upon imports of oil, iron, rubber, food, and other key materials essential to its economic well-being and military capability, these losses were catastrophic. When the Japanese surrendered at Tokyo Bay, its army and navy were essentially out of oil, gasoline, aluminum, and steel, and its people were increasingly hungry and malnourished. At its peak, counting backup personnel and staffs, the U.S. Navy submarine force numbered only about 50,000 men. When the final numbers were in, this force of less than 2 percent of the naval establishment had accounted for 55 percent of Japan's shipping losses.

The architect of the American submarine campaign was Admiral Charles A. Lockwood, an officer so solicitous of his crews' well-being that his men christened him "Uncle Charley." Lockwood, gregarious, short in stature, thin-lipped, with large, notable eyes, was for much of the war responsible for the strategic planning and tactical employment of all submarine operations in the Pacific. As Commander, Submarines, Pacific Fleet, he overcame obstacles that would have daunted most of his contemporaries: boats aging, obsolescent, and few in number at the start of the war; poor tactics; ineffective commanders; and, perhaps most incredible of all, torpedoes that would not work. It was Lockwood whose personal involvement resolved each of these issues. He fought for, and received, modern fleet submarines; developed more effective "wolf-pack" tactics; removed timid and unproductive skippers; and, though consistently opposed by the service's hierarchy, personally ordered and oversaw the testing that demonstrated shortcomings with the torpedoes. He succeeded to an extraordinary degree. By war's end, Lockwood's boats had sunk some 1,314 Japanese vessels—more than half of all ships lost during the war—constituting five million tons of enemy shipping. The magnitude of the losses irreparably severed Japanese supply lines and contributed materially to America's victory. At the time of Pearl Harbor, Japan had about 122,000 merchant marine personnel. By war's end, 116,000 had been killed, wounded, or were missing. About 70,000 of these casualties were inflicted during submarine operations.

On December 7, 1941, "Skip" Lockwood was in London serving as naval attaché, answering submarine-related questions and planning for the anticipated participation of U.S. vessels in the Battle of the Atlantic. In May 1942, orders took him, eager as always for operational command, to Australia to assume duties as Commander, Submarines, Southwest Pacific. Promotion to rear admiral followed soon after.

Lockwood took over an organization short of boats and chronically lacking in equipment and supplies. Morale was low, a factor attributable in part to the minimal success thus far achieved on war patrols. In 1942, throughout the entire Pacific theater, U.S. submarines had fired 1,442 torpedoes and sunk only 103 enemy ships of relatively low tonnage.

Lockwood, a man who thrived on personal interaction, began an approach that would characterize his leadership style throughout the war. He met every boat as it returned from patrol, talking with crew members, sitting down with them in ward rooms, and poring over patrol reports. In later days at Pearl Harbor, by then in command of all Pacific-based submarines, he would continue to personally meet return-ing patrols and provide the crew members with crates of ice cream, fresh fruit, and vegetables, as well as two weeks of rest and rehabilitation at the Royal Hawaiian Hotel—actions that endeared him to his sailors and led to his nickname. During the course of the war, Lockwood secured special-duty pay for his submariners, an extra stipend commensurate with the pay received by naval aviators.

Lockwood's initial interchanges with returning crews met with a common refrain: almost all believed their boats were equipped with defective torpedoes. Incredibly, because of bureaucratic impediments and prewar budget constraints, the Mark 14 torpedo had never been tested under operational conditions. Now, despite persistent crew complaints, the navy's Bureau of Ordnance refused to conduct official tests, blaming improper maintenance and poor marksmanship for the abysmal results.

Unwilling to accept the bureau's assessment, Lockwood conducted his own tests, stringing a fishing net across a portion of an inlet in Hawaii. Torpedoes fired at the net revealed that the "fish" were running 11 feet deeper than the depth set in the firing sequence. When Lockwood sent his results to Washington, the bureau labeled them "unscientific." Lockwood repeated his tests with more rigor and achieved the same results. Eventually, with the assistance of Admiral Chester Nimitz, commander in chief of the Pacific Fleet, the bureau conducted its own "official" tests, which revealed that, indeed, on average, the Mark 14s were running at a depth 10 feet deeper than set for. Compensating instructions were soon issued. By this time, the war was nine months old. Lockwood had corrected the depth problem in nine weeks.

As it turned out, Lockwood's interactions confirmed that the depth issue was only one of a set of problems with the Mark 14, each component masking yet another issue. Among other of the weapon's shortcomings: far too many were either duds or exploded prematurely.

While defective torpedoes were perhaps the most visible of the many issues that initially confronted Lockwood, problems with ineffective commanders were no less consequential. In the years leading up to World War II, the navy had overvalued the antisubmarine capabilities of its major adversaries. In particular, undue precision was ascribed to the capacity of potential to detect submarines by sonar or air surveillance and to the lethality of antisubmarine munitions. Peacetime exercises, most of them artificial and unrealistic, emphasized the submarine's supposed vulnerability to counterattack. As a result, submarine doctrine tended to be conservative. Too many submarine skippers, ingrained in the cautious tactics, shrank from aggressive employment of their boats.

In Australia and later at Pearl Harbor, Lockwood cleaned house, removing his more timid and unproductive commanders and replacing them with bold, innovative, highly aggressive skippers. Slowly morale among Lockwood's crews began to improve, accompanied by more frequent successes on patrols. Lockwood began sending his boats to interdict shipping lanes rather than posting them off enemy ports.

In January 1943, fate intervened in a major way in Lockwood's life. Admiral Robert H. English, Lockwood's superior as commander of Submarine Force, Pacific, was killed in an airplane crash. Though expressing misgivings, Lockwood was sent to Pearl Harbor as English's replacement. Still plagued by recurring torpedo issues, Lockwood ordered more tests, firing Mark 14s against submerged formations off Kahoolawe, a small island near Oahu. The torpedoes failed to explode.

Lockwood's men followed with still more tests, this time using overhead cranes to drop torpedoes with dummy warheads from various angles. The follow-on tests revealed beyond any doubt that the Mark 14's exploders were improperly designed and inadequately tested.

Still facing obstacles in the Bureau of Ordnance, Lockwood set off to Washington to take on the issue of poor torpedoes head-on. Neither his accusations nor his test results sat well with senior members of the bureau's hierarchy. Undaunted, Lockwood told one doubter that "if anything I have said will get the Bureau off its duff and get some action, I will feel my trip has not been wasted." Much to the bureau's chagrin, Lockwood's men then fabricated a new, lighter firing pin (the "contact pistol") and deactivated the torpedo's magnetic exploder features. The modification at long last solved the torpedo problem and gave American submarines a lethal, reliable weapon. The Bureau of Ordnance eventually introduced appropriate design changes.

Finally, conditions began to markedly improve. After 21 months of war, the major defects in the submarine's primary weapon had at last been identified and corrected. Despite opposition, defects with deep-running, magnetic exploders and the contact firing pin had all been fixed in the fleet by Lockwood.

The flow of boats, men, and equipment to Lockwood would also improve. During the early months of 1943, because of a shortage of boats and maintenance capacity, boats operating out of Pearl Harbor managed only 28 war patrols. By August 1944, 140 fleet boats were available for duty in the Pacific. Still, the introduction of new, late-version, long-range boats did not occur without further headaches for Lockwood. The engines on many of the new craft were initially defective, and the introduction of long-coveted electronic torpedoes was plagued with problems. The latter issue required extensive debugging and test firings, as well as a rigorous training program for fire-control parties.

During the summer of 1943, Lockwood sent his boats on daring raids into the Sea of Japan. The strikes resulted in some sinkings, though not as many as Lockwood anticipated, but the real effect was the consternation the raids caused the Japanese, who had assumed that shipping in their home waters would be invulnerable to attack. Their attempted countermoves never proved effective.

When analysts on his staff recognized that a preponderance of Japanese convoys transited the waters between Luzon in the Philippines and Formosa, Lockwood launched wolf-pack operations against enemy vessels. After initial expeditions, three U.S. submarines under the tactical command of the senior skipper formed packs that lurked along the convoy routes. Drawing lessons from the Allied countermeasures used against German wolf packs, Lockwood eliminated communication between headquarters and the boats at sea.

Introduction of the wolf-pack technique represented somewhat of a change of heart for Lockwood. However, the increasing size and better organization of convoys, accompanied as they were by stronger escorts, convinced him of their necessity. As the ocean floor beneath the Luzon Strait became littered with Japanese merchant vessels, the utility of the wolf-pack concept became apparent.

As the war progressed, Lockwood began forward-basing submarines at such places as Saipan, Guam, the Admiralty Islands, and Subic Bay in the Philippines. The advanced locations shortened the boats' voyages to the shipping lanes, increased their loiter times, and further tightened the noose on Japanese supply lines.

With naval operations expanding across the immense seascape of the Pacific, Lockwood was asked to provide "lifeguard duty" for air strikes against Japanese-held islands, an unconventional role that placed submarines close to enemy shores. Lives of countless downed airmen—including a future president of the United States, George H. W. Bush—were saved by Lockwood's submariners. Lockwood was promoted to vice admiral, the youngest in the Navy at that time.

A torpedoed Japanese ship photographed through the periscope of an American submarine. U.S. submarines sank more than a thousand Japanese merchant ships and a significant number of warships of the Japanese navy.

With the torpedo problem solved and Lockwood's purging of ineffective commanders, sinkings of enemy ships increased dramatically. Through 1944, the Japanese merchant fleet was decimated by staggering losses. Forced away from normal shipping lanes, Japan's ships sought sanctuary in ever shallower waters, where Lockwood's aggressive commanders pursued them relentlessly, sometimes scraping the bottom during their chases.

As successes multiplied, Lockwood persisted in his personal efforts to improve the capabilities of his boats and enhance the safety of his crews. He argued for and guided innovations such as homing and electronic torpedoes, improved countermeasures, better radars and periscopes, and larger deck guns. He became an especially strong advocate of mine-detecting FM sonar, believing the capability would improve the safety of his ships and men as they probed the heavily mined waters surrounding the Japanese homeland.

Innovations continued throughout the war. The latter stages of the conflict brought a spate of new equipment. Beginning in December 1944, the U.S. submarine force introduced a noise maker, a decoy device for boats undergoing depth charge attacks aimed at spoofing enemy sonar; a more efficient night periscope; a new short-range sonar; and a small electric acoustical torpedo.

Lockwood's submarines would play an ever-growing and decisive role in fleet operations as the war progressed. In the months ahead, his boats supported the invasion of the Marianas and were engaged in the Battles of the Philippine Sea, Palau Island, and Leyte before rendering exceptional service in the waters off Iwo Jima and Okinawa. By the end of the Marianas invasion in the spring and early summer of 1944 and continuing for the duration of the war, Lockwood's submarine operations transformed into several key mission areas:

- Intercept, report, and attack Japanese naval forces, troop convoys, tankers, and other supply ships based on Ultra (code-breaking) intercepts.
- Report movements of Japanese naval formations discovered without the aid of Ultra intercepts and attack those vessels.
- Provide advance reconnaissance on islands about to be attacked or invaded.
- Perform lifeguard support duty, especially during preliminary raids before the arrival of major elements of the American fleet.

Under Lockwood's leadership, operations in each of those areas were performed with increasing effectiveness, often achieving results that exceeded the most optimistic expectations. Results in the encounters that followed would further demonstrate Lockwood's flexibility and tactical skill. In the Philippine Sea, he shifted the submarine "box" about 100 miles farther south than initially planned. His move had the effect of placing several of his boats right on the middle of the enemy's main carrier group. As the Japanese ships were detected, one of Lockwood's boats, the *Albacore*, sank the Japanese carrier *Taihō*, the flag ship of Admiral Jisaburō Ozawa, the fleet commander. A short time later, the submarine *Cavalla* torpedoed and sank the aircraft carrier *Shōkaku*.

Heavy action in support of attacks on areas around Palau Island were ongoing through September and October 1944. These struggles overlapped with operations near Leyte as General Douglas MacArthur moved against Japanese forces in the Philippines. On October 20, Lockwood's boats intercepted Japanese forces attempting to transport troops from Mindanao to reinforce Leyte. American submarines sank two heavy cruisers and severely damaged a third. While the battle for Leyte was in progress, Lockwood sent two wolf packs to the Luzon Strait, directing them to form a scouting line to intercept Japanese forces leaving the area after battling with vessels under the command of Admiral William F. Halsey Jr.

At Iwo Jima in February 1945 and at Okinawa beginning in April, American submarines shielded landings and were especially active in mine detection and sweeping in advance of the invasion fleet. Lifeguard and lookout duty also drew special attention as the navy struggled against elements of the Japanese surface fleet and hundreds of kamikaze strikes.

In a last desperate gamble, the remaining major components of the Japanese surface fleet sortied from the Sea of Japan on April 6. Aimed at the American armada off Okinawa, the strike force included the giant battleship *Yamato*. So strained were the Japanese resources by that time that the *Yamato* sailed with only enough fuel for a one-way mission. Clearly, the assault was intended to be a desperate, last-gasp operation. Lockwood's subs on picket duty were waiting, however, and reported the movement of the enemy fleet.

Long before it could threaten the invasion flotilla, the *Yamato* was attacked and sunk by aircraft operating from carriers in the waters near Okinawa. Along with the *Yamato*, the cruiser *Yahagi* and four destroyers were sent to the bottom. The Japanese surface fleet was effectively destroyed.

By summer 1945, Lockwood's boats were operating with near-impunity along the entire coast of Japan. The assault on merchant shipping had caught the Japanese off guard; they never recovered from the devastating losses. On August 14, the submarine *Torsk* launched the last torpedoes fired in anger in World War II, sinking two Japanese frigates performing coastal defense duties—losses that likely constituted the last of the more than five million tons of Japanese shipping that now resided on the ocean floor. Within hours of that event, the Japanese officially accepted the Allied Powers' terms of surrender. Admiral Nimitz ordered U.S. naval forces to cease fire.

The cost had been high. Forty-nine U.S. submarines were lost in the Pacific during the course of the war. At about 22 percent—375 officers and 3,131 enlisted men out of about 16,000 deployed—the casualty rate for submariners was the highest of any American force. Still, under Lockwood's command, the U.S. rate was the lowest of any combatant submarine force in the navies of either the Allied or Axis Powers. The German undersea force lost 781 U-boats and 33,000 crewmen killed or captured out of 39,000 who sent to sea. The Japanese lost 130 submarines and the Italians 85.

When Nimitz invited Lockwood to attend the surrender ceremony on the USS *Missouri*, Lockwood made arrangements to have a dozen American submarines and a tender present in Tokyo Bay to visibly commemorate the role his boats had played in the Allied victory. As usual with Lockwood, his focus was on the sailors who had fought so well and accomplished so much.

Before and After

Lockwood was born in Midland, Virginia, on May 6, 1890, but grew up in rural Missouri. Appointed to the United States Naval Academy in 1908, Lockwood was a less-than-enthusiastic scholar, graduating in the bottom half of the class of 1912.

Eager to quickly acquire a command billet, Lockwood gravitated toward submarine service after graduation. By 1914, he was in command of submarine *A-2*, only the third submarine commissioned by the U.S. Navy. With only rare breaks, Lockwood would remain affiliated with undersea warfare for the remainder of his 35-year career. Lockwood's few nonsubmarine billets were notable for their significance and reflected the navy hierarchy's recognition of his potential. His tours included serving as naval adviser to Brazil and as an instructor at the Naval Academy, teaching seamanship and navigation. Later, he would be named naval attaché to Great Britain. Mostly, though, he spent his career in positions directly affiliated with submarines: even when not in direct command of a vessel, his billets involved submarine operations.

Although only five years out of Annapolis, Lockwood was named commander of the Asiatic Submarine Division, based in the Philippines. Tasked with escorting shipping in Manila Bay, Lockwood recognized deficiencies in the design and performance of U.S. submarines, a conviction that led to his advocacy for larger, more capable fleet submarines. In a pattern notable throughout his career, he turned down prestigious school assignments for a continued series of command billets on various submarines—he would command seven different boats until considerations of rank and experience compelled his assignments to key staff and operational positions.

Eventually, in 1936, he was given command of Submarine Division 13, and the following year was made chair of the Submarine Officer's Conference in Washington, DC. The latter position gave him a forceful platform for advocating his views on submarine design. Along with his own studies, Lockwood's test of a German submarine following World War I had convinced him of the potential for long-range offensive submarine operations (and also revealed the considerable gap in technological capabilities between the German boat and its closest U.S. counterpart).

Lockwood pushed for a true oceangoing submarine fleet that would be large in size, be equipped with the latest diesel engine technology, better target-computing devices, and a sizable deck gun, and have double the number of torpedo tubes. Lockwood saw "habitability" as a major consideration for his proposed class of submarines; thus, freshwater distillation and air conditioning would be important capabilities.

As would be the case with many of Lockwood's proposals, his suggestions were opposed by influential members of the navy hierarchy. The chairman of the navy's General Board, Admiral Thomas Hart, opposed the entire concept of fleet submarines, arguing instead for smaller boats that would be focused on coastal defense and be devoid of "luxuries" such as air conditioning. Lockwood, a gregarious, well-liked, and highly respected officer, countered by assembling a formidable coalition of like-minded advocates. Eventually, through shrewd political maneuvering and the determination that would so distinguish his leadership, he won approval for almost all of his design ideas, a large deck gun being the major exception. The classes of submarines that emerged from Lockwood's innovations – the *Balao* class entered service in mid-1943 and the *Tench* class in late 1944 – would later form the foundation of America's World War II submarine fleet.

In his last prewar staff assignment in Washington, Lockwood served as chief of staff, Submarine Force, U.S. Fleet. His subsequent posting took him to Great Britain to serve as America's naval attaché. He was in those duties when the United States entered World War II.

From his post as commander of the Pacific submarine fleet, the position he held when the war ended, Lockwood was named the navy's inspector general. The office fitted neither his gregarious personality nor his preference for dealing with problems through personal relationships. He disliked his duties intensely. On September 1, 1947, Lockwood retired from the navy. Years earlier, while still serving in the Pacific, he had advocated the creation of an Office of Deputy Chief of Staff of Naval Operations for Submarines, a proposal that eventually came to fruition in 1970. In retirement, he wrote several well-received fiction and nonfiction books about submarines and submarine warfare and served as technical adviser on submarine-related movies made in Hollywood.

The example of his leadership, particularly his concern for his crews, is one of Lockwood's enduring legacies in today's navy. After the war,

Lockwood wrote of those who served under him, saying, "They were no supermen, nor were they endowed with any supernatural qualities of heroism. They were merely top-notch American lads, well trained, well treated, well armed and equipped with superb ships."

True enough, perhaps, but many of those latter qualities—training, treatment, munitions, and equipment—resulted from Lockwood's personal involvement and leadership.

Lockwood died on June 7, 1967, and is buried alongside his World War II colleagues Chester Nimitz, Raymond Spruance, and Richmond Kelly Turner in San Francisco's Golden Gate Cemetery.

ROBERT L. EICHELBERGER

Eichelberger was the field commander who transformed General Douglas MacArthur's plans into battlefield victories. At Papua, New Guinea, he won the first U.S. victory against Japanese ground forces and later led operations elsewhere in New Guinea, at Hollandia, and on Leyte and Luzon, where he secured the capitulation of Japanese forces in the Philippines.

Lieutenant General Robert L. Eichelberger labored under the enormous shadow cast by General Douglas MacArthur, his superior in the command chain in the Pacific theater. Eichelberger was a low-key, competent, and highly respected officer whose accomplishments were seldom fully credited by the American media or the army/MacArthur publicity machine. In fact, Eichelberger was the field commander who transformed many of MacArthur's plans into victories on the battlefield.

During the course of the war, Eichelberger rose from division to corps commander and then led an army (the newly formed Eighth Army) that would build its legend in New Guinea and the Philippines.

At the Buna front in Papua, New Guinea, he won the first American victory against Japanese ground forces, revitalizing a stalled offensive. Buna would be a precursor to important victories elsewhere in New Guinea and to a lightning campaign that secured Hollandia as a major base for the Allies. At war's end, Eichelberger led operations in the southern Philippines and clearing operations on Leyte and Luzon where, on that island alone, he supervised the capitulation of more than 50,000 Japanese troops. His achievements were recognized by his presence aboard the USS *Missouri* to witness the Japanese surrender.

Eichelberger was serving as superintendent of the United States Military Academy when the United States entered World War II. Diverted to the West Point job at the last minute from a projected assignment as an assistant division commander, he was urged by army chief of staff George C. Marshall to make the academy curriculum more reflective of the army's immediate needs. During the months ahead, Eichelberger modernized the academy's programs and course offerings, reducing activities such as horseback riding and close-order drill. Combat training was emphasized, a portion of which was conducted in concert with National Guard units. A flight training facility, Stewart Field, was acquired, and cadets were indoctrinated in basic flight training. Eichelberger was promoted to major general in July 1941.

By the time the United States declared war on Japan, Marshall had come to believe that with the country in a shooting war, Eichelberger's obvious talents could be far better utilized elsewhere. In March 1942, Eichelberger was given command of the 77th Infantry Division at

Fort Jackson, South Carolina. The posting was a brief one, in June he was named commander of I Corps. Initially nominated to command American forces in Operation Torch, the Allied invasion of North Africa, Eichelberger guided the three-division force through extensive amphibious training in the Chesapeake Bay area in August. Eichelberger's orders were abruptly changed yet again as Marshall assigned him and his I Corps headquarters staff to the Southwest Pacific, where Eichelberger would work under the direct command of MacArthur. It was not an assignment that Eichelberger looked forward to. Acquainted with MacArthur from an earlier assignment, Eichelberger knew him as an officer who was difficult to work for.

Promoted to lieutenant general in October, Eichelberger set out to get an initial reading on the two American units—the 32nd and the 41st Infantry Divisions—that would constitute his I Corps command. (I Corps, in turn, fell under the command of the Australian First Army.) Eichelberger's initial impressions were not favorable. He told MacArthur and his staff that neither division had been trained to fight in the jungle, instead they were being prepared using the standard syllabus taught in the United States. Until those deficiencies were corrected, he was skeptical that the divisions could hold their own against the veteran Japanese troops they would be facing.

Eichelberger's apprehensions proved valid when the 32nd Division, overconfident but poorly trained and led, was defeated at Buna-Gona. The 32nd's performance was a catalog of things gone wrong: poor staff work, faulty intelligence, and insufficient preparation were only the most visible indicators of an organization woefully unprepared for combat. On MacArthur's orders, Eichelberger flew to Buna to assume direct control of the battle. In his book, Eichelberger recounts a scene where MacArthur told him, "Bob, I want you to take Buna or not come back alive."

In late November 1942, Eichelberger flew to Buna to take command of all U.S. troops in the area. He relieved the division commander and several other officers. In one instance, convinced the officer would fight, he appointed a captain to run a battalion. He was consistently at the front, moving among the troops. As a signal to his soldiers that their commander was present, he conspicuously displayed his three-star insignia even though that made him a prime target for Japanese snipers. Although his troops grew to admire him, they were initially taken aback by his forceful leadership style, his replacement of familiar officers, and high casualties, and their respect was grudgingly awarded. The troops named the division's cemetery near Buna "Eichelberger Square."

The assault had begun on November 16, when Allied forces were sent against Japanese-held enclaves at Buna, Sanananda, and Gora. They would face 6,500 Japanese troops, many of them veterans of fighting in China, Hong Kong, and Java. The Japanese made masterful use of the terrain and used intervals in the fighting to construct hidden, camouflaged fortifications. Coconut-tree-log bunkers and pillboxes were superbly hidden in the jungle and supported overlapping fields of fire.

The terrain on New Guinea generally, and Buna specifically, ranks among the most horrific encountered by American soldiers in any of the nation's wars. The immediate landscape was virtually a swamp cut by several streams and closed in on the periphery by dense, almost impenetrable foliage. The surrounding jungle and the configuration of the terrain made it difficult to flank the three major strongholds that formed the core of the Japanese emplacements. The ever-present intense heat was exacerbated by debilitating humidity. Rains were frequent and heavy, with downpours sometimes measuring as much as 10 inches. Both sides suffered greatly from disease and lack of supplies and food. At the outset, U.S. forces rationed ammunition and for a time were relegated to a portion of a C ration carton each day.

As postwar scholars would note, it was clearly an environment that called for heavy supporting fire to reduce the strongpoints. The problem was that none was available. The navy declined to assist because of poorly charted waters and restricted maneuverability in nearby waters. The tenuous overland supply route and almost nonexistent roads greatly limited the amount of heavy ordnance that flowed to the battlefield. American units began the battle with almost no artillery and only a few mortars borrowed from nearby Australian units.

When Eichelberger reached the battlefield and assessed the situation, he ordered a two-day stand-down to rest the troops and restore some organization to the chaos. Additional reconnaissance was ordered as well. On November 24, he officially relieved the 32nd Division's commander, although he came to express sympathy for him, given the conditions that officer had faced.

When two consecutive division commanders were wounded, Eichelberger assumed personal command of the division. Over the next 30 days, he lost 30 pounds—an indication of the conditions faced by the combatants in the Buna region.

Eventually Eichelberger began receiving artillery pieces and some Stuart light tanks. A few reinforcements began to trickle in as well. Eichelberger's troops finally captured Buna on December 14, although heavy fighting raged through the surrounding area until January 1943. As elsewhere in New Guinea, the Buna struggle was waged under ghastly conditions. Casualty rates exceeded those sustained during the fierce struggle on Guadalcanal. "Jungle rot" was pervasive, afflicting men, machines, weapons, and clothing. At one point during the campaign, the illness rate among American units reached 66 percent.

When the region was finally in Allied hands, it was discovered that Japanese troops had been dying from disease at the rate of 20 soldiers per day. Evidence of cannibalism was discovered among some Japanese units whose members had eaten the bodies of American POWs.

The cost to the 32nd Division was high: 767 dead, 1,689 wounded, and 8,287 hospitalized with tropical diseases. Though not as major in scope as many of the titanic struggles that would follow, Buna was a significant achievement—the first significant battle won by American troops in the Southwest Pacific.

The following month, Lieutenant General Walter Krueger's Sixth Army arrived in Australia. For the next several months, Eichelberger found himself relegated to training newly arrived units, preparing them for future operations. In the organizational scheme, Eichelberger's corps headquarters was placed subordinate to Krueger's Sixth Army operation, an arrangement that some historians have attributed to MacArthur's petulance at Eichelberger's having received some notoriety for his achievements during the Buna campaign. One scholar asserted that Eichelberger was "rewarded for his success by being assigned to train troops in Auckland for a year in near obscurity. There wasn't room in the Southwest Pacific command for two Army heroes."

That conjecture is difficult to assess. It should be noted that on occasion MacArthur publicly lauded Eichelberger, labeling him "a commander of the first order, fearless in battle." MacArthur turned down War Department requests to move Eichelberger from the Southwest Pacific to command billets with the First and Ninth U.S. Armies in the ETO.

After the war, MacArthur complimented Eichelberger for being one of the few officers who got along well with Australian military leaders. Many American officers objected to serving under Allied commanders, believing it to be detrimental to promotion and career prospects. Those considerations apparently never entered Eichelberger's calculus; he cultivated excellent relationships with Australian counterparts. Eichelberger's personal correspondence, though, makes it evident that he found many aspects of his service with MacArthur disagreeable and was at times incensed by MacArthur's machinations.

Early in 1944, Eichelberger was named to command Operation Reckless, a two-division landing operation at Hollandia. Reckless was well named. It was a risky venture that bypassed Japanese defenses at Hansa Bay but put Allied forces outside the range of supporting land-based air cover. Instead, aircraft carriers of the Pacific Fleet would provide air support to the invasion forces. The more limited loiter time of the fleet assets necessitated a campaign plan with relatively restricted timelines.

Eichelberger was up to the task, planning the operation in meticulous fashion and sending his units through an arduous training program that stressed physical fitness, initiative, small-unit tactics, and amphibious landings. Though not without difficulties, aided by surprise the operation met with notable success.

June 1944 saw Eichelberger again used in the "firefighter" role. The 41st Infantry Division had landed at Biak on May 27. The battle was not going well for the Allies. The invasion of Saipan loomed on the near horizon, and MacArthur had promised that the airstrips around Biak would be available to support the landings. Eichelberger found that intelligence had underestimated the strength of the Japanese, who were present in significant numbers, dug into caves overlooking the airfields.

In addition to its importance in supporting operations on Saipan, Biak was a key component of MacArthur's drive to eliminate major Japanese resistance on New Guinea, thus clearing the way for invasion of the Philippines. The battle would be historically notable in another way as well: it was the first instance in which the Japanese allowed uncontested landings for the purpose of luring the invading forces into a kill zone some miles inland. It was a tactic that in the coming months would be replicated with fearful results at such places as Iwo Jima and Okinawa.

Biak, an island located near the western edge of New Guinea, dominated key waters nearby. The Allies' goal, obvious to the Japanese, would be the capture of several airfields situated in the island's interior. Once there, the invaders would face a deadly honeycomb of caves, pillboxes, and interlocking artillery and motor fire, as well as a company of light tanks.

Allied forces waded ashore on May 27. Devoid of Japanese opposition, initial landings went well. By late afternoon, 12,000 troops of the 41st Infantry Division were ashore along with 12 Stuart tanks, artillery pieces, five hundred vehicles, and assorted supplies.

The 41st pushed quickly inland, reaching the edge of one of the airstrips the following day. There they ran into a Japanese fortress, taking fire from caves and other positions located on elevated terrain that wrapped around the low ground where the landing strips were. The Allies' initial surge was halted; troops were pinned down and were finally extricated with severe difficulty.

With the 41st making marginal progress or in some places retreating, Eichelberger assumed personal command of the battle on June 15 after relieving the division commander and having sent a regimental combat team to reinforce the unit's efforts. Eichelberger changed the focus of the attack, giving priority not to the airfields themselves but to clearing the caves and ridges that sheltered them. Eichelberger's well-trained troops eventually prevailed, though the experienced Japanese units facing them extracted a heavy toll—474 killed and 2,428 wounded. The Japanese fought to annihilation, with only 450 surviving out of the

11,000 initially engaged. MacArthur awarded Eichelberger a Silver Star for his performance at Biak.

During the course of the campaign, MacArthur named Eichelberger to command the Eighth United States Army. The newly formed unit took control of operations on Leyte in the Philippines on December 26, relieving Walter Krueger's Sixth Army. Although intelligence reports had indicated that the remaining Japanese force was limited to about five thousand soldiers, Eichelberger's troops encountered continuous resistance. By the time the island was cleared of opposition the following May, an additional 24,000 enemy soldiers had been killed.

In the meantime, in January elements of the Eighth Army had landed on Luzon. Eichelberger took personal command of the operation that combined with Sixth Army units in a giant pincer movement to envelop Manila. As the wings converged, Eichelberger sent the 11th Airborne Division on a lightning dash toward the city. He later took the surrender of more than 50,000 Japanese troops on Luzon. MacArthur awarded him another Silver Star.

In the closing months of the war, Eichelberger sent the Eighth Army against Japanese-held islands in the southern Philippines. Altogether, 14 major and 24 minor amphibious operations cleared the large island of Mindanao, as well as Mindoro, Palawan, Marinduque, Panay, Negros, Cebu, and Bohol. Though isolated resistance continued on Luzon and Mindanao—and would do so until the end of the war—capture of the southern islands provided bases for airstrikes throughout the South China Sea region.

The Japanese surrender aboard the USS *Missouri* afforded Eichelberger his first look at the Japanese mainland. In the years ahead he would come to know the landscape quite well while leading the Eighth Army as it performed occupation duty on the Japanese home islands.

Before and After

Eichelberger was born March 9, 1886, in Urbana, Ohio. An indifferent student in high school and during a brief sojourn at Ohio State University, he received an appointment to West Point through the good graces of an Ohio congressman who had been his father's law partner. At the academy, his leadership skills were noted, but again his academic performance was not exceptional. In 1909, he graduated 68th in a class of 103.

Following graduation, issues along the border with Mexico prompted a quick series of moves. After a brief time at Fort Benjamin Harrison in Indiana, Eichelberger and his unit, the 10th Infantry, were sent to San Antonio, Texas, as part of the Maneuver Division, formed to conduct operations during the undeclared war with Mexico. Six months later he was posted to the Panama Canal Zone. After a brief return to the United States at Fort Porter, New York, that unit, the 22nd Infantry, was sent to the Mexican border, this time based at Douglas, Arizona. In September 1916, now a recently minted first lieutenant, he became professor of military science and tactics at the Kemper Military School in Boonville, Missouri.

As with many of his colleagues, for Eichelberger the United States' entry into World War I in April 1917 brought a succession of accelerated moves and promotions. Promoted to captain in May, he soon moved to battalion command at Fort Douglas, Utah, and Camp Pike, Arkansas, where he was later made senior infantry instructor at an officer's training camp. In February 1918, Eichelberger was assigned to the War Department General Staff in Washington. He was promoted to major a month later.

In July, Eichelberger's boss in Washington, Brigadier General William S. Graves, was appointed commander of the 8th Division, based at Palo Alto, California. Graves took Eichelberger with him as his assistant chief of staff for operations. After the 8th was initially alerted for movement to France, its assignment was changed to Siberia. Amidst the chaos of the Russian Civil War, troops from several Allied nations were sent there to safeguard the mountains of supplies and munitions given to Russia prior to the February 1918 Brest-Litovsk Treaty that ended Russia's participation in World War I. General Graves was assigned to command the American Expeditionary Force Siberia. Eichelberger's job was changed to assistant chief of staff for intelligence.

Once deployed, American forces were situated mainly around Vladivostok in the Far East, at Archangel in the northwestern portion of European Russia, and at Murmansk on the Kola Bay in the extreme northwest, close to the country's borders with Norway and Finland. At its peak strength, the American force numbered about 13,000 soldiers— two full infantry regiments sent from the Philippines and elements of three more from Camp Fremont, California.

Cautioned to maintain strict neutrality, American leaders in Russia found themselves thrust into a confused, highly volatile imbroglio. Eichelberger, appointed as a member of the ten-nation Inter-Allied Military Council, quickly found that political and diplomatic pressures, as well as military considerations, influenced interactions among the nations. He was convinced that U.S. objectives in Siberia were not universally shared by their major Allies. Differences between Allies were not the only difficulties faced by Eichelberger. There were also frequent, sharp disagreements between the State and War Departments of his own government. Nonetheless, Eichelberger persevered and was highly lauded for his performance.

Though the U.S. involvement was not conceived as having a direct combat role, Eichelberger was decorated with the Distinguished Service Cross for at least three acts of heroism during his time in Russia. He single-handedly covered the extraction of a platoon under fire, entered partisan lines to secure the release of four Americans held captive, and secured a firing line under heavy assault. His personal bravery and "presence" were cited in each instance.

Eichelberger's exemplary performance in Russia earned him not only U.S. medals but several from Allied nations, including a particularly prestigious one from Japan. Before Allied troops were withdrawn from Siberia in April 1920, he worked closely with Japanese troops and was impressed by their discipline and training.

Reduced to his permanent rank of captain in June 1920 (but promoted to major the following day), Eichelberger was sent from Russia to the Philippine Department as assistant chief of staff for intelligence. The following spring he was named to lead the intelligence mission to China, where he established offices in Peking (Beijing) and Tientsin. In May 1921, he returned to the United States with a posting to the War Department General Staff as an intelligence officer in the Far Eastern Section.

In 1925, Eichelberger transferred to the Adjutant General's Corps. After a brief assignment at Fort Hayes, Ohio, he was nominated for attendance at the Army Command and General Staff College at Fort Leavenworth, Kansas, where his colleague in the seat next to him was Dwight D. Eisenhower. Eichelberger remained at the school as its adjutant general before attending Army War College.

In 1931, Eichelberger went to West Point as the academy's adjutant. In April 1935, now a lieutenant colonel, he became secretary of the War Department General Staff, a job that brought him for the first time in contact with the army's chief of staff, General Douglas MacArthur. Seven years later their paths would cross again, this time in a major way, in the Southwest Pacific. While in the War Department, Eichelberger transferred back to the infantry and in August 1938 was promoted to colonel. Given command of the 30th Infantry Regiment at the Presidio of San Francisco, Eichelberger led the unit through a series of major training exercises over the next two years as the United States tortuously geared up for war.

Eichelberger was a newly promoted brigadier general (October 1940) awaiting a projected assignment to deputy division commander billet when General Marshall diverted him to duties as superintendent of the United States Military Academy. In March 1942, having extensively revised the curriculum at West Point, Eichelberger was sent to the Southwest Pacific, where he went to war with MacArthur.

Eichelberger's initial postwar service was leading the Eighth Army in its occupation duties in Japan. He retired from the army in 1948. For the next several years, until overcome by ill health, he wrote articles, consulted, and lectured on his wartime experiences in the Far East from his home in Asheville, North Carolina. In 1954, he was promoted to four-star general.

On September 26, 1961, Eichelberger died in Asheville from complications following surgery. He is buried in Arlington National Cemetery.

Deeper in the Shadows ...

CLIFTON A. F. SPRAGUE

In one of World War II's most remarkable feats of leadership, in a battle fought near Samar Island in the Philippines, Sprague, with only a tiny force of escort carriers, destroyers and destroyer escorts, fought off a major Japanese fleet consisting of 23 ships that included four battleships, the Yamato – the largest of its type ever built – three heavy cruisers, two light cruisers and eleven destroyers. Despite being overwhelmingly out-manned and out-gunned, Sprague's intrepid leadership prevented the Japanese force from disrupting U.S. landings on Leyte.

Vice Admiral Clifton Albert Frederick ("Ziggy") Sprague is best known for his remarkable leadership during a single episode—a battle fought near Samar Island in the Philippines on October 25, 1944. Desperately outnumbered and outgunned, his small force of six escort carriers, three destroyers, and four destroyer escorts fought off a 23-ship Japanese fleet that included among other battleships the *Yamato*, the world's largest, as well as heavy cruisers, light cruisers, and destroyers, all bent on shattering American forces landing in the Philippines.

In numbers and strengths of the opposing forces, the struggle was grossly one-sided, the apparent mismatch further complicated by the fact that the American naval units in the immediate area were taken by surprise. Somehow Sprague's intrepid leadership, abetted by the resourcefulness of his skippers and sailors, enabled his tiny force—forever immortalized by its call sign "Taffy 3"—to prevail.

Sprague's role in the larger Battle of Leyte Gulf evolved when the Japanese shammed Admiral William F. Halsey Jr., commander of the immense U.S. Third Fleet, into sailing away from the immediate area in pursuit of a decoy force. The resulting chaos took Halsey far afield from Leyte Gulf, where naval operations as well as Allied landings were ongoing. Halsey's movement left passage to the interior gulf through the San Bernardino Strait unguarded, open to the Japanese naval units that began transiting it during the night of October 24.

After leading Halsey astray, the Japanese plan was to attack and destroy American landing forces and transports, which would be stripped of convoy and airpower by Halsey's absence. (Halsey had taken ten aircraft carriers with him.) With Halsey absent from the scene, the assault troops and supporting vessels would be attacked by Vice Admiral Takeo Kurita's Center Force approaching from the west, as well as by a second armada led by Admiral Shōji Nishimura coming from the south.

During the daylight hours of October 24, Third Fleet aircraft had struck Kurita's force, which had been detected by U.S. submarines the previous night. Kurita's vessels were severely battered, and the giant battleship *Musashi*, a sister ship to *Yamato*, was sunk. Kurita momentarily reversed course, a move Halsey interpreted as a full retreat. Now convinced that the main threat came from the so-called Northern Force—in reality a decoy fleet consisting of one fleet carrier and three light carriers minimally equipped with 108 aircraft scattered between them, two older battleships, three light cruisers, and nine destroyers—Halsey gave chase. He took with him five fleet carriers and five light carriers with more than six hundred aircraft, six new battleships, eight cruisers, and 40 destroyers. Halsey's force eventually caught and overwhelmed the decoys, whose destruction had served the purpose of enticing the Third Fleet away from the area of the intended major fight.

While Halsey was running down the decoys, Kurita, with his Center Force, had turned around and under the cover of darkness made his way undetected and unobstructed through the San Bernardino Strait.

Only light American naval forces initially stood in the way of Kurita's massive flotilla. Arrayed north to south, the small units were code-named Taffy 1, 2, and 3. The northernmost, the one directly in harm's way, was Taffy 3, commanded by Ziggy Sprague. First contact was made at 6:46 a.m., when the oncoming Japanese ships opened fire.

Pulitzer Prize–winning author William Tuohy begins his narration of the battle with the words "At 0716, Ziggy Sprague ordered his destroyers to attack the Japanese main body. The tin cans launched one of the most gallant attacks of the whole war." Indeed, the next two hours would be filled with some of the most valiant moments in American naval history.

When the Japanese fleet was in sight, Sprague turned his slow escort carriers, seeking to distance them from the oncoming enemy vessels. The move had another purpose as well: the carriers' only armament was mounted at the aft end of the ships, enabling Sprague to use that added bit of firepower while at the same time reducing the ships' profiles.

Sprague ordered the use of smoke screens and, as the battle progressed, astutely used smoke and nearby rain squalls to hide his small, fast-moving destroyers and destroyer escorts, which darted in and out of the sheltering obscurations. Brought under attack by the massive firepower of the Japanese heavy cruisers and the *Yamato*'s 18-inch guns— the world's largest battleship weapons—Sprague's destroyers struck back with five-inch guns and torpedoes. Using speed and zigzagging erratically, Sprague's "tin cans" slashed into the enemy formation. The battle area soon became a maelstrom of rain, smoke, explosions, geysers, and burning ships as Sprague's vessels cut in and out through the Japanese fleet, twisting and turning to avoid return fire, at times narrowly missing

BATTLE OFF SAMAR
October 25, 1944

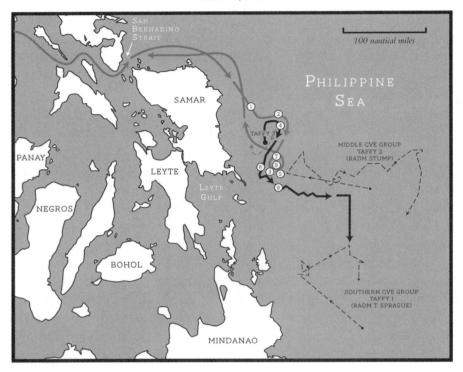

At 0300, a large Japanese force commanded by VADM Takeo Kurita entered San Bernadino Strait unobserved. With ADM William F. Halsey and major elements of the U.S. Third Fleet having been lured away from the area, only light U.S. forces remained to oppose the Japanese thrust aimed at disrupting American landings on Leyte. The effect numerically was to create one of the greatest mismatches in naval history. Kurita's force consisted of four battleships, including the Yamato, the largest battleship ever built, six heavy cruisers, two light cruisers, and eleven destroyers. Opposing that armada was a small U.S. force code named Taffy 3 consisting of six escort carriers, three destroyers, and four destroyer escorts armed and configured mainly for anti-submarine warfare and close support of infantry. The Yamato alone displaced more than all the vessels in Taffy 3 combined.

Taffy 3 commander, RADM Clifton Sprague, drew the Japanese into a tail chase. Using smoke, darting in and out of rain squalls, and taking advantage of air strikes, superior fire control systems, and the daring and aggressiveness of U.S. skippers, Sprague inflicted heavy damage and created chaos among the Japanese units at times causing the Japanese commander to lose tactical control. The fury of the battle convinced Kurita that he was facing a superior force. Unsure of Halsey's location, at 0911 he issued a withdrawal order.

(1) 0645 • Japanese force comes up on Taffy 3 achieving tactical surprise. 0700 Yamato opens fire. 0710 USS Johnston begins returning U.S. fire.

(2) 0727 • Kumano retires; Suzuya sunk.

(3) 0836 • Chokai sunk.

(4) 0855 • USS Hoel sunk

(5) 0857 • Chikuma sunk

(6) 0907 • USS Gambier Bay sunk

(7) 1005 • USS Samuel B. Roberts sunk.

(8) 1016 • USS Johnston sunk

(9) 1051 • After the surface battle ends, USS St. Lo is struck by kamikaze attack (the first of the war) and sank at 1123.

collisions not only with the Japanese vessels but with other American ships engaged in the swirling melee.

Sprague's ships and the aircraft aboard his small carriers were intended and equipped mainly to provide support for ground troops. Thus, the ordnance available to them was less than well suited to the task at hand. Both ships and planes lacked armor-piercing shells; they were armed instead with conventional bombs, munitions, and high explosives. Some carried depth charges for a corollary role in antisubmarine warfare. Sprague sent all of them anyway.

Seeking to buy enough time for his escort carriers to escape and to disrupt and delay the Japanese until help arrived, Sprague's audacious attack disconcerted the Japanese. At one point in the battle, the *Yamato*, Kurita's flagship, had to maneuver away from the fight to avoid a spread of three torpedoes fired by an American destroyer that had burst through the outer screen. Not for the last time, the Japanese commander lost tactical control of the battle as his ships struggled with little success to regroup in the chaos.

Technology contributed to the Americans' success. U.S. destroyers were aided by radar-directed fire-control systems that enabled the vessels to fire their weapons more quickly and accurately even in the midst of violent maneuvers. Though the Japanese weapons were larger and potentially more lethal, they were aimed by slower and less accurate optical range finders.

Ironically, the American destroyers and destroyer escorts were so thin-skinned that many of the Japanese armor-piercing shells penetrated clear through the vessels without exploding. So much redundancy was built into the U.S. ships that they were able to remain in the fight despite being struck repeatedly. Many received multiple major hits before being sunk or abandoned.

Meanwhile, aircraft from Sprague's escort carriers hammered the Japanese ships. TBM Avengers, FM-2 Wildcats, and F6F Hellcats, though carrying ordnance suited for close support of ground troops, struck repeatedly. When bombing, strafing, and torpedo runs had exhausted munitions and when all remaining depth charges had been expended, U.S. planes launched "dry run" strikes at the attacking force.

In combination, it all worked. The ferocity of Sprague's assault convinced Kurita that he was facing major elements of the American fleet. Having learned by this time that Nishimura's Southern Fleet had been defeated the day before and unsure when Halsey might return, Kurita broke off the fight.

His own substantial losses likely also factored into the decision to withdraw. Three of his heavy cruisers were sunk or had to be scuttled, and a fourth limped away, having had its bow blown off. All of Kurita's battleships except the *Yamato* received considerable damage.

The price Taffy 3 paid for its victory was substantial. One escort carrier, the *Gambier Bay*, was lost to surface attack. Another, the *St. Lo*, sank after Taffy 3 was struck by the first attack made by kamikaze aircraft. Two destroyers, the *Hoel* and the *Jackson*, and a destroyer escort, the *Roberts*, were also lost. The *Hoel's* story was descriptive of many: the ship took forty hits before going down. After-action reports said the crew "performed their duties coolly and efficiently until their ship was shot from under them." Four other destroyers or escorts were damaged, and aircraft losses were heavy. More than a thousand Americans were dead, making the casualty count comparable to other far more noted battles in the Pacific.

Sprague's battle off Samar had major consequences. His was the last major surface engagement between the American and Japanese fleets during World War II. The victory, and the resulting conquest of the Philippines, separated the Japanese from their major sources of oil in Southeast Asia. After the battle, the Japanese fleet—the most powerful force sent to sea by Japan since the Battle of Midway—sailed home. Except for an attempted suicide mission by the *Yamato* during the Battle of Okinawa, most Japanese vessels, starved for fuel, remained in port until the war ended. Samar was the final defeat for the Japanese navy.

Sprague was awarded the Navy Cross for his leadership during the battle. Taffy 3 received a Presidential Unit Citation.

Before and After

Clifton Sprague was born in Dorchester, Massachusetts, on January 8, 1896. He entered the United States Naval Academy in 1914, graduating in 1917—a year early because of the demands of World War I—ranked 43 of 199. After a first assignment on the gunboat *Wheeling* on convoy-escort duty in the Atlantic and the Mediterranean, Sprague held various positions on the destroyer *Manley* and on the newly commissioned battleship *Tennessee*.

Late 1920 brought a position that would shape Sprague's career for his remaining time in the navy. In December, he reported to the Naval Air Station at Pensacola, Florida, as a student pilot. As it turned out, he was a natural. Soon after receiving his gold wings as a naval aviator, he was named squadron commander of an air unit at Pensacola. The following months brought other aviation-related assignments with the Atlantic Fleet. In November 1923, Sprague was posted to Naval Station Anacostia, in Washington, DC, where his duty took several forms. Interspersed with Operations and Executive Officer obligations, it included service as test pilot doing research and experiments that contributed to the development of the catapult system later used on American aircraft carriers. Assigned as test pilot in 1926 to Naval Air Station Hampton Roads, Virginia, for the next two years he assisted famed inventor Carl Norden, designer of the Norden bombsight, with improvements to the aircraft carrier arresting gear that would be employed on the *Lexington* and the *Saratoga*, both designed from scratch as the navy's first fleet carriers.

Sprague's next assignment was a logical follow-on to his work at Hampton Roads. In March 1928, he reported to the *Lexington* as flight deck officer and assistant air officer. Sprague was aboard the "Lex" until 1929, when he was posted to a two-and-a-half-year tour of duty at the United States Naval Academy.

December 1931 took him to an assignment with a squadron based on the seaplane tender *Wright*, homeported at Norfolk, Virginia. The *Wright*'s deployments took Sprague and his squadron first to Panama and then to Hawaii. In February 1934, Sprague was the first navy pilot to make a round-trip flight between Hawaii and Midway Island.

After a two-year tour (May 1934 to July 1936) as an operations officer at the Norfolk, Virginia, naval air station, Sprague was posted as an air officer on the carrier *Yorktown*. Sprague made the first two landings on the new vessel and was the first to test its catapult systems. He would remain with the ship for the next three years.

Highly regarded by his peers, he was sent in June 1939 for special-ized study at the Naval War College. The three-month course would be the first of two such schools—the second coming the following year—bracketed around his first sea command, on the oil tanker *Patoka*.

With war looming, Sprague took command of the seaplane tender *Tangier* in 1941, homeported at Pearl Harbor. The ship was in port on December 7, 1941, berthed on the northwestern side of Ford Island. Sprague's vessel was one of the first to open fire. The *Tangier* fought through both morning raids and shot down three of the attacking aircraft. Promoted to captain, Sprague skippered the *Tangier* through operations on New Caledonia in early 1942.

A series of consequential assignments then followed as America's role in the war intensified. The first occurred in mid-1942, when, as air officer of the Gulf Sea Frontier, Sprague helped counter the U-boat threat to America's southeastern coast. In the spring of 1943, he left to take command of the Naval Air Center in Seattle, Washington. Nine months later, he was assigned as commander of the newly commissioned fleet carrier *Wasp*.

With Sprague in command, the new ship was sent immediately to the Pacific. Actions against Marcus and Wake Islands quickly ensued, followed by support for the invasion of Saipan and the Battle of the Philippine Sea. On July 9, 1944, Sprague was promoted to rear admiral and two weeks later was named commander of Carrier Division 35. In September, his flotilla supported landings on Morotai in eastern Indonesia's Maluku Islands.

Sprague's magnum opus, the Battle of Samar, took place in October. Reassigned as commander of Carrier Division 26 in February 1945, Sprague led his new command in providing close air support for Marine landings on Iwo Jima. Similar operations took place a month later as U.S. forces invaded Okinawa.

Sprague's service with Carrier Division 26 was of brief duration. In late April, he was given command of Carrier Division 2—a task group comprising fast carriers that Sprague sent against targets in the Japanese home islands of Kyushu, Honshu, and Hokkaido. Four days after the Japanese surrender, Sprague, aboard his flagship *Ticonderoga*, sailed his carrier division into Tokyo Bay.

Postwar duties first took Sprague to Washington, DC, for a series of high-level briefings. Early in 1946, he took command of a naval air group at San Diego and during the subsequent several months supported nuclear tests on Bikini Atoll.

In August 1946, Sprague was assigned to Corpus Christi, Texas. His duty titles there – first as Chief, Naval Basic Air Training and subsequently as Commander, Naval Air Advance Training – recognized his status as one of the Navy's preeminent naval aviators.By appearance and personality, Sprague was well suited for his training command slots. He was universally respected as a thorough professional, and his forte during the war had been in leading young, inexperienced airmen and sailors, with extraordinary success. His leadership style was informal; shipmates recalled him making time to stroll the decks where he chatted easily with all ranks. A bit chunky in appearance, Sprague was well liked by his sailors, who saw him as "chubby, thorough, and conscientious."

From May to October 1948, Sprague held one final, brief seagoing command as commander of Carrier Division 6, operating in the Mediterranean with his flag about the carrier *Kearsarge*. Command of naval districts at Naval Air Station Coronado in San Diego and Kodiak Island, Alaska (where he also served as commander of the Alaskan Sea Frontier) followed before his retirement from the navy in November 1951.

Sprague died on April 11, 1955, at San Diego, California. He is buried at Fort Rosecrans National Cemetery in Point Loma, California.

WILLIAM H. TUNNER

Tunner led airlift operations over the "Hump," supplying Allied forces on the Chinese mainland. Though flying over the world's tallest mountains and buffeted by extremes of weather, Tunner created an air bridge that was "China's lifeline to the outside world," keeping China in the war while tying up a million Japanese troops who would otherwise have been available for employment against Allied forces elsewhere in the East. A notably gifted manager, in the face of severe logistical and maintenance obstacles Tunner doubled the amount of tonnage flown to China while reducing accident rates among aircrews.

The phrase "in the shadows" describes William H. Tunner's World War II service rather well. Though the forces he led made major, war-shortening contributions to the Allied victory, his legacy is less well known than many of his U.S. Army Air Forces contemporaries. To a considerable extent, "in the shadows" characterizes the theater Tunner operated in as well. The China-Burma-India (CBI) Theater has historically received less attention than Europe and the Pacific. Compounding it all is that Tunner's achievements involved transport aircraft. Despite the remarkable contributions of cargo and air mobility units, the public and indeed some military writers and historians have not always attributed the credit to them that bomber and fighter outfits more routinely received.

Nearly coincident with the strike on Pearl Harbor, Imperial Japanese Army forces launched attacks on Burma as well. Within three months the Burma Road, rightly labeled "China's lifeline to the outside world," was closed. Treacherous and winding, the road formed the chief supply route into China from the United States and Great Britain. Shutting it down choked off vital supplies to Chinese forces and American units operating on the Chinese mainland. Burma's abundant resources—tin, oil, and rice—made the country a lucrative target for Japanese conquest. Burma was also a key to Japan's larger ambitions: it was the gateway to India, the jewel in the crown of the British Empire.

Though not without opposition from Allies and some of his military advisers, President Franklin D. Roosevelt determined at the outset to support the Chinese in their struggle, believing that they would tie down a million or so Japanese troops and bleed them of weapons and matériel that would otherwise be available for use against the Allies on islands throughout the Pacific. With the Burma Road closed, an airlift provided the only viable alternative.

The task would be particularly daunting. Though the range was not great—five to six hundred miles—the planes would be flying over and around some of the tallest mountains in the world. Perpetually snow-covered and subject to violent extremes of wind and weather, the Himalayas posed an enormous challenge to the air bridge to China that the Allies hoped to establish. Compounding the dangers of flying in perhaps the world's most formidable terrain were squadrons of Japanese fighters based close by.

As initially conceived, plans called for supplying five thousand tons a month to China, flying over "the Hump," as the route quickly became known. American C-46s and C-47s would initially bear the brunt of the effort. By December 1943, tonnage had exceeded that goal, earning a Presidential Unit Citation for the forces involved, the first time a noncombat unit had received the award.

Still, the airlift challenge presented a moving target. As greatly increased numbers of men, planes, and matériel flowed into the theater, the need for additional airlift expanded accordingly. To aircrews and maintenance personnel, it was like racing all out to stay even with an ever-accelerating train. Even when a figure of 10,000 tons a month was reached, the sustainment effort was increasingly stressed.

August 1944 brought Tunner to the CBI Theater to take command of the India-China Division of the brand new Air Transport Command. Immediately, almost *everything* changed. Living conditions for the crews, filthy and unkempt prior to his arrival, were cleaned up. Formal parades were held each Saturday for crews not flying or on alert. Shaves, haircuts, and pressed uniforms were mandatory. The troops marched and complained—and morale improved.

"Quiet" quarters were established for crews on night duty. Mobile post-exchange trucks, possibly a first anywhere in the world, took food and drinks to the flight line. Mess halls were kept open around the clock.

Jungle survival training received great emphasis; Tunner reorganized search-and-rescue squadrons to extract airmen who went down in the seemingly endless miles of jungle. Eventually four B-25s, a C-47, and a small liaison plane, all painted yellow, with specially trained crews, were devoted to the effort. Correspondence courses were established, allowing interested crew members to acquire college credits. Tunner even encouraged passes to allow airmen to take administrative hops and see the sights of India.

Equal attention was devoted to the equipment. Maintenance, a nightmare of partially trained technicians, climate-induced difficulties, and chronic shortages of supplies before Tunner's arrival, received a total makeover.

However, the operating conditions faced by Tunner's maintenance crews would always remain formidable. At some locations, the very high temperatures forced aircraft maintainers to work at night lest they suffer second-degree burns form touching the metallic skins of their aircraft. On occasions when heat was not a primary culprit, quite often it was rain—monsoons of it—that challenged repair activities. At bases where permanent hangars were not available, crews had to jerry-rig tarp-covered shelters. In dry months, dust posed a pervasive problem, as many of the runways, taxiways, and parking pads were unpaved. Fine grit, if left unattended, took a heavy toll on engines and flight controls.

Still, as was typical of Tunner, he tackled the maintenance problems head-on. One of his staff recalled: "Planes brought in for maintenance would pass through three to ten stations as if on a factory production line. At each station, a plane would go through different maintenance functions. A rigorous inspection completed the procedure. If approved, each aircraft would be test-flown before being sent back to the line."

Tunner seemed to be everywhere. He personally intervened to accelerate the flow of supplies. He launched a mosquito-eradication effort using a stripped-down B-25 to spray the surrounding countryside. He discovered that many pilots were flying up to 165 hours a month, accumulating unnecessary flight hours so they could become more quickly eligible for reassignment back to the States. The flight surgeon advised him that half of the crews were flying tired and that some accidents had been caused by operational fatigue. Tunner immediately extended the tour length of every pilot in the theater to a full year and increased the number of flight hours required for rotation. Tunner later said, "It didn't make the pilots happy, but it kept quite a few of them alive."

Indeed, collectively Tunner's measures brought dividends in terms of more cargo carried and lower accident rates, which had been extreme before his arrival. In the final analysis, Himalayan weather and the horrific flying conditions that often resulted from it accounted for more injuries and deaths than any other factor.

Though the mountains themselves and the weather around them were the major dangers, the unarmed transports also faced periodic threats from marauding Japanese fighters. Fortunately for many, cloud formations were often close by, enabling the C-46s and C-47s to duck in and out of cloud banks.

Late 1944 brought newer four-engine C-54s into the theater. Eager to exploit the capabilities of the larger cargo carriers, Tunner adjusted flight paths to provide more direct routes to China. Though the new routes took his crews across 150 miles of Japanese-held territory, Tunner's observations after several weeks in theater led him to conclude that the threat would be minimal. He secured protection for the transports from nearby American fighter units and the C-54s were little troubled.

Coordination of traffic by different types of aircraft flying from an assortment of bases scattered throughout the area caused Tunner and his staff to carefully deconflict flight paths, speeds, altitudes, and timing. At its peak, the airlift employed 640 aircraft. They flew mainly from six major bases in Assam Province in northeastern India and 13 strung out along an Indian railway system. Their routes took them into six Chinese airfields in the area of Kunming.

Facilities throughout the theater varied enormously. Chabua Air Base in Assam, for example, was all-weather capable and featured permanent buildings and relatively modern equipment and flight operations. At the other extreme was a small, British-controlled airfield near Jiwani, with a handful of American personnel assigned. Located inland from Karachi not far from the Iranian border at the extreme western end of the theater, Jiwani's runway was a dry creek bed used mainly for stopover and emergency operations. Some of the installation's utility buildings were improvised from cargo containers; power came from a single generator shack.

By the end of the war, Tunner's innovations had so improved performance that in a single day—August 1, 1945, five days prior to Hiroshima—his crews flew 1,118 round-trips, ferrying 5,327 tons of weapons, munitions, fuel, and other war matériel. On that day a plane crossed the Himalayas every minute and twelve seconds. Every four minutes, a ton of supplies and equipment landed in China, all without a single accident.

Altogether, during the course of the lift, 650,000 tons of supplies were flown over the Hump. Tunner's goals on arrival—to increase tonnage and reduce the horrific accident rate—were achieved beyond expectations. Indeed, accident rates were cut by 75 percent while airlift tonnage was more than doubled.

The air bridge over the Himalayas demonstrated a heretofore little seen attribute of the soon-to-be U.S. Air Force: the capability to deliver massive amounts of men and matériel over great distances under unfavorable conditions to people in harm's way. That unmatched capacity continues to serve the nation well to the present day.

Before and After

Tunner was born July 14, 1906, in Elizabeth, New Jersey. After graduating from West Point with the class of 1928, he chose aviation as his branch of service. Early assignments took him to a variety of stateside bases and acquainted him with several aircraft types, including transports such as the Fokker Trimotor. In subsequent years, Tunner logged time as an instructor pilot, worked in personnel staff officer duties, served as an operations officer and adjutant, and flew observation planes in the Panama Canal Zone and at stateside bases.

An assignment to Air Corps Tactical School in 1939 was a signal that his potential was recognized by the aviation hierarchy. A recruiting command slot followed the school posting, followed in turn by a position as a personnel officer on what today would be called the Air Staff.

With war looming, 1941 became a pivotal year in Tunner's career. One of the first officers assigned to the brand-new Air Transport Command (for a brief time originally called the Ferrying Command), Tunner advanced rapidly through adjutant, staff officer, executive officer, and command duties. Originally envisioned mainly as an organization focused on ferrying aircraft just off the assembly line to operational units around the country, the nature of the war and its worldwide scope rather quickly transformed its major role into supporting combat units around the globe.

Moving factory-new planes to receiving units would remain an important part of the Air Transport Command's mission, however. In April 1942, Tunner set up a unit within the command that was eventually designated the Ferrying Division. Notably, Tunner employed highly qualified female pilots to fly the planes. After merger of two groups, the combined organization became the renowned Women's Airforce Service Pilots (WASP).

Promoted to brigadier general in June 1943, he remained at Air Transport Command headquarters until assigned to lead airlift operations in the China-Burma-India Theater. His arrival there in September 1944 began the transformation that sustained Allied operations in the region.

Postwar assignments kept Tunner in airlift-related billets, first as Air Transport Command inspector general and then in a series of division commands. Promotion to major general came in July 1946.

When the U.S. Army Air Forces became a separate service, the U.S. Air Force, in September 1947, several organization- and mission-related adjustments were made within the defense hierarchy. Foremost among them was combining the transport services of the air force and navy into the Military Air Transport Service. Tunner was named deputy commander of operations for the new organization in March 1948. He was serving in those duties when he was chosen to lead transport operations associated with the Berlin Airlift, a deepening five-week-old crisis that threatened the fragile peace in the opening stage of the Cold War.

As he did in the CBI Theater, Tunner brought order out of chaos in a performance so masterful that, by its end, airlift operations were bringing more supplies into Berlin than the city had been receiving before land, rail, and water routes were shut off. *Everything* had to be flown into the city: food, salt, fuel, medical supplies, coal, generators, tools, equipment, and countless other items large and small—all necessary to sustain the world's fifth-largest city. Even forage to sustain Berlin's three thousand milk-producing cows was brought in by air. Animals in the Berlin zoo were also sustained by Tunner's airmen.

Tunner arrived in the city on July 28. As in China, almost everything immediately changed. Tunner divided the day into 1,440 minutes after having determined that 480 landings—one every three minutes—were necessary in every 24-hour period. He reorganized the three air corridors into the city, designating one as an exit-only route. There was to be no slowing down; if an aircraft missed a landing, it flew through the exit corridor back to its departure base where it resumed its place in the pattern. Planes flew at three-minute intervals, each flying at a steady two hundred miles per hour. The plan, as one staff officer described it, was to make the operation "as inflexible as a metronome." So steady was the pace that pilots did not leave their aircraft after landing. As in China, they were served by mobile canteens that brought snacks and drinks to crew members. Repair facilities were streamlined, and Tunner's planners adeptly integrated airlift types from several different countries into the flight pattern. In January 1949, Tunner introduced a complete integration of Allied air operations. Astute crew-rotation policies improved safety and kept crews alert. Crew training prior to arrival in Germany was bulked up as well.

The transparent success of the airlift embarrassed the Soviet Union. Finally, ground, rail, and water corridors were reopened. On September 30, 1949, after 15 months of operations, the airlift ended. On 277,000 flights into Berlin, American and Allied crews under Tunner's leadership had delivered 2,300,000 tons of cargo and flown 124,421,000 miles. As many observers noted, Berlin was the first Allied victory of the Cold War.

Berlin would not be Tunner's last command of major airlift operations. Nine months after the last flight departed from Rhein-Main Air Base, another crisis developed halfway around the world. On June 25, 1950, North Korean forces invaded South Korea. Within days Tunner flew to the area and quickly formed a unit, the Combat Cargo Command, that delivered cargo, transported 155,294 troops, evacuated 83,000 casualties, and supported General Douglas MacArthur's amphibious landing at Inchon and the parachute drops that followed. MacArthur awarded him a Distinguished Service Cross on the spot. When U.S. Marines made their legendary fighting withdrawal from the Chosin Reservoir, Tunner's airmen dropped bridge sections and bridging equipment to help maintain their route.

Major postings followed to close his career: deputy commander, Air Materiel Command; commander, United States Air Forces in Europe; deputy chief of staff for operations, Headquarters United States Air Force; and, in July 1958, a final assignment for which surely no officer in the military was more highly qualified—commander, Military Air Transport Service. In the latter role, he brought the first jet transport (the C-141) into the air force's inventory. In congressional hearings held early in 1960 to examine the nation's airlift requirements, Tunner did a masterful job of educating decision makers on the need for improved capabilities to complement the nation's emerging "Flexible Response" strategy.

Tunner retired as a lieutenant general on May 31, 1960. He died at age 76 on April 6, 1983. He is buried at Arlington National Cemetery.

A SPECIAL CASE: THE CODE BREAKER
JOSEPH J. ROCHEFORT

Rochefort ran America's Bletchley Park–like operations in the Pacific, organizing, leading, and inspiring an elite group of code breakers who cracked Japanese diplomatic and naval codes. The station's efforts contributed directly to the victory at Midway and facilitated Allied successes in surface and submarine warfare throughout the theater. His code-breaking expertise is made all the more implausible by the fact that he was a high school dropout who happened to become a cryptanalyst only because a shipmate observed that he was good at crossword puzzles and cards.

By its very nature, success in code-breaking requires integration of several elements: insight, analytic ability, and mathematical skill prominent among them. Almost always, it involves a collegial effort. It is, therefore, difficult to single out individuals whose contributions set them apart from the collective achievements of the larger group. That is certainly true in the Pacific theater where the accomplishments of a cadre of U.S. Navy code breakers was truly extraordinary, contributing in very direct and substantial ways to the eventual Allied victory. But, within that small, exceptional band, one individual—the group's leader, a brilliant, driven, insightful genius—must surely be recognized.

The path that originally brought Joseph J. Rochefort to the navy's cryptanalysis function reads like something out of a novel. Years before, in 1925, a fellow shipmate had noted Rochefort's otherworldly ability with crossword puzzles and complex card games and suggested him for a job in the navy's miniscule cryptanalysis operation. It was a simpler time, and that was all that it took. Still, Rochefort regarded himself foremost as a sailor and throughout his career aspired to shipboard duties. Indeed, in his 23-year-career prior to Pearl Harbor, he spent a combined 9 years in intelligence-related functions and 14 aboard warships. Rochefort was not a Naval Academy graduate, a circumstance that often inhibited advancement in the class-conscious navy. Most incredible of all, perhaps, was that he was not even a high school graduate.

Rochefort reported for duty as chief of the cryptanalysis section— code name Station Hypo (for "Hawaii," using the phonetic alphabet then employed by the navy)—at the naval base at Pearl Harbor on June 2, 1941. Promotion to commander followed in October. Station Hypo was located in the basement of the administration building of the Fourteenth Naval District Headquarters. The site was quickly nicknamed "the Dungeon" by the handpicked team Rochefort was allowed to assemble by his boss, Captain Laurence Safford. In operation, the crew—composed of cipher specialists, linguists, cryptanalysts, and traffic analysts—was outwardly somewhat irreverent, freewheeling, and, by one characterization, a bit oddball. Dress codes and military formalities were not foremost considerations in Rochefort's leadership style. The basement was cold and damp. Rochefort himself sometimes wore a smoking jacket over his uniform blouse to ward off the chill. He was also often seen wearing slippers, a circumstance likely associated with his work habits: he often spent days at a time in the basement, working around the clock and sleeping on a cot in the office as message traffic and other demands permitted. Neither his appearance nor his leadership style endeared him to the navy hierarchy, a circumstance that in the months ahead would act to his detriment.

Nor did his personality make him a popular favorite. Rochefort was not belligerent, flamboyant, or unprofessional in his conduct; he did not, however, suffer fools lightly. Quiet and soft-spoken, he was stubborn and fiercely independent and had a biting, acerbic wit that was not warmly received by contemporaries and superiors who felt the heat. Though he was respected for his abilities, during the course of his career his comments acquired for him several eventually high-ranking acquaintances who regarded him with varying degrees of disfavor.

Within Station Hypo he was known for his epic work habits and analytic talent, as well as for his gifted leadership of an unusually talented group of eccentrics. "His attitude," said colleague, "was you can accomplish almost anything as long as nobody cares who gets credit."

Early on, even before Station Hypo's major work in code decryption began to have an impact, Rochefort and his team devised techniques that would contribute substantially to the navy's success in the Pacific War. On January 27, 1942, Rochefort and his analysts were responsible for the first Japanese warship sunk during World War II. Using less-than-optimum RDF equipment and intercepts of radio transmissions, Rochefort plotted the course of three Japanese submarines returning to Japan from their patrols along the West Coast of the United States. (Before departing, they had fired shots at an oil refinery near Los Angeles.) Alerted to the submarines' route, an American submarine, the *Gudgeon*, waited at the point of intercept projected by Rochefort. The Japanese arrived right on schedule. The *Gudgeon* fired a spread of three torpedoes, sinking the Japanese submarine *I-173*. It was the first vessel to be destroyed as a direct result of radio intelligence.

The sinking was the first of Station Hypo's considerable successes in tracking enemy submarines. It was a pattern that would continue through the war. Their achievements enabled American commanders to route their vessels out of harm's way and facilitated countermeasures that disrupted operations of the Japanese submarine fleet.

Lacking for a time a copy of the codebook associated with JN-25, the main Japanese naval code (incredibly, it was lost for a time in transit from Washington), Station Hypo was initially directed to focus on the less-used Japanese flag officers' code. Work on JN-25 in the meantime was assigned to the Philippines cryptanalysis station. Three days after Pearl Harbor, those orders were changed, and Rochefort and Station Hype began work on JN-25.

To that mission, Rochefort brought analytic ability, fluency in the Japanese language, and insights derived from staff officer experience with fleet operations and high-level strategy. All would serve him well. As events would show, however, what made him truly remarkable was his "unique and irreplaceable ability to take fragmented recoveries of the contents of a small portion of Japanese operational traffic and somehow connect the shards into an accurate picture of Japanese intentions and plans."

By early 1942, U.S. Navy analysts, in concert with British and Dutch specialists operating from scattered locations in the region, had made tentative inroads into deciphering Japanese communications traffic. It is likely that at the time only about 10 percent of the encryptions were readable, severely limiting its utility as a basis for prediction or as actionable intelligence.

The deciphering task provided a daunting challenge for Rochefort and his team, who were already working 12-hour shifts around the clock, with Rochefort seemingly there all the time, guiding, and—always—goading. Unlike the German codes, which used machines such as Enigma to encipher messages, the Japanese navy used "book" ciphers, which replaced common words and phrases with nine-character sets of letters and numbers.

Text not contained in the codebook's 90,000 words and phrases were encoded character by character. Receivers of book-code communications looked up each of the sets of numbers and letters in the codebook and reassembled the messages. In addition to periodically changing the codebook, the Japanese added an additional level of security—called "superenciphering"—by enciphering the code groups themselves. Thus, even when the superenciphering overlay was stripped to reveal the nine-character alphanumeric sets, the meaning of each of those code groups still had to be ascertained.

Deciphering JN-25 was a formidable exercise in problem solving. While Rochefort and his crew of borderline (or beyond) geniuses were renowned for their prodigious memories, they were also aided by a relatively recent innovation. One of the team members, Lieutenant Commander Thomas H. Dyer, was a pioneer in automatic tabulating machines. With Dyer's expertise, the group made extensive use of IBM punch-card sorting technology to find messages with specific code-group combinations. Eventually, the Americans began to reverse-engineer the cipher tables, enabling messages or message portions to be read more quickly and completely. Readable portions improved over time, and by April 1942 about 30 percent of JN-25 was deciphered, allowing more finite assessments and reporting.

Though much of the total code package remained unbroken, Rochefort's extraordinary gift for molding bits and pieces of Japanese message traffic into a comprehensive picture enabled him to advise Admiral Chester W. Nimitz, commander in chief of the U.S. Pacific Fleet, of an impending Japanese attempt to capture Port Moresby, New Guinea. Rochefort correctly identified the base from which the Japanese force would be drawn (Rabaul, New Britain Island) and the date of the planned attack (May 7). Nimitz responded by moving American naval units, including the carriers *Lexington* and *Yorktown*, to the area and sending additional land-based aircraft to reinforce Port Moresby. The resulting Battle of the Coral Sea was a tactical draw in which both sides sustained significant losses. The aftermath, however, was a strategic victory for the United States: the Japanese abandoned their attempt to capture Port Moresby.

Meanwhile, events were ramping up that would result in Rochefort's most notable success. Analysts began picking up signs that the Japanese were preparing for a major operation. Included in the intercepts was the hint that a smaller diversionary attack might also be part of the campaign scheme.

Indeed, Japanese forces were in fact assembling to implement a scheme devised by the chief of the Japanese navy, Fleet Admiral Isoroku Yamamoto. Yamamoto's plan aimed at capturing Midway Island and involved a concurrent diversionary invasion of the Aleutians as well. Taking Midway would deny the Americans use of the island as a refueling base for submarines and surface vessels, while providing a site from which Japan could launch long-range air strikes against American military installations in the Hawaiian Islands.

Equally as intriguing for Yamamoto was the possibility that an attack on Midway might draw the remaining U.S. sea forces in the Pacific into the "decisive military engagement"—a battle of annihilation, long espoused in Japanese naval doctrine. Destruction of the American fleet, Yamamoto believed, might result in a cease-fire in place or a negotiated peace that would allow the Japanese to retain their conquests.

Missing initially from the intercepts of Japanese transmissions was specific information regarding the location and timing of the attack. Rochefort's assessment that Midway was the likely target was adamantly disputed by naval intelligence officials in Washington. Analysts working for the chief of naval operations, Admiral Ernest J. King, were convinced that the Japanese target would be elsewhere, with Johnson Island as a major possibility. Army analysts were inclined to favor the West Coast of the United States as the objective. There was disagreement about the timing as well. Rochefort believed it would most likely occur in early June. Analysts in Washington felt strongly that it would not take place until mid-June or possibly toward the end of the month. The resulting feud would have repercussions for Rochefort later on.

Definitive support for Rochefort's assessment was initially lacking. A key element concerned an unknown component labeled "AF" in a JN-25 code group. Rochefort believed "AF" referred to Midway. Rochefort accepted an idea from Jasper Holmes, a Station Hypo staff member, to send an unencrypted message mentioning a water supply failure on Midway. Rochefort and his crew hoped that the message would provoke a Japanese response, thus identifying "AF" as Midway and revealing it as the target. With Nimitz's approval, the message was transmitted. The Japanese took the bait, broadcasting instructions to load additional water distillation equipment for "AF." Midway was established as the target. Also, the Japanese message seemed to indicate that the attack would occur before mid-June.

Washington was still not convinced of the timing of the attack. The date-time group of the "AF" message was superenciphered, and Admiral King's analysts held fast to the belief that the strike would occur later in the month. Already working around the clock, Rochefort's crew intensified their efforts to pin down the date. During a "normal" day in May, Station Hype decrypted, translated, reviewed, analyzed, and reported about 140 messages. During the final days leading up the battle, several hundred decrypts were processed every 24 hours. Finally, on May 26, an intercept was decrypted that established the date as June 4 or June 5. Rochefort had not only determined the target and date of the attack but had also correctly identified the strength and composition of the attacking force and its general route to Midway.

Nimitz, to his lasting credit, trusted Rochefort's assessments. On June 4, an outnumbered and outgunned American fleet, superbly led by Admiral Raymond A. Spruance, surprised the Japanese force, sinking all four Japanese fleet carriers. In an incredible few minutes, the course of the war in the Pacific was forever changed.

Rochefort's crew would also break the three separate codes used by Japanese merchant vessels (called *maru*). The *maru* codes provided daily position reports for merchant ships at sea, exposing them as prey for the wide-ranging American submarine fleet commanded by Admiral Charles Lockwood. By the end of the war, virtually the entire Japanese merchant fleet was destroyed or confined to port, starved of fuel.

Station Hypo analysts would also be instrumental in the April 14, 1943, downing of the aircraft transporting Admiral Yamamoto to the Solomon Islands. By then, however, Rochefort was long gone. In one of the most unusual personnel actions of World War II, not long after his war-shortening contributions at Midway, he was removed from his duties at Station Hypo and reassigned elsewhere.

Meanwhile, Admiral Nimitz had nominated Rochefort for the Distinguished Service Medal to recognize his Midway-related achievements. Nimitz, perhaps most of all, understood that Rochefort and his team in the Dungeon had contributed enormously to the victory. When the nomination package reached Washington, the awarding of the medal was denied by Admiral King at the recommendation of his staff.

It is likely that Rochefort was not taken aback by King's action. Given the friction between the two staffs, he had been wary that the nomination would simply cause trouble.

Nonetheless, it is difficult to assess Rochefort's reassignment and the denial of the medal as anything but vindictive in nature. Contemporaries before and after stated that giving Rochefort the medal would have acknowledged, in the Washington staff's view, that it had blundered in its forecast of the attack's location and timing. By several accounts, the naval intelligence hierarchy in Washington not only removed Rochefort from command of Station Hypo but then tried to take credit for Rochefort's code breaking and assessments. Admiral King's staff convinced him that success at Midway had resulted from a "team effort" and that, in reality, "they [the Washington office] had done the bulk of the work." Then, too, a senior adviser to King, one of those who recommended against the medal, had a negative history with Rochefort, having crossed paths with him over the years.

Whatever the reasons, after a brief billet elsewhere at Pearl Harbor, Rochefort was on his way to Washington by the end of October 1942 for a temporary assignment. Within a month, he was reposted to San Francisco, where he was placed in charge of a new intelligence center with responsibility for the Alaska–California coastal region. That posting was to be only the first in a series of short-duration assignments that engaged Rochefort until the end of the war: August 1943, Eureka, California—overseeing the commissioning of a floating dry dock; March 1944, Washington, DC—testifying before a Pearl Harbor investigation board; April 1944, Washington, DC—command of the Far Eastern Section of the U.S. Navy Office of Naval Intelligence; and November 1944, Washington, DC—command of the Pacific Strategic Intelligence Section, an assignment that led, in May 1945, to a request for him to brief Admiral King on Japan's war matériel situation.

Rochefort was promoted to captain in September 1944. As the war drew down, he renewed his request for transfer to sea duty. Though it was initially accepted, in March 1945 unexpected orders to serve as a witness in an investigation into the Pearl Harbor attack precluded a shipboard assignment. Rochefort would never return to sea duty. As one code breaker colleague noted, Rochefort's assignment to the floating dry dock "was Joe's first and only [ship] command. A dry dock—Joe's reward for providing the most important intelligence information in the history of naval warfare."

One scholar later summed up Rochefort's World War II saga, saying it was "the story of a talented, sometimes abrasive, but always effective officer battling the bureaucracy and unjustified criticism in the tradition-bound Navy."

Midway, where his efforts made possible an American victory and changed the course of the war in the Pacific, remains his indelible legacy.

Before and After

Joseph Rochefort was born May 12, 1900, in Dayton, Ohio. In 1918, he dropped out of high school and, in April of that year, enlisted in the navy, serving initially as an electrician.

When his ambitions to join the navy's flying corps did not come to fruition, Rochefort transferred to a navy reserve organization in New York City. After serving as a mechanic on a passenger liner contracted by the navy, he was sent to the Stevens Steam-Engineering Training School in Hoboken, New Jersey. He was commissioned as a temporary ensign on graduation in June 1919. In April 1921, he transferred from the reserve establishment to the regular navy, an exceptionally rare accomplishment in that era. From the time he enlisted in the navy until the advent of World War II, Rochefort spent a total of 14 years on sea duty. He served on a wide range of vessels: tankers, minesweepers, battleships, destroyers, and cruisers. His duties were equally as diverse and included among them engineer officer, chief engineer, executive officer, navigator, and operations officer. From 1929 to 1932, he received Navy-sponsored Japanese language training. In the mid-1930s, Rochefort served aboard the USS *California* as right-hand man for the commander of the U.S. Navy battle fleet, Admiral Joseph Reeves.

Reeves was an officer legendary for his lack of tact. Though his own personality would exacerbate the issue, many of the adversaries who later sought retribution against Rochefort first crossed paths with him as he was carrying out Reeves's often impatient, difficult directives. Conversely, Rochefort's presence on Reeves's staff involved him deeply in fleet operations and high-level strategy, providing insights which he exploited in a superb fashion at Station Hypo.

Nine of the interwar years were spent in intelligence-related duties. In 1925, the executive officer aboard the USS *Arizona*, Commander Chester C. Jersey, noted Rochefort's exceptional talent working cross-word puzzles and intricate card games. When Commander Jersey was assigned the following year to Washington, he recommended Rochefort for a vacant position on the navy's cryptanalysis staff (which at the time consisted of one person). The appointment brought Rochefort in con-tact with then–Lieutenant (later Captain) Laurence F. Safford, the Navy's one-person code-breaking bureau chief.

Safford, sometimes termed "the father of U.S. cryptology," became somewhat of a legend in his own right. As a young officer he was named head of research in the navy's Code and Signal Section. Some of his first work involved extracting information from a stolen Japanese codebook. He later established a system of intercept stations focused on collecting covert Japanese message traffic and with other colleagues did extensive work in building cryptographic machines. In 1941, it was Safford, again serving as chief cryptanalyst in Washington, who placed Rochefort at Pearl Harbor as head of Station Hypo.

When Rochefort reported to his new duties, Safford trained him for six months, mainly by giving him cryptograms to solve. When Safford was reassigned early in 1926, Rochefort took over the function super-vising the miniscule staff. Shortly after his arrival Rochefort worked with, and was mentored by, Agnes Meyer Driscoll. Driscoll, sometimes referred to as "Madame X" by her coworkers, had entered the navy as a chief yeoman at the end of World War I. Except for a two-year interval, she worked as a cryptanalyst for the next 30 years. Fluent in Japanese, with degrees in mathematics and physics, Driscoll helped develop a cipher machine and led the effort to decrypt the Japanese device that transmitted coded messages between Japanese naval attachés. She began breaking Japanese manual codes early in her career and was working on JN-25 when World War II began.

Later Rochefort's career path would intersect with other intelligence officers whose names remain famous in intelligence circles. His key assistant at Station Hypo was Lieutenant Commander (later Captain) Thomas Dyer. Also initially trained by Agnes Driscoll, Dyer became known as the "father of machine cryptanalysis" for his use of IBM tabulating machines to assist in the process of breaking codes and ciphers. His work in this area contributed in a major way to decrypting JN-25 prior to Midway.

The liaison between Rochefort and Station Hypo and Admiral Nimitz was Commander (later Admiral) Edwin Layton. A Japanese speaker—he had served two years as assistant naval attaché in Japan—Layton was a gifted, veteran intelligence officer twice assigned to the navy's Office of Intelligence in Washington. As a member of Nimitz's staff, he was responsible for all intelligence operations in the Pacific and for evaluating Japanese military capabilities and the empire's intentions. A friend and confidant of Rochefort, he communicated Station Hypo's assessments to the commander in chief of the Pacific Fleet. Nimitz trusted him and Rochefort and used Rochefort's findings to prepare for Midway. Years later, Layton, along with others at Station Hypo, would articulate Rochefort's contributions to the victory at Midway to the American public and Department of Defense officials. Their cumulative efforts helped make the case for awarding the Distinguished Service Medal and documented Rochefort's shabby treatment by senior officials in the navy hierarchy.

Disappointed that a sea billet was foreclosed as a possibility, Rochefort retired effective January 1, 1947.

And then he did something extraordinary. He got his high school diploma.

Citing his cryptanalysis skills, foreign language ability, and years of varied experiences in the navy, he applied for and received his graduation certificate. He then rather quickly launched into a college career, taking international relations, Russian, and advanced mathematics courses. His work toward a college degree ended with the outbreak of the Korean War in 1950. Rochefort was recalled to active duty and placed in charge of the Intelligence Section of the Fleet Evaluation Group. He was subsequently sent to the Naval War College, where he translated Japanese documents for a war college study of the Battle of Leyte Gulf.

In March 1953, Rochefort retired for a second, final time. He returned to his studies at the University of Southern California and subsequently dabbled a bit in real estate ventures. He served as consultant for the films *Tora! Tora! Tora!* and *Midway*.

As years passed, momentum grew for correcting the record and recognizing Rochefort's contributions to victory in the Pacific War. In addition to Admiral Edwin Layton, Rochefort's former colleagues at Station Hype, especially including Jasper Holmes and Admiral D. "Mac" Showers, launched an extended twenty-plus-year campaign, which continued long after Rochefort's death, aimed at redeeming his legacy.

Over time, their combined efforts revealed his sordid treatment by senior officials in the navy hierarchy and helped make the case for awarding the Distinguished Service Medal. Finally, in 1985, 43 years after Midway, the long-standing wrong was rectified. Rochefort was approved for posthumous awarding of the medal. The following year, President Ronald Reagan personally presented the medal to the Rochefort family in a White House ceremony attended by Vice President George H. W. Bush and other senior dignitaries. The award's citation, so long in coming, said that the intelligence information provided by Rochefort's unit "served as the singular basis for the fleet commander in chief to plan his defenses, deploy his limited forces and devise strategy to insure U.S. Navy success in engaging the Japanese forces at Midway."

More honors would follow. Later in 1986, Rochefort was awarded the Presidential Medal of Freedom. In 2000, he was inducted into the National Security Agency/Central Security Agency Hall of Honor. In 2012, the Captain Joseph J. Rochefort Building—not terribly far from the location of the Dungeon, where he had served the navy and the nation so well—was dedicated at the National Security Administration facility in Hawaii.

CLOSING THOUGHTS

The battles of the leaders whose stories were told in this volume shared an important characteristic: all were fought on foreign soil or on the great oceans and sea lanes of the world. Although war would touch the future states of Alaska and Hawaii, unlike the conflicts that beset the nation during its first century of existence, no battles were fought on ground in any of the contiguous forty-eight states or on the nation's lakes or waterways.

The forces they led during the not-quite-50-year period between the beginning of the Spanish-American War and the end of World War II retained generally the same descriptive titles and, for the most part, similar structures. The army, for example, continued to be organized in platoons, companies, battalions, brigades/regiments, divisions, and corps. The navy's general structure also stayed essentially the same, although the alphabet-soup nomenclature of forces below the fleet level differed considerably over time.

Beyond the labels, however, much changed during those five decades. World War I brought orders-of-magnitude increases in the destructiveness and lethality of machine guns and artillery, an occurrence perhaps best illustrated by the *60,000* casualties suffered by the British army in a *single day* at the Somme.

The same conflict saw the introduction of submarine warfare on a major scale. Indeed, had the scale of Allied losses sustained during the peak month of April 1917 (880,000 tons) persisted, the war might well have taken a different turn. U-boats sank five thousand Allied merchant vessels during the course of the war.

"The war to end all wars" also saw the dawn of aerial combat. Beginning with modest employment as airborne scouts, as the conflict continued and technology improved aircraft were increasingly employed in offensive roles, taking on counterair, ground-support, and bombardment missions. Numbers expanded exponentially as well (though none of the aircraft flown in combat by American pilots were designed or built in the United States). In September 1918, Billy Mitchell led 1,500 Allied aircraft in an air-ground offensive at Saint-Mihiel. The end of the war left the future and organizational status of the nation's air arm unclear. The military establishment would wrestle with questions related to employment and structure of its air service for many years. Only in 1947 did the U.S. Air Force become a separate branch of the armed forces.

On September 15, 1916, tanks were used in battle for the first time. The models later used by American units were French-made; as with combat aircraft, none were built in the United States. When those first primitive vehicles lumbered onto a battlefield in France, the event foreshadowed the armored formations and mobile warfare that would be more fully unveiled a quarter of a century later.

When that war came, the scale of the conflict would surpass that of all previous wars. All of the world's oceans and all of its continents save Antarctica were drawn to one degree or another into the maelstrom that was World War II. Though not deployed in overwhelming numbers, jet aircraft were used for the first time. Long-range bombers destroyed opponents' national infrastructure and industrial capabilities and, coincident with those attacks, devastated many of the world's great cities as well. For the first time, significant numbers of troops and enormous quantities of supplies were transported directly to combat zones via aircraft. Aerial warfare also manifested itself as a critical component of sea power. Floating aerodromes—technological marvels of the day—with immortal names such as *Hornet*, *Wasp*, *Lexington*, and *Enterprise* carried crews and craft toward the sound of the guns. The ETO saw the advent of other weapons new to the annals of warfare: the German V-1 guided missiles and V-2 rockets that rained terror on London, Antwerp, and other targets.

Most consequential of all—not just for military planners but indeed for future generations—was the use of the weapon that ended the war. Atomic weapons brought an entirely new dimension to human conflict, along with continuing discussions regarding deterrent value, efficacy of use, "weapon of last resort," and many more.

Interestingly enough, when the United States entered the war, a weapon at the opposite end of the spectrum, the infantryman's rifle, was one of the few areas in which U.S. forces held a technological edge. Introduced in 1936, the M1 Garand replaced the M1903 Springfield and gave American infantrymen a distinct advantage over adversaries who continued to use slower-firing bolt-action rifles.

Sometimes overshadowed in discussions of weapons and their relative effects was a final "after-action" truth gleaned from experiences in World War II. Indeed, so pervasive was its influence that it undergirded the nation's entire array of war-making capabilities. To a greater degree than earlier conflicts, the *industrial capacity* of a modern nation-state played a determining role in influencing the outcome of the war. By the time of V-E and V-J Days, the United States was producing a B-24 bomber every 63 minutes, 24 hours a day, seven days a week, 365 days a year. Altogether, American plants produced more than 303,000 airplanes, nearly double that built by any other nation. By mid-1943, three Liberty Ships were being launched every day. The Liberty Ships were but a small segment of the 124,000 vessels of all types built by American shipyards during the course of the war. The enormous industrial strength of the United States buttressed and complemented an increasingly capable fighting machine whose power and potential eventually outstripped the capabilities of friends and foes alike.

The manner in which the nation went to war also evolved. The forces assembled by the United States after the declaration of war with Spain consisted of an embarrassingly small regular army establishment augmented by hastily put together militia units. Forty-three years later, the nation entered World War II with a regular army that had, finally, been increased in size over the previous two years but remained substantially smaller than the forces fielded by belligerent nations. (As late as the summer of 1939, three months before the onset of war in Europe, the U.S. Army had ranked 19th in size among the armies of the world, trailing even Portugal.) The mobilization process, thanks to a barely passed conscription law, was by then built around a draftee force. Sixty-one percent of the American soldiers who served in World War II were conscripts.

America's industrial capacity was a major determinant in the Allies' victory in World War II. At the Willow Run plant near Detroit, Michigan, a B-24 bomber was produced every 63 minutes, 24 hours a day, seven days a week.

While the procedures used by the United States to enter a conflict were substantially modified, the manner in which the country left a war stayed generally constant. Massive, rapid demobilization remained a consistent feature. Twelve million Americans were in uniform when World War II ended. By mid-1947, only a million and a half remained.

The end of the conflict found the United States as the world's dominant power, a nation of unparalleled strength with an industrial output that far surpassed that of any other nation or combination of nations. That robust, overwhelming power combined with sole possession of atomic weapons and, for a brief time, the apparent absence of a credible threat fueled an attempt to do "defense on the cheap" with drastically reduced

A line of Victory ships at a West Coast shipyard. From mid-1943, three Victory ships were launched every day. During the course of the war, American shipyards produced 124,000 vessels of all types.

military budgets and force sizes. Five years later, the nation would pay a price for that approach during the initial days of the Korean War.

For the armed forces of the United States, the aftermath of World War II brought the most notable change to the defense structure in the nation's history. America entered the war with a military establishment composed of separate fiefdoms and without anything resembling a Joint Chiefs of Staff (JCS). The scope and complexity of modern war made apparent the need for a permanent body to plan and coordinate joint services matters and to provide collective advice to the nation's political leadership. Passed on September 18, 1947, the National Security Act, as amended over the years, led to the establishment of the Department of Defense and institutionalized a JCS organization with supporting staff.

Prompted by difficulties encountered during 1983 operations in Grenada, more recent adjustments via the Goldwater–Nichols Act (1986) enhanced the influence of the JCS chairman, who was designated as the principal military adviser to the national command authority, while a second major provision specified that the operational chain of command runs from the president to the secretary of defense directly to combatant commanders.

Operations in Panama in 1989 brought the first, successful test of structural changes brought by the Goldwater–Nichols legislation. Those provisions remain in effect, guiding the employment of American forces to the present day.

REFERENCES

Spanish-American War: Road to War
"splendid little war"
>   Thomas, Evan. *The War Lovers*. New York: Back Bay Books, 2010, p.
>   12. The original cite is in a letter from John Hay to Theodore Roosevelt
>   dated July 27, 1898.

"You supply the pictures, I'll supply the war."
Leckie, Robert. *The Wars of America: Vol 2—San Juan Hill to Tonkin*. New
    York: Harper & Row, 1968, p. 21. However, there is some controversy
    surrounding the wording and the quote itself. Joseph W. Campbell (*Yellow
    Journalism: Puncturing the Myths, Defining the Legacies*. Westport, CT: Praeger,
    2003, p. 72) asserts that the quote is apocryphal, arguing that the notorious
    telegram was never sent. Evan Thomas (Thomas, p. 161) accepts the quote
    as factual but renders it "You furnish the pictures and I'll furnish the war."

Leonard Wood
"dynamo of organization"
>   Thomas, p. 262.

"worth the cost of the war"
>   McCallum, Jack. *Leonard Wood: Rough Rider, Surgeon, Architect of American
>   Imperialism*. New York: New York University Press, 2006, p. 173.

"15 men in a smoke-filled room"
>   McCallum, p. 283.

William T. Sampson
"You may fire when ready, Gridley."
>   Freidel, Frank. *The Splendid Little War*. Boston: Little, Brown, 1958, p.
>   22. Writing considerably later, Admiral Dewey offers a slightly differ-
>   ent version of the quote: "You may fire when you are ready, Gridley"
>   (Dewey, Admiral George. "The Battle of Manila Bay," *War Times Journal*,
>   accessed June 19, 2014.) See also McSherry, Patrick, "The Battle of
>   Manila Bay (Cavite)," for a detailed description of the encounter and
>   the context of the quote within the battle (www.spanamwar.com/mbay.
>   htm, accessed March 22, 2016).

"The fleet under my command"
    Thomas, p. 344.
"simply criminally negligent"
    McCallum, p. 107.

Frederick Funston
"the man who saved San Francisco"
    National Park Service. *Frederick Funston: The Man Who Saved San Francisco.*
    http://www.nps.gov/prs/history/bios/funston.htm, accessed May 28,
    2014.

Leonard Wood
"Wood at his best was altruistic ..."
    McCallum, p. 298.

John J. Pershing
"I have made many very strong personal friends"
    Lacey, Jim. *Pershing.* New York: Palgrave Macmillan, 2008, p. 39.

World War I: The Road to War
"too proud to fight"
    Leckie, p. 93. The quote is from a speech ("Address to Naturalized Citizens
    at Conventional Hall, Philadelphia") given by President Woodrow Wilson
    on May 10, 1915.

William S. Sims
"continuous aim firing"
    "William Snowden Sims," *Encyclopedia Britannica.* www.britannica.com/
    biography/William-Snowden-Sims, accessed March 24, 2016.

George C. Marshall
"organizer of victory"
    Cray, Ed. *General of the Army: George C. Marshall Soldier and Statesman.*
    New York: W.W. Norton, 1990, p. 515.

William "Billy" Mitchell
"almost treasonable administration of national defense"
    Sharp, Harold S. "The Court-martial of Billy Mitchell," *Footnotes in
    American History.* Metuchen, NJ: Scarecrow Press, 1977, pp. 430–33. The

initial quote was from an interview in San Antonio, Texas, later published by the *New York Times*. See also Maksel, Rebecca. "The Billy Mitchell Court-Martial." *Air & Space Magazine*, July 2009.

Omar Bradley
"in the wrong war, at the wrong place"
Bradley, Omar N. "Testimony before the Senate Committees on Armed Forces and Foreign Relations, May 15, 1951" *Military Situation in the Far East*. Washington, DC, 1951. Part 2, p. 732.
"GI's general"
Nichols, David. *Ernie's War: The Best of Ernie Pyle's World War II Dispatches*. New York: Simon & Schuster, 1986. p. 358
"conspicuous for his ability to handle people"
Cray, p. 106.

Terry Allen
"Never in my life have I seen a man so worshipped"
Aster, Gerald. *Terrible Terry Allen*. New York: Ballantine, 2003. p. x.
"Major General Terry Allen was one of my favorite people"
Whitlock, Flint. *The Fighting First: The Untold Story of the Big Red One on D-Day*. Boulder, CO: Westview. 2005. p. 17
"A soldier doesn't fight to save suffering humanity"
Aster, p. 127.
"El Guettar was the first solid"
Aster, p. 169.
"The air would turn blue as the two friends"
Aster, p. 167.
"captured every man in the audience"
Aster, p. 183.
"trashed clubs"
Aster, p. 184.
"of all the American soldiers arrested the previous month"
Atkinson, Rick. *An Army at Dawn*. New York: Henry Holt, 2002. p. 82.
"had the longest, most arduous and most successful combat record"
Aster, p. 271.
"cleared 8,000 square miles of Europe"
Aster, p. 321.
"The 1st Infantry Division during Allen's leadership"
Aster, p. xii.

"as far as I know, Terry Allen was the only general"
  Aster, p. 161.
"Among the division commanders, none excelled"
  Whitlock, pp. 19–20.
"the embodiment of an inspirational commander"
  McManus, John C. *The Dead and Those About to Die.* New York: Penguin, 2014.
"It meant something to sweating, tired, bone-weary"
  Aster, p. 232.
"the finest division commander"
  Atkinson, p. 520.

Raymond A. Spruance
"Spruance is the smartest officer in the Navy."
  Tuohy, William. *America's Fighting Admirals.* St. Paul, MN: Zenith, 2007. p. 81.
"Now that we have ample data"
  Morison, Samuel Eliot. *History of United States Naval Operations in World War II (Vol. 4): Coral Sea, Midway, and Submarine Actions, May 12 1941–August 1942.* Boston: Little, Brown, 1988. p. 142.
"one of the greatest fighting and thinking admirals in American naval history"
  Buell, Thomas B. *The Quiet Warrior: A Biography of Admiral Raymond A. Spruance.* Annapolis, MD: Naval Institute Press, reissue edition, 2009. p. 166.
"seedbed for victory"
  Tuohy, p. 216.
"As the primary objective of American forces"
  Tuohy, p. 271.

Elwood R. "Pete" Quesada
"traffic desert"
  Hughes, Thomas A. *Overlord: Pete Quesada and the Triumph of Tactical Air Power in World War II.* New York: Free Press, 1995. p. 151.
"I simply can't imagine any other officer who would have given us as much help"
  Hughes, p. 226.
"The American fighter-bombers destroyed us"
  Galland, Adolph. *The First and the Last.* New York: Bantam, 1978. p. 242.

"nothing conventional about Quesada . . . a fine unpretentious field soldier"
    Hughes, p. 157.
"This man Quesada is a jewel"
    Hughes, p. 162.
"unlike most airmen"
    Bradley, Omar. *A Soldier's Story.* New York: Henry Holt, 1951. p. 249.
"I have never seen such affection between air and ground commanders"
    Hughes, p. 302.
"future wars will require"
    Hughes, p. 63.
"The public acts in faith"
    Time. "The Right Man for the Right Job," February 22, 1960.
"a rare bird: a military man with a lively and uncluttered mind"
    Time Magazine. "Right Man."
"a dashing, cooperative leader"
    Hughes, p. 303.
"an officer of engaging personality"
    Hughes, p. 67.
"although Quesada could have passed"
    Bradley, p. 337.
"suffered by comparison"
    Hughes, p. 234.

J. Lawton Collins
"Had we created another ETO Army"
    Wade, Major Gary. "Conversations with General J. Lawton Collins." U.S.
    Army Command and General Staff College, Fort Leavenworth, KS, 1983.
    p. 2.
"a tremendous believer in doing everything we could in the combined arms"
    Hughes, p. 161.
"a coordinated attack and that means infantry, artillery, air, and engineers"
    Hughes, p. 161.
"some of the wildest melees of the war"
    Hughes, p. 222.
"after an hour I had no communication with anybody"
    Keegan, John. *The Second World War.* New York: Viking, 1989. p. 334.
"the toughest fighting since the *bocage* days in Normandy"
    Hughes, p. 260.

"reevaluation of our plans"
  Millett, Allan R. (ed.) *A Short History of the Vietnam War.* Bloomington: Indiana University Press, 1978. p. 137.

Charles A. Lockwood
"a little known war: the U.S. submarine offense"
  Blair, Clay, Jr. *Silent Victory: The U.S. Submarine War against Japan.* Philadelphia and New York: J. B. Lippincott, 1975. p. 17.
"if anything I have said will get the Bureau off its duff"
  Blair, p. 403.
"They were no supermen, nor were they endowed with any supernatural qualities"
  Lockwood, Charles A. *Sink 'Em All: Submarine Warfare in the Pacific.* Boston: E. P. Dalton, 1951.

Robert L. Eichelberger
"Bob, I want you to take Buna or not come back alive."
  Eichelberger, Robert L. *Our Jungle Road to Toyko.* New York: Viking, 1950. p. 21.
"rewarded for his success by being assigned to train troops in Auckland"
  Tuohy, p. 173.
"a commander of the first order, fearless in battle"
  MacArthur, Douglas. *Reminiscences.* New York: McGraw-Hill. 1964. p. 157.

Clifton A. F. "Ziggy" Sprague
"At 0716, Ziggy Sprague ordered his destroyers to attack the Japanese main body."
  Tuohy, p. 312.
"performed their duties coolly and efficiently"
  Tuohy, p. 312.
"chubby, thorough, and conscientious"
  Boatner, Mark M., III. *The Biographical Dictionary of World War II.* New York: Presidio, 1996. pp. 524–25.

William H. Tunner
"China's lifeline to the outside world"
  Gilbert, Bill. *Air Power.* New York: Kensington, 2003. p. 81.
"Planes brought in for maintenance"
  Gilbert, p. 92.

"It didn't make the pilots happy"
Gilbert, p. 92
"as inflexible as a metronome"
Collier, Richard. *Bridge across the Sky*. New York: McGraw-Hill, 1978.
p. 101.

Joseph J. Rochefort
"His attitude was you can accomplish anything"
"Officer Who Broke Japanese War Code Gets Belated Honor," *New York Times*, November 17, 1985.
"unique and irreplaceable ability"
"Joe Rochefort's War: Deciphering a Code Breaker." http: //www. historynet.com/joe-rocheforts-war-deciphering-a-code-breaker.htm. p. 1.
"a team effort . . . they [the Washington office] had done the bulk of the work"
Blair, p. 262.
"Joe's first and only command"
Blair, p. 263.
"the story of a talented, sometimes abrasive"
Penke, Hayden (ed.). "Intelligence Officer Bookshelf," *Studies in Intelligence*. Washington, DC: Center for the Study of Intelligence, Central Intelligence Agency. September 2012. p. 95.
"served as the singular basis"
"Officer Who Broke Japanese War Code Gets Belated Honor," *New York Times*, November 17, 1985.

SELECTED BIBLIOGRAPHY

Spanish-American War: General References
Dolan, Edward F. *The Spanish-American War.* Minneapolis, MN: Twenty-First Century Books, 2001.
Freidel, Frank. *The Splendid Little War.* Boston: Little, Brown, 1958.
Hendrickson, Kenneth E., Jr. *The Spanish-American War.* Westport, CT: Greenwood, 2003.
Keller, Allan. *The Spanish-American War: A Compact History.* Portland, OR: Hawthorne, 1969.
Leckie, Robert. *The Wars of America: Volume 2 – San Juan Hill to Tonkin.* New York: Harper & Row, 1968.
O'Toole, G. J. A. *The Spanish-American War: An American Epic.* New York: W. W. Norton, 1986.
Thomas, Evan. *The War Lovers.* New York: Little, Brown, 2010.
Trask, David F. *The War with Spain in 1898.* Lincoln: University of Nebraska Press, 1996.

Leonard Wood
Hamblen, Joseph. *The Career of Leonard Wood.* Charleston, SC: Nabu Press, 2010.
Lane, Jack C. *Armed Progressive: General Leonard Wood.* Lincoln: University of Nebraska Press, 2009.
McCallum, Jack. *Leonard Wood: Rough Rider, Surgeon, Architect of American Imperialism.* New York: New York University Press, 2006.
Thomas, Evan. *The War Lovers.* New York: Little, Brown, 2010.

William T. Sampson
Brasford, James C., ed. *Admirals of the New Steel Navy: Makers of the American Naval Tradition, 1880–1930.* Annapolis, MD: Naval Institute Press, 1989.
Trask, David F. *The War with Spain in 1898.* Lincoln: University of Nebraska Press, 1996.
West, Richard F. *Admirals of the American Empire.* Lincoln: University of Nebraska Press, 1996.

The Philippine Insurrection: General References

Arnold, James R. *The Moro War.* London: Bloomsburg Press, 2011.

Boot, Max. *The Savage Wars of Peace: Small Wars and the Rise of American Power.* New York: Basic Books, 2003.

Feuer, A. B. *America at War: The Philippines 1898–1913.* Westport, CT: Greenwood, 2002.

Linn, Brian McAllister. *The Philippine War of 1899–1902.* Lawrence: University of Kansas Press, 2000.

Silbey, David J. *A War of Frontier and Empire: The Philippine-American War 1899–1902.* New York: Farrar, Straus & Giroux, 2007.

Quesada, Alejandro, and Stephen Walsh. *The Spanish-American War and the Philippine Insurrection.* Oxford, UK; Osprey, 2007.

Frederick Funston

Bain, David Howard. *Sitting in Darkness: Americans in the Philippines.* Boston: Houghton Mifflin, 1984.

Crouch, Thomas W. *Leader of Volunteers: Frederick Funston and the 20th Kansas in the Philippines 1898–1899.* Lawrence, KS: Coronado, 1984.

———. *A Yankee Guerrillero: Frederick Funston and the Cuban Insurrection, 1986–1897.* Memphis, TN: Memphis State University Press, 1975.

Funston, Frederick. *Memories of Two Wars: Cuba and Philippine Experiences (1911).* Whitefish, MT: Kessinger, 2009.

Leonard Wood

See "Spanish-American War" chapter.

John J. Pershing

Lacey, Jim. *Pershing.* New York: Palgrave Macmillan, 2008.

Smith, Gene. *Until the Last Trumpet Sounds: The Life of General of the Armies John J. Pershing.* New York: Wiley, 1999.

Smythe, Donald. *Guerrilla Warrior: The Early Life of John J. Pershing.* New York: Scribner, 1973.

———. *Pershing: General of the Armies.* Bloomington, IN: Indiana University Press, 2007.

Vandiver, Everson. *Black Jack: The Life and Times of John J. Pershing.* College Station: Texas A&M University Press, 1977.

World War I: General References

Gilbert, Martin. *The First World War: A Complete History*. New York: Henry Holt, 1994.

Guernsey, Irwin Schofield. *A Reference History of the War*. New York: Dodd, Mead, 1920.

Keegan, John. *The First World War*. New York: Alfred A. Knopf, 1999.

King, Jere Clemens. *The First World War*. New York: Walker, 1972.

MacMillan, Margaret. *The War That Ended Peace: The Road to 1914*. New York: Random House, 2013.

Philpott, William. *War of Attrition: Fighting the First World War*. New York: Overlook, 2014.

Reynolds, Francis J., and Allen L. Churchill. *World's War Events (Vol. III)*. New York: P. F. Collier, 1919.

Strachan, Hew. *The First World War*. New York: Viking, 2004.

Tuchman, Barbara. *The Guns of August*. New York: Random House, 1962.

Special thanks to the U.S. Army Center of Military History.

Hunter Liggett

Farrell, Robert H., ed. *In the Company of Generals: The World War I Diary of Pierpont L. Stackpole*. Columbia: University of Missouri Press, 2009.

Liddell Hart, Basil H. *Reputations Ten Years After*. Boston: Little, Brown, 1928.

Liggett, Hunter. *A.E.F.: Ten Years Ago in France*. New York: Dodd, Mead, 1928.

———. *Commanding an American Army: Recollections of the World War*. Boston: Houghton Mifflin, 1925.

Spiller, Roger J., ed. *Dictionary of American Military Biography*. Westport, CT: Greenwood, 1984.

William S. Sims

Allard, Dean C. "Admiral William S. Sims and the United States Naval Policy in World War I." *American Neptune*, April 1975.

Cherpak, Evelyn M., compiler. *Register of the Papers of William S. Sims*. Annapolis, MD: Naval War College Historical Collection, 2002.

Little, Branden, and Kenneth I. Hagan. "Radical, but Right: William Sowden Sims (1858–1936)." In *Nineteen Gun Salute: Case Studies of Operational, Strategic, and Diplomatic Naval Leadership during the 20th and Early 21st Centuries*, edited by John B. Hattendorf and Bruce Elleman. Newport, RI, and Washington, DC: Naval War College Press and Government Printing Office, 2010.

Morison, Elting E. *Admiral Sims and the Modern American Navy.* Boston: Houghton Mifflin, 1942.

Simpson, Michael. "William S. Sims, U.S. Navy, and Admiral Sir Lewis Bayly, Royal Navy: An Unlikely Friendship, and Anglo-American Cooperation." *Naval War College Review,* spring 1988.

Sims, William S. *Victory at Sea.* Charleston, SC: Nabu Press, 2011 (originally published in 1921).

Special thanks to the Naval Historical Center.

James G. Harbord

Garraty, John Arthur and Mark Christopher Carnes, eds. "James Harbord," *American National Biographies.* New York: Oxford University Press, 1999.

Harbord, James G. *The American Army in France, 1917–1919.* New York: Little, Brown, Little, 1936.

―――. *Leaves from a War Diary: Major General James G. Harbord.* New York: Dodd, Mead, 1925.

McHenry, Robert, ed. "James Harbord." *Webster's American Military Biographies.* New York: Merriam-Webster, 1999.

Robert L. Bullard

Bullard, Robert L. *American Soldiers Also Fought.* London: Longmans, Green, 1935.

―――. *Personalities and Reminiscences of the War.* New York: Doubleday, 1925.

Millett, Allan R. *The General: Robert L. Bullard and Officership in the United States Army 1881–1925.* Westport, CT: Greenwood, 1975.

Reynolds, Francis J., and Allen L. Churchill. *World's War Event.* New York: P. F. Collier, 1919.

Dwight D. Eisenhower

Ambrose, Stephen. *Eisenhower: Soldier and President.* New York: Simon & Schuster, 1991.

Blumenson, Martin. *Eisenhower.* New York: Ballantine, 1979.

D'Este, Carlo. *Eisenhower: A Soldier's Life.* New York: Henry Holt, 2002.

Eisenhower, David. *Eisenhower: At War 1943–1945.* New York: Random House, 1986.

Perry, Mark. *Partners in Command.* New York: Penguin, 2007.

Wicker, Tom, and Arthur M. Schlesinger. *Dwight D. Eisenhower.* New York: Times Books, 2002.

John A. Lejeune
Bartlett, Merrill L. *Lejeune: A Marine's Life, 1867–1942.* Annapolis, MD: Naval Institute Press, 1996.
Lejeune, John A. *The Reminiscences of a Marine.* Pittsburgh: Dorrance, 1930.
"Major General John Archer Lejeune, USMC." In *Who's Who in Marine Corps History.* Washington, DC: United States Marine Corps History Division.

Douglas MacArthur
MacArthur, Douglas, and Sam Sloan. *Reminiscences.* New York: McGraw-Hill, 1964.
Manchester, William. *American Caesar: Douglas MacArthur 1880–1964.* New York: Little, Brown, 1978.
Perrett, Geoffrey. *Old Soldiers Never Die: The Life of Douglas MacArthur.* Avon, MA: Adams Media Corporation, 1997.
Windrow, Martin, and Francis K. Mason. *A Concise Dictionary of Military Biography.* New York: Wiley, 1975.
Yockelson, Mitchell. *MacArthur: America's General.* Nashville, TN: Thomas Nelson, 2011.

George C. Marshall
Chambers, John Whiteclay III, ed. *The Oxford Companion to American Military History.* Oxford and New York: Oxford University Press, 2000.
Cray, Ed. *General of the Army: George C. Marshall, Soldier and Statesman.* New York: W. W. Norton, 1990.
Pogue, Forrest C., and Gordon Harrison. *George C. Marshall, Vol. I: Education of a General, 1880–1939.* New York: Viking, 1963.
Marshall, George C. *Memoirs of My Services in the World War, 1917–1918.* Boston: Houghton Mifflin, 1976.

William "Billy" Mitchell
Chambers, John Whiteclay III, ed. *The Oxford Companion to American Military History.* Oxford and New York: Oxford University Press, 2000.
Futrell, Robert F. *Ideas, Concepts, Doctrine: Basic Thinking in the United States Air Force 1907–1960.* Maxwell AFB, AL: Air University Press, 1989.
Greer, Thomas H. *USAF Historical Study: The Development of Air Doctrine in the Army Air Arm, 1917–1941.* Maxwell AFB, AL: Air University Press, 1955.
Hurley, Alfred F. *Billy Mitchell: Crusader for Air Power.* Bloomington: Indiana University Press, 2006.

Jeffers, Paul. *Billy Mitchell: The Life, Times and Battles of America's Prophet of Air Power.* Minneapolis: Zenith Press, 2006.

George S. Patton
Blumenson, Martin. *Patton: The Man behind the Legend, 1885–1945.* New York: William Morrow, 1985.
———. *The Patton Papers: 1940–1945.* Boston: Houghton Mifflin, 1974.
D'Este, Carlo. *Patton: A Genius for War.* New York: HarperCollins, 1995.
Farago, Ladislas. *Patton: Ordeal and Triumph.* Yardley, PA: Westholme, 1964.
Smith, David A. *George S. Patton: A Biography.* Westport, CT: Greenwood, 2003.

Omar Bradley
Bradley, Omar N. *A Soldier's Story.* New York: Henry Holt, 1951.
Bradley, Omar N., and Clay Blair. *A General's Life: An Autobiography by General of the Army Omar N. Bradley.* New York: Simon &Schuster, 1983.
DeFelice, Jim. *Omar Bradley: General at War.* The Generals. Washington, DC: Regency History, 2014.
Jordan, Jonathan W. *Brothers, Rivals, Victors: Eisenhower, Patton, Bradley, and the Partnership That Drove the Allied Conquest in Europe.* New York: New American Library, 2012.
Petterchuk, Janice A. *The Soldier's General: Omar Bradley and the United States Military in Peace and War.* Ann Arbor, MI: Legacy Press, 2014.

World War II: General References
Ambrose, Stephen, ed. *New History of World War II.* New York: Viking, 1997.
Atkinson, Rick. *An Army at Dawn: The War in North Africa, 1942–43.* New York: Henry Holt, 2002.
———. *The Day of Battle: The War in Sicily and Italy, 1943–44.* New York: Henry Holt, 2007
———. *The Guns at Last Light: The War in Western Europe, 1944–45.* New York: Henry Holt, 2013.
Bookman, John T., and Stephen T. Powers. *The March to Victory.* Rev. ed. Niwot: University of Colorado Press, 1986.
Cowley, Robert, ed. *No End Save Victory: Perspectives on World War II.* New York: G. P. Putnam's Sons, 2001.
Keegan, John. *The Second World War.* New York: Viking, 1989.
Keegan, John, gen. ed. *World War II: A Visual Encyclopedia.* London: PRC Publishing, 1997.

Morison, Samuel Eliot. *The Two Ocean War: A Short History of the United States Navy in the Second World War.* Boston: Little, Brown, 1963.

Murray, Williamson, and Allan R. Millett. *A War to Be Won: Fighting the Second World War.* Cambridge, MA: Belknap Press of Harvard University Press, 2000.

Taylor, A. J. P. *The Second World War: An Illustrated History.* London: Penguin, 1975.

Toland, John. *The Rising Sun: The Decline and Fall of the Japanese Empire, 1936–1945.* New York: Random House, 1970.

Roberts, Andrew. *The Storm of War: A New History of the Second World War.* London: Penguin, 2009.

Terry de la Mesa Allen

Astor, Gerald. *Terrible Terry Allen.* New York: Ballantine Books, 2003.

Atkinson, Rick. *An Army at Dawn: The War in North Africa, 1942–1943.* New York: Henry Holt, 2002.

———. *The Day of Battle: The War in Italy and Sicily, 1943–1944.* New York: Henry Holt, 2007.

Jones, Philip D. *Dictionary of American Military Biography.* Westport, CT: Greenwood, 1984.

McManus, John C. *The Dead and Those About to Die.* New York: Penguin, 2014.

Terry de las Mesa Allen Papers, 1907–1969, MS 307. C. L. Sonnichson Special Collections Department, University of Texas at El Paso.

Whitlock, Flint. *The Fighting First: The Untold Story of the Big Red One on D-Day.* Boulder, CO: Westview, 2004.

Raymond A. Spruance

"Admiral Raymond A. Spruance, USN." *Biographies in Naval History.* Annapolis, MD: Naval History and Heritage Command. http://www.history.navy.mil/bios/spruance.htm. Accessed August 29, 2014.

Borneman, Walter. *The Admirals.* New York: Little, Brown, 2012.

Buell, Thomas B. *The Quiet Warrior: A Biography of Admiral Raymond A. Spruance.* Annapolis, MD: Naval Institute Press, reissue edition, 2009.

Correll, John T. "The Turkey Shoot." *Air Force Magazine,* April 2016.

Forrestel, Emmet Peter. *Admiral Raymond A. Spruance, USN: A Study in Command.* Washington, DC: Government Printing Office, 1966.

Toland, John. *The Rising Sun: The Decline and Fall of the Japanese Empire, 1936–1945.* New York: Random House 1970.

Tuohy, William. *America's Fighting Admirals*. St. Paul, MN: Zenith Press, 2007.

Westwell, Ian. *World War II Commanders*. New York: Metro Books, 2008.

Elwood R. "Pete" Quesada

Craven, W. F., and J. L. Cate, eds. *The American Air Forces in World War II, Vol. III, Europe: Argument to V-E Day, January 1944 to May 1945*. Washington, DC: Office of Air Force History, 1979.

Dorr, Robert F., and Thomas D. Jones. *Hell Hawks! The Untold Story of the American Fliers Who Savaged Hitler's Wehrmacht*. New York: Zenith, 2010.

Hughes, Thomas A. *Overlord: General Pete Quesada and the Triumph of Tactical Air Power in World War II*. New York: Crown, 1995.

Kahn, Richard H. and Joseph P. Harahan, *Air Superiority in World War II and Korea: An Interview with Gen. James Ferguson, Gen. Robert M. Lee, Gen. William W. Momyer, and Lt. Gen. Elwood P. Quesada*, Office of Air Force History, Washington, DC., 1983.

"The Right Man for the Right Job." *Time*, February 22, 1960.

United States Air Force Official Biography, Lieutenant General Elwood Richard Quesada. Air Force Public Affairs, Washington DC.

J. Lawton Collins

Bradley, Omar and Clay Blair. *A General's Life: An Autobiography by General of the Army Omar M. Bradley*. New York: Simon & Schuster, 1983.

Collins, Joseph Lawton. *Lightning Joe: An Autobiography*. Baton Rouge, LA: Louisiana State University Press, 1979.

————. *War in Peacetime: the History and Lessons of Korea*. Boston: Houghton Mifflin, 1969.

Hughes, Thomas A. *Overlord: Pete Quesada and the Triumph of Tactical Air Power in World War II*. New York: Free Press, 1995.

"Joseph Lawton Collins." Arlington National Cemetery website. Accessed November 25, 2014.

Wade, Gary. "Conversations with General J. Lawton Collins" Global Studies Institute, U.S. Army Command and General Staff College, Fort Leavenworth, Kansas, 1983.

Charles A. Lockwood

Blair, Clay. *Silent Victory: The U.S. Submarine War against Japan*. Philadelphia: J. B. Lippincott, 1975.

Defense Media Network. "The Mark 14 Torpedo Scandal." http://www.defensemedianetwork.com/stories/torpedo-scandal-rear-adm-charles-lockwood-the-mark-14-and-the-bureau-of-ordnance/. Accessed October 7, 2014.

Freedom Documents. "Charles A. Lockwood, Jr., Vice-Admiral (1890–1967)." http://www.freedomdocuments.com/Lockwood.html. Accessed October 7, 2014.

Lockwood, Charles A. *Down to the Sea in Subs: My Life in the U.S. Navy.* New York: W. W. Norton 1967.

Lockwood, Charles A. *Sink 'Em, All: Submarine Warfare in the Pacific.* Boston: E. P. Dalton, 1951.

"Lockwood, Charles Andrew Jr. (1890–1967)." Pacific War Online Encyclopedia. http://pwenmcycl.kgbudge.com/L/o/Lockwood_Charles_A.htm. Accessed October 7, 2014.

Morrison, Samuel Eliot. *History of United States Naval Operations in World War II: Volume 14, Victory in the Pacific.* Annapolis, MD: Naval Institute Press, reissue edition, 2012.

Robert L. Eichelberger

Chwialkowski, Paul. *In Caesar's Shadow: The Life of General Robert Eichelberger.* Westport, CT: Praeger, 1993.

Eichelberger, Robert L., and Emma Gudger Eichelberger. *Dear Miss Em: General Eichelberger's War in the Pacific, 1942–1945.* Westport, CT: Praeger, 1972.

———. *Our Jungle Road to Tokyo.* New York: Viking, 1950.

Fath, William H. "Intrepidity, Iron Will, and Intellect: General Robert L. Eichelberger and Military Genius." Master's thesis, U.S. Army Command and General Staff College, Fort Leavenworth, KS, 2004.

Shortal. John F. *Forged by Fire: Robert L. Eichelberger and the Pacific War.* Columbia: University of South Carolina Press, 1987.

Clifton A. F. Sprague

Boatner, Mark M., III. *The Biographical Dictionary of World War II.* New York: Presidio, 1996.

Cox, Robert Jon. *The Battle off Samar: Taffy III at Leyte Gulf.* 5th ed. Wakefield, MI: Agogeebic Press 2010.

Hornfischer, James D. *The Last Stand of the Tin Can Sailors.* New York: Bantam, 2004.

Tuohy, William. *America's Fighting Admirals.* St. Paul, MN: Zenith Press, 2007.

Wukovits, John F. *Devotion to Duty: A Biography of Admiral Clifton A. F. Sprague.* Annapolis, MD: Naval Institute Press, 1995.

William H. Tunner
Collier, Richard. *Bridge across the Sky.* New York: McGraw-Hill, 1978.
Gilbert, Bill. *Air Power.* New York: Kensington, 2003.
Hoppe, Billy J. *Lieutenant General William H. Tunner in the China-Burma-India "Hump" and Berlin Airlifts: A Case Study in Leadership and Development of Airlift Doctrine.* Maxwell AFB, AL: Air War College, Air University, 1995.
"Lieutenant General William H. Tunner." United States Air Force Bibliography. www.//www.af.mil/information/bios. Accessed March 3, 2015.
Plating, John D. *The Hump: America's Strategy for Keeping China in World War II.* College Station: Texas A&M University Press, 2011.
Tunner, William H. *Over the Hump.* New York: Duell, Sloan & Pearce, 1964.

Joseph J. Rochefort
Blair, Clay, Jr. *Silent Victory: The U.S. Submarine War against Japan.* Philadelphia and New York: J. B. Lippincott, 1975.
Budiansky, Stephen. *Battle of Wits: The Complete Story of Codebreaking in World War II.* New York: Simon & Schuster, 2000.
Carlton, Eliot. *Joe Rochefort's War: The Odyssey of the Codebreakers Who Outwitted Yamamoto at Midway.* Annapolis, MD: Naval Institute Press, 2013.
Farago, Ladislas. *The Broken Seal.* New York: Bantam, 1968.
Hastings, Max. *The Silent War: Spies, Ciphers, and Guerrillas, 1939–1945.* New York: HarperCollins, 2016.
Holmes, J. Wilfred. *Double-Edged Secrets.* Annapolis, MD: Naval Institute Press, 2012.
Layton, Edwin T. *And I Was There: Pearl Harbor and Midway; Breaking the Secrets.* New York: William Morrow, 1985.

INDEX